John Graves Simcoe, 1752–1806

John Graves Simcoe, 1752-1806
A Biography

Mary Beacock Fryer and Christopher Dracott

DUNDURN PRESS
TORONTO · OXFORD

Editor: Dennis Mills
Design: Scott Reid
Printer: Transcontinental Printing Inc.
Front Cover photograph: John Graves Simcoe courtesy of the Ontario Government Art Collection. Artist: George Berthon

Canadian Cataloguing in Publication Data

Fryer, Mary Beacock, 1929-
      John Graves Simcoe, 1752-1806: a biography

Includes bibliographical references and index.
ISBN 1-55002-309-8

1. Simcoe, John Graves, 1752-1806. 2. Lieutenant governors — Ontario — Biography. I. Dracott, Christopher. II. Title.

FC3071.1S55F79 1998   971.3'02'092   C98-931572-X
F1058.S79 1998

1 2 3 4 5 BJ 02 01 00 99 98

We acknowledge the support of the **Canada Council for the Arts** for our publishing program. We also acknowledge the support of the **Ontario Arts Council** and the **Book Publishing Industry Development Program** of the **Department of Canadian Heritage.**

Care has been taken to trace the ownership of copyright material used in this book. The author and the publisher welcome any information enabling them to rectify any references or credit in subsequent editions.

Printed and bound in Canada.

 Printed on recycled paper.

Dundurn Press
8 Market Street
Suite 200
Toronto, Ontario, Canada
M5E 1M6

Dundurn Press
73 Lime Walk
Headington, Oxford
England
OX3 7AD

Dundurn Press
2250 Military Road
Tonawanda, NY
U.S.A. 14150

CONTENTS

INTRODUCTION

John Graves Simcoe, the subject of this work, was a brilliant soldier and an imaginative tactician. He rose in rank from humble ensign to lieutenant general in the British Army. He was also an administrator of government, civil and military. His adult life divides into three phases.

The first, and probably the most heroic, was his service as a daring commander of the Queen's Rangers, a regiment of Provincial troops (men who remained loyal to the Crown) during the American Revolution.

Second came his service as the first lieutenant governor of Upper Canada (now Ontario). This province was established in 1791 in what remained of British North America after the Treaty of Separation of 1783, which gave the Thirteen Colonies their independence. In this role he was the imaginative innovator, whose plans were often frustrated by budget-conscious superiors.

The third phase was his command of the Western District of England (mainly the counties of Cornwall, Devon and part of Somerset) as the 19th century opened. Simcoe was responsible for the defense of these counties in the face of constant threats from France; in fact, he was the senior general on that part of the home front.

PREFACE

To tell the complete story of John Graves Simcoe required the work of two authors, one resident in Britain, the other in Canada. In the latter country, Simcoe is lionized as the founder of a province, but his military acumen is often overlooked; in the former he is less well known, beyond a certain fame in the vicinity of Honiton. He was a man of influence locally; his home, Wolford Lodge, was only a few miles outside the town. Christopher Dracott is the Briton, resident near Hemyock, Devon, not far from the site of the Simcoe house (that later burned down and was rebuilt). Mary Beacock Fryer is the Canadian, resident in Ontario.

Chris became fascinated by Simcoe after he retired as a Detective Chief Superintendent at New Scotland Yard. In 1979, two things happened. He purchased a home in Devon, and his son emigrated to Canada and settled in Toronto, Ontario. In both places Chris discovered John Graves Simcoe.

Mary, growing up in Brockville, Ontario, became acquainted with Simcoe somewhat earlier. One of Simcoe's associates during the American Revolution was Christopher Billop, the colonel of the Staten Island Militia. Billop was a second cousin by marriage of Mary's American Loyalist great-great-great-grandfather, Caleb Seaman. Caleb had enlisted in the cavalry troop of the New York Volunteers, a Provincial regiment Simcoe knew well.

Chris's strength lies in his knowledge of Devon, his perception of the countryside with its landmarks, and his access to records of Simcoe and his family's many friends who lived there. Some of the families still own the houses the Simcoes visited before and after the Canada years. Chris is the present chairman of the John Graves Simcoe/Wolford Chapel Advisory Committee. Mary is the author of several books on Provincial Corps of the British Army, American revolutionary era. One is *King's Men: the soldier founders of Ontario*. She has also written of Simcoe's wife, Elizabeth, and of their son Francis.[1]

PART I
BEGINNINGS

Throughout most of John Graves Simcoe's life, a backdrop on the world's stage was the conflict between Great Britain and France. The hostilities embraced both the rivalry between the two imperialist powers over North American colonies and the shifting alliances in Europe. Simcoe's childhood saw the triumph of Britain over France on the Plains of Abraham, which ended with the loss of most of the French empire in the western hemisphere. That event set the stage for the mood of independence that surfaced within Britain's own Thirteen Colonies. With the French menace largely gone, the colonists felt secure and ready to take control of their own governments.

The American success in turn helped spark the flame of republicanism in imperial France, and the revolution that ended the French monarchy. The instability that followed made France susceptible to the aspirations of a Corsican officer in the French Army named Napoleon Bonaparte.

Simcoe was directly involved in both the American Revolution and the Napoleonic Wars: as a regimental commander in the British Army that attempted to subdue the American rebels in arms, and as a defender of his home territory against French invasion.

ONE

"YOUNG GRAVES"

John Graves Simcoe was not a native Devonian. He was born in the village of Cotterstock, Northamptonshire, on 25 February 1752, and baptized on 5 March in the parish church of St. Andrew's. His parents were Captain John Simcoe, Royal Navy, and Katherine Stamford. He was their third child. Two elder brothers had died young. Pawlett William was baptized at Cotterstock on 28 April 1750, and buried on 29 May. The second son, John, was recorded as buried in 1751. A fourth son, Percy William, was born at Cotterstock in 1754.[1]

For John Graves's godfather, Captain Simcoe chose his fellow captain in the Royal Navy, Samuel Graves. A letter sent by Captain Graves, from Maddox Street in London on 9 May 1752 hints that this son was called after his godfather, to distinguish him from Captain Simcoe. Closing his letter, Captain Graves wrote that all sent compliments to "you and Mrs. Simcoe and infant Graves."[2]

Captain John Simcoe had been born at Staindrop, County Durham, in January 1710. His mother was Mary, and his father was William, a local parson. In 1730 John enlisted as a midshipman in the Royal Navy, and by 1737 he had attained the rank of lieutenant. Ten years later, in 1747, he was appointed captain of a frigate, HMS *Prince Edward*. That same year he married Katherine Stamford in the Abbey Church of Walcott (or Walcot) in Bath, (now in Avon County, but then in the county of Somerset).[3]

In Georgian England, Bath was an exceedingly popular place to visit. People from all over the country came to see the Roman Baths and to "take the waters." To go to Bath for the season was, in Georgian parlance, "all the ton" in society circles. At the many parties and balls, mothers would introduce their unmarried daughters into society, hoping to find eligible, preferably wealthy, husbands for them. Not so wealthy young men would also be on the lookout for young heiresses to marry. Neither Katherine Stamford nor Captain John Simcoe, were particularly wealthy, merely "comfortably placed."

In 1747 John Simcoe was granted a coat of arms by the Garter and Clarencieux King of Arms. In the College of Arms records he is shown as of Chelsea, in the County of Middlesex.[4] At that time Chelsea was a pleasant village situated on the banks of the River Thames, a short journey by road or water from London. Chelsea is known worldwide for the Royal Hospital, being the home of the Chelsea Pensioners in their distinctive red uniforms, the Chelsea Flower Show, even a football club. How long John Simcoe lived in Chelsea is unknown, but by 1748 he and his wife had taken up residence in Cotterstock, a delightful village in Northamptonshire. Their home was Cotterstock Hall. According to notes made by their grandson, Henry Addington Simcoe, the family "hired" Cotterstock Hall.[5]

Very early, Captain Simcoe gave thought to the education and future conduct of his two surviving sons. In 1754, when young Graves was only two and Percy a babe in arms, he wrote down nineteen maxims entitled "Rules for your Conduct."[6] While some of the advice was religious or sheer patriotism, much was common sense. He warned his sons that he who did not learn to obey could never become qualified to command, and that an officer should never order an inferior to perform any task he could not do himself. The captain may have been aware that the life of a naval officer on active command might not be long. He needed to leave his sons a legacy should he not be there to guide them.

In 1756 war broke out between Britain and France, (known as the French and Indian War in North America). By 1759, in his ship *Pembroke*, Simcoe was sailing towards Quebec, escorting troop transports required for General James Wolfe, commander of land forces. Aboard as the *Pembroke*'s sailing master was James Cook, then being guided by Simcoe in the art of navigation. All summer Wolfe had been bombarding the heavily fortified Beauport shore. With the coming of autumn, he had arrived at a plan that would succeed, by moving his troops upriver in the smaller vessels of his fleet. He was able to land them below the Plains of Abraham, thereby taking the French commander, Montcalm, from behind and forcing his surrender. By that time Captain John Simcoe was dead. He had contracted pneumonia in May, and had been buried at sea off the Island of Anticosti. Young Graves was then only seven, and Percy five.[7]

Captain John Simcoe did not leave a will, and Letters of Administration granted to his wife were never administered. Further letters were granted to John Graves Simcoe in March 1786, but no evidence suggests that Mrs. Katherine Simcoe was a wealthy widow. She was comfortable no doubt, but no more than that.[8] A memorial placed in St. Andrew's Church, Cotterstock, bears this inscription:

> To the memory of John Simcoe Esq. late commander of His Majesty's ship Pembroke who died in ye Royal Service upon that important expedition against Quebeck in North America in the year 1759, aged 45 years. He spent the greatest part of his life in the service of his King and Country ever preferring the good of both to all private views. He was an accomplished officer esteemed for his great abilities in naval and military affairs, of unquestioned bravery and wearied diligence. He was an indulgent husband and tender parent and sincere friend, generous and benevolent to all. So that his loss to the public as well as to his family cannot be too much regretted this monument is erected in honour of his memory by his disconsolate widow Katherine Simcoe 1760. Underneath lie Pawlett William and John sons of the above John and Katherine Simcoe.

Captain Simcoe's correct age was forty-nine, not forty-five. People rarely seemed to keep accurate records of their ages in this period of history. Unfortunately the marriage entry at Walcott does not give his age.

Soon after the death of her husband, Katherine moved, with her two young sons, to the cathedral city of Exeter, in Devon. When he was not at sea in his ship HMS *Duke*, Captain Samuel Graves lived at Hembury Fort House, only a few miles from Exeter. His intermittent presence probably had a bearing on her decision, although she may have had other friends in the vicinity. Katherine had selected one of the most delightful cities in England. Founded by the Romans c. A.D. 50, Exeter lay in the heart of the territory of the Celtic Dumnonii tribe from whose name comes the County of Devon. The cathedral dates from the 14th century. In the Cathedral Close, both Katherine and her elder son were destined to end their lives, but exactly where they first lived in Exeter is unknown.

John Graves became a pupil at the ancient Exeter School and went from there to Eton in 1765. In later years he became a founding member of the Exeter School Old Boys Association.[9] The year before he went to Eton, his young brother Percy drowned in the River Exe. The Exeter *Flying Post*, dated 29 June 1764, reported the tragedy:

> Last Thursday evening Master Simcoe about twelve years of age going into the water with other boys was drowned at a place called Sandy Point between Exwick and Head Wear. After he was taken out of the water endeavour was used for bringing him to life again by rubbing his body with salt etc. etc. but without success.

Quite likely his elder brother was one of the other boys who went into the water. Even if he had not been a witness to the horror, the loss of young Percy at age ten, not twelve, had a severe impact on him. Overnight he had become an only child.

On 16 September 1765, Simcoe entered historic Eton College, situated on the banks of the River Thames near Windsor, in Berkshire. He was a medium-sized boy with dark hair and brown eyes. He spoke with more than a hint of broad Devon, with traces of the Midlands.[10] No doubt, encouraged or coerced by the masters, he would soon lose much of his regional accent and sound like a proper Etonian.

His mother paid an entrance fee of two guineas. The school records show that his tutor was Benjamin Heath, an assistant master at Eton from 1763 to 1771. The Eton College Register reveals that Simcoe boarded in a house called "Gulliver's." The "Dame" or keeper of the establishment was a lady named Bagwell.[11] (Gulliver's is now divided into small family homes for the masters and is situated on the Eton side of the college precinct.)

Several of his fellow scholars were from Devon; two of them became his close friends. The first, Vicary Gibbs, was the son of an Exeter surgeon, George Abraham Gibbs. The family lived in Cathedral Close and there Vicary was born. When Gibbs left Eton, he went on to study law. He became a distinguished advocate and at the peak of his career he was appointed as England's attorney general. He remained a lifelong firm friend of Simcoe's.

The second of his particular friends was Jeremiah Milles, son of a Dean of Exeter Cathedral. Like Gibbs, Milles chose a legal career but he abandoned it quite early in life, following his marriage to a wealthy heiress. Milles's brother Thomas, also a lawyer, became another of Simcoe's valued friends and was one of several trustees of his will.[12] A poem by William Boscawen written to "Colonel Simcoe on his return from San Domingo" suggests that here was yet another close friend.

Simcoe was unlucky in his headmaster. Dr. John Foster was a brilliant classical scholar, but very unpopular with the Eton boys, and a notorious flogger. A man of small stature, he was also the son of an Oxford tradesman, and both features made him a subject of scorn by young gentlemen. In his *History of Eton College*, C. M. Lyte described "The Rebellion of 1768" which began on 2 November when Simcoe was in the fifth form.[13] The cause of the outburst was, apparently, a dispute between assistant masters and sixth-form "Praeposters" (who had monitorial authority over fellow pupils). The dispute led to the sixth-form, together with some boys from the fifth and fourth forms, marching from Eton to Maidenhead where they spent the night at Marsh's Inn, no doubt taking full advantage of the tavern's hospitality.

An account of the whole incident was subsequently written by Jeremiah Milles, who was then in the sixth form. (Milles' account was a source for Lyte's.) Whether Simcoe was involved is a matter of debate. Certainly, events of his later life imply that if he stood up for himself as an adult, would he have done any less as a youth? On 27 November 1768, Vicary Gibbs wrote, "I have a particular reason for not saying anything of the rebellion. If I see you in the hollidays [sic] I will give you a full account. Don't mention this to anyone."[14]

This letter, addressed to Simcoe at Exeter, tends to indicate that he was away from Eton at the time, or that Gibbs preferred not to discuss in writing Simcoe's role. Perhaps Gibbs' legal instincts were already coming to the fore. He enquired whether Simcoe intended returning to Eton, or going to Oxford sooner than he had expected.

William Boscawen's poem to "Colonel Simcoe" suggests that both he and Simcoe were deeply involved:

> With you [Simcoe] rebellion's chance I tried
> Old Foster's threats, his arm defied
> And dar'd his empire mock
> But oh, how short our glory's fate
> How few escaped *The Block*.[15]

The rebellion occurred over 2–3 November, and Gibbs's letter was dated the 27th. This allowed time for Simcoe to have returned to Eton and, like many other rebels, taken Foster's flogging at the birching block, and to have arrived in Exeter before Gibbs was writing to him. Had he simply gone home unpunished, Foster would undoubtedly have expelled him, a disgrace he could not afford because it would damage his future prospects. He probably decided not to return to Eton because, never a happy place, it had become intolerable to him.

Simcoe matriculated at Merton College, Oxford, on 4 February 1769. According to *Alumnii Oxonienses*, Simcoe was a "Commoner" under Warden Henry Barton during what turned out to be a brief stay at Oxford University. Many sixteen-year-olds are undecided over which career to pursue. Close friends such as Gibbs and Milles, already contemplating the legal profession, were not following in their fathers' footsteps. At first, Simcoe, too, was leaning towards the law. On 10 February 1769, only days after matriculating at Oxford, he enrolled as a law student at Lincoln's Inn, one of London's Inns of Court.[16] These Inns are voluntary societies that have the power to call law students to the English Bar to become barristers. Enrollment was the extent of Simcoe's aspirations.

He might well have chosen a naval career, out of respect and admiration for the father he scarcely knew. Never very strong, he may have decided, with his mother's help, that life at sea might prove too strenuous for him. Evidence indicates that he suffered from asthma and bronchial difficulties later on, and in their letters his friends often enquired about his violent headaches. On the other hand, an overwhelming desire to make his own mark might have led him to an allied profession rather than into direct competition with Captain John Simcoe. Whatever his reasoning, his mother purchased an ensign's commission for him in the 35th Regiment of Foot. The commission was dated 27 April 1770, when he was eighteen years of age.[17]

Some secondary sources recount that Simcoe spent time with a military tutor after he left Oxford. He may have done so, or filled the fifteen-month gap studying history, his favourite subject. Equally well his choice of the army may have been influenced by a somewhat older man and close friend. Edward Drewe was already serving as a lieutenant with the 35th. Some records of this regiment are missing, but it was stationed at Plymouth, Devon, in December 1769, four months before Simcoe received his first commission. When, on 12 March 1774, Simcoe was promoted to lieutenant, again by purchase of the commission, Drewe was promoted to captain.[18] Drewe's father, also named Edward, was a brother of another friend, Francis Drewe (1712-1773) of the Grange and Broadhembury.[19] Edward Jr. was an outspoken critic of certain absurd aspects of the training stressed in military manuals, and of the inappropriate uniforms designed by some of the wealthy colonels. Such officers purchased their commissions and designed and paid for the regimental dress from their own pockets. Somewhere, Simcoe learned, field uniforms at least should be chosen for practicality and safety, ideas which Drewe advocated.

Whatever his reasons, Simcoe had chosen a profession in which he could excel. He might have made an equally competent lawyer, but he might also have found that he preferred the field of battle to that in the courtroom. Perhaps the most telling comment came from Vicary Gibbs, who wrote to Simcoe on 2 August 1775: "as it was impossible for us both to reach the highest pitch of glory in the same profession our good fortune ordained that you should alter your original intention and prefer the field to the forum."[20]

TWO

"The Field, Not the Forum"

Simcoe passed the first four years of his military career in England, Wales, and Ireland. For him life was pleasant, and not too demanding, even though he was conscientious about learning his job. He was able to spend a reasonable amount of time in his home city of Exeter, enjoying a busy social life and making new friends. In 1773 he became a Freemason, joining the Union Lodge, which met at the Globe Tavern in Cathedral Close. (The Globe was destroyed by enemy action during the Second World War.) One of his proposers for the Freemasons was "Brother Cholwich," a member of a well known and respected Devon family. A boy named Cholwich who had been at Eton with Simcoe was probably this same person. Apart from these early references, little evidence suggests that Simcoe was a particularly active member.[1]

When he was travelling around the country with his regiment, he maintained a regular correspondence with friends. Extant letters, in collections, of those received by Simcoe, give much insight into the activities of his friends, as well as his own. On 18 April 1774, Jeremiah Milles wrote to Simcoe, who was then serving in Wales, outlining his ambitions to be a barrister, describing his many visits to Exeter, and bringing his friend up to date on happenings in that city. Milles also mentioned Simcoe's forthcoming journey from Wales to Ireland.[2]

By that time, Simcoe had received his promotion, by purchase, to lieutenant in the 35th Foot.[3] He would be going to Ireland because his regiment had received a posting to the garrison at Dublin. In certain parts of Ireland, garrison duty meant being among hostile people, particularly in Roman Catholic areas. Dublin, however, was a popular posting because of the social life that revolved around the "court" of the lord lieutenant and the commander of British forces.

Another friend, James White wrote, in July 1774, addressing his letter to Simcoe at Dublin Barracks. White was responding to a letter in which Simcoe outlined his military wanderings in Snowdonia, North Wales. He also reminded Simcoe of his portrait, before which White would often stand and contemplate. White did not say where the picture was located, but most likely it hung in Mrs. Simcoe's home. The earliest known portrait of Simcoe is a full length one, showing him, at about aged twenty, as an ensign in the 35th (Royal Sussex) Regiment, hair powdered, red coat faced orange, with silver lace. The portrait was attributed to the artist Zoffany. [4] (A copy of the ensign portrait is now in the Samuel E. Weir collection at Niagara-on-the-Lake, Ontario.)

Vicary Gibbs wrote Simcoe on 28 April 1774. Still at Oxford and hoping to receive his Bachelor's degree by Christmas, Gibbs also admitted contemplating Simcoe's likeness. He recalled that it was in "Mrs. Simcoe's room." Gibbs mentioned his own health problems — pains in his chest, which he attributed to a "sedentary life." He still intended to study law. If Simcoe had second thoughts about leaving Oxford, he had no cause for regrets; military leadership seemed tailored for him. Gibbs wrote again in November, complaining of having been laid up with a fever after travelling around the country on horseback. He also mentioned Simcoe's talent for writing poetry. While some might belittle the strength of his muse, undaunted, he continued to write poems through his lifetime. Aware of Simcoe's deep interest in military heros, Gibbs discussed the campaigns of Alexander and Caesar. In a letter Milles sent early in 1775, he made reference to his friend's "violent headaches." Simcoe's health worsened over the ensuing years, but it rarely prevented him zealously carrying out his duties.[5]

By the time Simcoe received this letter, the vast differences between Great Britain and her Thirteen Colonies in North America were coming to a head. Difficulties were centred on Boston, the most important trading port on the Atlantic seaboard. On 5 March 1770 the Boston

Massacre had inflamed feelings against British troops. The Boston Tea Party, on 16 December 1773, was a strong protest against any "taxation without representation." Dressed as "Indians," certain Bostonians boarded the cargo ships, removed the tea and threw it into the harbour. In response, Parliament passed the Boston Port Bill in May 1774. Boston would be shut down until the colonists had paid for the destroyed tea. In July the government dispatched a fleet under the command of Simcoe's godfather, Samuel Graves, a rear admiral since 1772. By the time the fleet began an attempted blockade of the port, Graves had been placed in command of the American Station of the Royal Navy and promoted vice admiral.[6]

Meanwhile, the army was mobilising to reinforce the British garrison at Boston, as well as major key points. Among the many troops, the 35th Regiment embarked in transports bound for Boston. On 17 June more than 2,000 British troops under Generals William Howe, Henry Clinton, and John Burgoyne set out to drive away hordes of rebels who were entrenching themselves on high points around Boston, including Breed's Hill and Dorchester Heights. Badly mauled on Breed's Hill, the British force retired after driving away the rebels. Part of the 35th Regiment was with the British defenders, but Simcoe was still aboard his transport and did not land until the 19th. Captain Edward Drewe, who was with the men of the 35th at Breed's Hill, was severely wounded and soon invalided home. What became known as the Battle of Bunker Hill was in fact fought on Breed's Hill, which the rebels had fortified by mistake; they had been ordered to place the defences on Bunker Hill.

Admiral Graves's efforts to close the port at Boston were being thwarted. He arrived with an inadequate fleet, too few ships for the purpose, and many of them unsuitable. The large war ships carried heavy guns appropriate to bombarding the city, but he required small maneuverable vessels to patrol the many points that allowed rebel-owned small boats, often oared, to slip through unchecked.[7]

On 22 June, Simcoe wrote his first letter home to his mother and gave his own interpretation of events at Breed's Hill. Like Britons and Loyalists, he never referred to the enemy as "Patriots" but as "rebels":

> Dear Madam,
> We arrived here on the 19th being the last ship of the fleet. Two days before our arrival the dreadful scene of civil war commenced. for at a distance we saw the flames of Charlestown [today part of Boston] and steered into harbour by it's [sic] direction.

On our arrival we learned that the rebels had taken possession of the heights on the opposite side, from whence the town at that time was blockaded by numbers, was endangered. To force this was absolutely necessary and it was done in the most glorious manner — an action by the confession of veteran jealousy that exceeds whatever had before happened in America and equalled the legends of romance. It proves to me how very narrow are the limits of experience. Our light infantry was commanded by Drewe, whose behaviour was such as outdoes any panegyrick by every confession.[8]

Simcoe hoped the "check" at Breed's/Bunker Hill would lead to an "effectual reconciliation" with the rebels. Like many officers, particularly those of very senior rank, Simcoe thought the "civil war" would be of short duration.

Edward Drewe was so moved by his experience at the battle, and by his friendship with John Graves Simcoe, that he wrote a lengthy poem about both subjects. His work was included in a collection of poems published in 1792 by their mutual friend, the West Country historian, Richard Polwhele. He described Drewe's effort as an "Elegaic Piece." Drewe followed with a short statement, "On the authors leaving Boston in 1775 for the cure of his wounds sustained at Bunkers Hill." A few verses serve to show the strength of the relationship between himself and Simcoe:

> Oh Dorilas and must we part?
> Alas the fatal day
> and must I leave thee, generous youth
> and tempt the raging sea?
> Must we entwine the firmest link,
> In friendship's golden chain?
> 'Tis so stern Destiny decrees;
> and friendship pleads in vain.
>
> In infancy, ere reason dawn'd
> We felt her sacred beam
> 'twas Love instinctive filled the spot
> Where now dwells pure esteem
> And as we ripen'd into man
> that love was still the same;

Save that the spark, in childhood nursed
Glow'd with a stronger flame.

Say, had thy Edward e'er a grief
That was not mourned by thee:
Or hadst thou e'er a secret joy
Which brightens not in me?

Each thought each act, seem'd but to flow
From one united mind;
So close had friendship's magic pow'r
Our mutual hearts entwined.

When late fell Discord, rear'd her torch
O'er Boston's hapless land;
Unmov'd we left our weeping friends
At Honour's high Command.[9]

More of the same followed. Theirs was indeed a close relationship. Fortunately, the two lived in an age where such words dedicated by one man to another did not imply anything other than true and loyal friendship.

While Drewe was returning home, Simcoe remained in Boston. He was full of suggestions for the conduct of the war. In the journal he later published, writing in the third person, he advocated, among other innovations, recruitment of "negroes" and making full use of the loyal colonists:

> His intimate connection with that most upright and zealous officer the late Admiral Graves who commanded at Boston in the year 1775 and some services which he was pleased to entrust him with, brought him acquainted with many of the American Loyalists; from them he learned the practability of raising troops in the country whenever it should be opened to the King's forces; and the propriety of such a measure appeared to be self evident. He therefore importuned Admiral Graves to ask General Gage that he might enlist such negroes as were in Boston and with them put himself under the direction of Sir James Wallace, who was actively engaged in Rhode Island, and to whom that

colony had opposed negroes: adding to the Admiral who seemed surprised at his request, "that he entertained no doubt he should soon exchange them for whites." Gen. Gage, the Admiral's application informed him that the negroes were, not sufficiently numerous to be servicable and he had other employments for those at Boston.[10]

By the autumn of 1775, Admiral Graves's recommendations did not carry much weight. He was discredited when he failed to stop traffic in and out of Boston harbour, even though the fault lay with the inadequacy of his fleet. London bureaucrats rarely understood the exigencies of conditions in the field. However, the War Office was making plans to recruit white-skinned loyal colonials and copper-skinned aboriginal tribes. The British Indian Department would strive to keep the native warriors on the side of the Crown. Loyalists would be recruited to serve in Provincial Corps of the British Army. Four military departments would be established in places where the army could be in firm control, a safe haven for provincials when not operating against the rebels.

New York City, on Manhattan Island, as well as Long island and Staten Island, would form the Central Department, which would be in command of the other departments. The Northeastern would be Nova Scotia, headquarters in Halifax. The Northern Department would be the Province of Canada, headquarters Quebec City. The Southern would be Florida, headquarters Saint Augustine. Provincial Corps would be attached to each department. The first task facing the British Army would be capturing and securing New York. In October, General Gage resigned. He had never liked fighting against the people whom he regarded as his own. The new commander in chief in North America was General William Howe.

On 27 December 1775, Simcoe purchased a captaincy in the 40th Foot. He required alterations to his uniform. His facings would now be buff, his lace of gold.[11] He would command the Grenadier Company, a post that usually went to the senior captain. The Grenadiers were the tallest and strongest men in the regiment, intended to be sent in wherever a position needed to be strengthened. Minimum height for a grenadier was five feet, nine inches, and where possible all commissioned officers would be that tall. However, in the Britain of the late 18th century rules could be broken owing to corruption within the system. Having the funds, or knowing the right people, could override the rules. Admiral Graves may have been the one to help out, as Simcoe may not have met the height requirements. Boot heels and a tall bearskin cap would, of course, mask a certain shortcoming.

News soon arrived from Jeremiah Milles, who wrote from London's Inner Temple. He informed Simcoe that Edward Drewe had been made a Freeman of the City of Exeter for his exploits at Bunker/Breed's Hill. Milles wrote again in March, by which time his father had purchased him a set of chambers in Lincoln's Inn, heartland of the legal profession. Milles had decided to call a spare room in his chambers "Simcoe's apartment." Simcoe had certainly inspired loyalty in his friends. He himself, despite supervising the training of his grenadiers, had considerable time for letter writing.

In January 1776, Admiral Graves was recalled, owing to his failure to carry out orders from London. The fault still lay with the home government, who were blind to his problems, and had never allowed him enough equipment to perform adequately. The new naval commander was Admiral Richard Howe, the commander in chief's brother. In Boston the British Army had reached a stalemate. With land routes firmly in rebel hands, General Howe began making plans to evacuate the army by sea. The evacuation of the army was accelerated when the rebels brought guns from the recently captured Fort Ticonderoga, and seized Dorchester Heights that overlooked the city.

While the army in Boston was pinned down, the action had moved to an attempt by the rebels, under Richard Montgomery and Benedict Arnold, to capture Canada. Montgomery had moved from Lake Champlain and the Richelieu River to Montreal. Arnold had led an expedition from the Kennebec River, in what is now Maine, directly towards the fortress of Quebec, overlooking the St. Lawrence. An attack on New Year's Eve failed. Montgomery was killed, and Arnold wounded. Later, Arnold led a retreat to Montreal to await reinforcements.

Meanwhile, in Boston, accommodation for troops and officers alike was crowded. On 13 March, Simcoe wrote to his mother:

> It is past two o'clock in the morning. I am Captain of our Picquet [party of sentries]. In one corner of the room on one half of my bed made (luxury indeed) of clean straw, lies an officer asleep with his feet towards the fire. He snores, but not in one drone, but in several modulations. My bayonet is stuck in the table, the socket of which serves as a candlestick to the night light. One half of my chair is now burning in the fire and the other, when I shall have finished this letter will be

applied to the same use, serving rather to light the room than to warm it, there being no want of fuel from a multitude of wooden houses and coal. Underneath me is a Capt. Bradstreets: on the same floor my company repose almost drowning the solo of my companion with an almost anti-musical concert. Scattered in the room lie many excellent and valuable books, picked up in the street by my sergeant, where they were thrown in the trunk that contained them to form part of a barricade.[12]

One can hear, even smell, that small room somewhere in Boston. Simcoe, a lover of books, was affronted by such wanton destruction of so valuable a resource. Odd is his reference to his bayonet. Officers were not expected to carry them nor to make use of muskets; that was for the rank and file, although officers of flank companies carried fusils. On 17 March, four days after Simcoe had finished his letter, the British Army began to evacuate Boston. Guarded by Admiral Howe's ships of war, and riding in unarmed transports, the troops moved to Halifax, to be ready for a renewed assault on the colonies.

Reinforcements arrived in Quebec from Britain, before much help reached Benedict Arnold. The military governor of Canada, General Guy Carleton, had cleared the province of rebels by June. Among his officers were the Baron von Riedesel, commander of German troops, and John Burgoyne, who had been on a leave of absence from Boston. Americans still scornfully refer to all the Germans as "Hessians" and mercenaries. However, they were also subjects of King George III in his capacity as Elector of Hanover.

In July Jeremiah Milles wrote again, noting that Simcoe's comrade in arms, Edward Drewe, could usually be seen in Moll's Coffee House in Cathedral Close. By that time the British Army was leaving Halifax, bound for the relief of New York City, and General George Washington had taken command of the rebels' Continental Army. On 4 July the rebels proclaimed their Declaration of Independence. A few weeks later an expedition under General Henry Clinton failed to capture Charleston, South Carolina.

In August General Howe opened his campaign against New York and New Jersey. On the 27th the British drove the rebels out of Long Island. By 15 September, following the Battle of Harlem Heights, Howe had occupied New York City. Simcoe's future friend, General Alexander Leslie, commanded the British troops at Harlem Heights. Howe could now establish his Central Department. On 28 October, Howe and Leslie drove Washington out of White Plains, north of New York on the Hudson River. The 40th Regiment was involved in most of these actions, but Simcoe did not leave a record of his participation. In the midst of the energetic campaign, Simcoe's mother, Katherine, died. The Exeter *Flying Post* in the 28 June issue reported: "Saturday last died at her house in the Close Mrs. Simcoe, much lamented by her friends."[13]

When or how Simcoe received the news is not known, but Jeremiah Milles wrote a letter of condolence dated 19 October 1776. Milles reported that his brother, Dick, had been ordained by the Bishop of Exeter, and that a mutual friend, Tobias Cholwich, was standing for Parliament. This was probably the "Brother Cholwich" who had proposed Simcoe as a Freemason several years earlier. On his part, while grieving at being unable to comfort his mother in her last days, Simcoe was very much occupied with the war and he had scant time to dwell on events at home. Early in 1777 Simcoe received several important letters from Devonshire. One was from William Pitfield, a friend of the family and the apothecary responsible for drugs at Exeter Hospital. Pitfield, who was among the city's leading citizens, was in charge of some of Mrs. Simcoe's affairs. In a letter of condolence he wrote:

> Your poor mother's death was truly a release her last disorders were so exceedingly painful that no friend could wish her continuance. She made all provisions a good woman could for the payment of her debts.[14]

Pitfield sought Simcoe's instructions regarding a woman named Tozer, who had been in his mother's service and in receipt of an annuity from her. He wondered whether Simcoe wished to continue the annuity, although Pitfield thought that this was not necessary. Mrs. Simcoe also owed Pitfield £100. He had been able to sell some of her effects for £50, and he requested Simcoe to send him a draft for the balance. Little evidence suggests that Mrs. Simcoe was more than comfortably off. The sum of £950 for her son's captaincy must have been a considerable drain. (The cost of the captaincy was £1,500, but he would have obtained £550 from the sale of his lieutenancy.)

Also corresponding with Simcoe at this time was Admiral Samuel Graves. On his return to England he had gone into virtual retirement at Hembury Fort House, near Honiton in east Devon. Graves admitted to his godson that he had no further naval ambitions and was content to remain at his country estate. Widowed some years before, he had then married in 1769 Miss Margaret Spinckes of Aldwinkle,

Northamptonshire, an heiress in her own right. Growing up in Aldwinkle with her grandmother, Jemima Steward Spinckes, was Miss Elizabeth Gwillim, a wealthy girl who was orphaned at birth. Her father, Colonel Thomas Gwillim, had died on duty in Germany sometime after she was conceived. Elizabeth was baptized on 22 September 1762. Her mother was buried on the 23rd.[15] She was a frequent visitor to Hembury Fort House, and almost from the start the admiral looked upon her as a future Mrs. Simcoe. In May 1776, her fourteenth year, her Grandmother Spinckes died. Miss Gwillim then came to reside most of the time in Devonshire with the Graves.

On 11 September 1777, the 40th Regiment was involved in the hard-fought and costly British success on the banks of the Brandywine Creek, in Pennsylvania, not far from Philadelphia. Simcoe was severely wounded, but the nature of these wounds was not revealed. Some of the highest casualties on that campaign were borne by a Provincial Corps called the Queen's Rangers. Many British officers were scornful of the colonials, but the most astute recognised that the guerrilla hit-and-run tactics at which the Provincials excelled, could do far more damage against the rebels than set-piece battles of the European manner. Simcoe was one of the latter. His conviction grew as word arrived that General "Gentleman Johnny" Burgoyne was in trouble. He was in command of an army of British, German, Canadian and Provincial troops that had descended from Montreal.

Popular myth states that Burgoyne was supposed to come south and affect a junction with General Howe, who would come north towards Albany. In fact, Burgoyne was aware, before he left Canada, that Howe would move on Philadelphia. Burgoyne's orders were that he was to reach Albany and place himself under Howe's command. Military etiquette decreed that General Carleton, now Sir Guy, could not lead the expedition because he was senior to Howe.[16] A junior general was required because New York (province/state) was Howe's territory.

By October, Burgoyne found his army surrounded and outnumbered at Saratoga. On the 17th he surrendered to rebel General Horatio Gates. Howe had taken Philadelphia on 26 September, since when Simcoe had been convalescing in that city. So was the commander of the Queen's Rangers, Major James Wemyss. The corps was temporarily under Lieutenant Colonel John Randolph Grymes, but headquarters was considering a permanent replacement for Wemyss. At age twenty-five Captain John Graves Simcoe saw his opportunity.

PART II
THE DASHING PARTISAN

The American Revolutionary War lasted from 1776, with the Declaration of Independence, until after the Treaty of Separation in 1783. The war was not confined to Britain and her rebelling colonies. Both sides acquired allies, which complicated the tensions.

In May 1776, the Continental Congress, the rebels' governing body to conduct the war, sent a mission to Paris, led by Benjamin Franklin, in quest of support. In August, Britain began recruiting in several German states. In April 1777, the young French aristocrat, the Marquis de Lafayette, arrived in the colonies with a party of French volunteers. Spain declared war on Britain in June 1779, on the assurance that France would help her recover Gibraltar.

In 1780, France, Spain, Austria, Prussia, Denmark, and Sweden formed a League of Armed Neutrality, and in November, Britain declared war on Holland to prevent that country joining the league. Britain was also fighting in India to prevent the French, Dutch and Portuguese, or Indians, seizing the assets of the East India Company. Empress Catherine II (The Great) of Russia was also in a conquering mood.

Britain recruited Germans, and then Loyalists resident in the colonies, as a source of support for the limited number of British regular troops she could commit to North America. They were organised into four military departments, established as headquarters for the conduct of the war. Along the frontier were aboriginal nations who traded with the officers of the British Indian Department stationed at Niagara, Detroit and other posts. Encouraging Indians to take to the war path was fairly simple. They resented the way frontiersmen were encroaching on the lands that had been guaranteed, by treaty, to be closed to white settlement.

The rebel Continental Congress established the Continental Army, regulars commanded by George Washington. Militia units in the various colonies, usually dating from before the rebellion began, tended to support the Continentals, but they were divided. Some units were mainly rebels, but Loyalists were stronger in others. Most Loyalists who served joined Provincial Corps of the British Army that were stationed in the military departments — troops that took to the field against the rebels, sometimes with British regulars, at other times by themselves. Loyalists resident close to department headquarters turned out with the militia when such headquarters were threatened with attack. A few units, the Staten Island Militia, for example, left their home turf. Several times they crossed into New Jersey to do battle with the rebels. The longer the war continued, the greater was British dependence on her loyal Provincials, a fact seldom understood. Afterwards, British officers often blamed the failure of the war on the lack of Loyalist support, but in fact it was considerable.

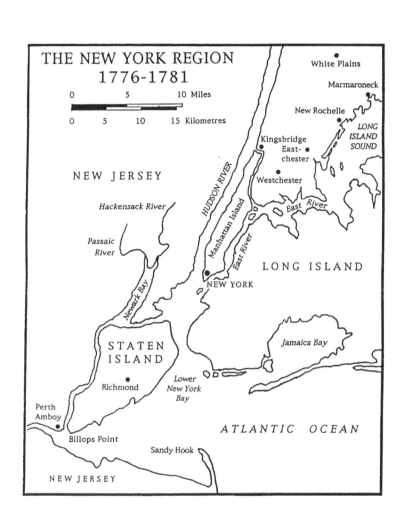

THE NEW YORK REGION
1776-1781

0   5   10 Miles

0   5   10   15 Kilometres

White Plains

Marmaroneck

New Rochelle

LONG ISLAND SOUND

NEW JERSEY

Kingsbridge

East-chester

Hackensack River

HUDSON RIVER

Westchester

East River

Passaic River

Manhattan Island

East River

LONG ISLAND

Newark Bay

NEW YORK

STATEN ISLAND

Jamaica Bay

Richmond

Lower New York Bay

Perth Amboy

ATLANTIC OCEAN

Billops Point

Sandy Hook

NEW JERSEY

THREE

The Green Jackets

John Graves Simcoe's Queen's Rangers had the reputation as one of the most effective regiments that served the British cause during the American Revolutionary War. Among others in the Central Military Department who qualified for such praise was the British Legion, led by Banastre Tarleton. Author Stephen Jenkins called Simcoe, Tarleton, Andreas Emmerich and Oliver DeLancey "the ablest and most dashing partisans of the British army...."[1] The first two, an enterprising, daring Simcoe and a positively reckless Tarleton, were British professional officers; Emmerich and DeLancey were Americans, the first of Dutch/German descent, the second of a French Huguenot family. Emmerich led "Chasseurs," riflemen; DeLancey raised three battalions of infantry and held Provincial rank as a brigadier general. With a few exceptions the men who followed all four regimental commanders were Americans who had remained loyal to the King.

At first, green was the colour of the coats worn by Provincial Corps. These corps were inferior to the British regular regiments; they were not included in The Army List. Officers of like rank were considered one rank lower than officers in regular units. At first, they were not entitled to receive half-pay when their corps were reduced, nor were they entitled to pensions if they were disabled. In the case of Simcoe and Tarleton, both were on The Army List, but with the ranks they held in the army, or in their regular regiments.

As time passed, and many of the Provincial Corps proved their worth, benefits were gradually extended, and officers and men were issued with red coats of the British regulars. Not every regimental commander welcomed the change to red. One who rejected this supposed honour was John Graves Simcoe. Men operating as irregulars were safer in green, which was bright in the springtime, at the start of the yearly campaigns, and faded so that it blended into autumn foliage. Green had other advantages as well. Certain rebel regiments also wore green, and Simcoe's Rangers were able to move among the enemy without being identified automatically as British soldiers. At first, the corps was light infantry. Gradually, light cavalry — Simcoe chose to call them "Hussars" — were added, and a kilted Highland company uniformed in "old government" tartan, the sett first worn by the Black Watch following the Jacobite rising of 1745–46. Even then, all the Queen's Rangers retained their green jackets.[2]

When Banastre Tarleton received command of the British Legion, a combined force of infantry and cavalry, he, too, retained green coats. Thus the men of the British Legion were nicknamed "Tarleton's Greens."[3]

Robert Rogers and the First and Second Queen's Rangers

The name Queen's Rangers originated during the Seven Years' War, when the legendary Robert Rogers (1731–1795) received a warrant to raise companies of rangers to operate with greater mobility than conventional infantry. They were uniformed, as far as is known, in green. (Rogers was the recipient of the Hollywood treatment in the 1940 film *Northwest Passage*, based on the book by Kenneth Roberts. Spencer Tracey played Rogers, sporting a little cap, blue but, in shape, similar to those worn by American soldiers in the Second World War. It in no way resembled any hat thought to have been used by 18th century rangers.)

Rogers did not invent ranger methods; these had been used on the American frontier for some years, but he did perfect their tactics. The first requirement for a ranger was that he be able to endure severe hardship for long periods of time, miles from the comforts of civilisation. Whereas most regular troops and Provincials went into winter quarters when the weather turned bitter, rangers often operated all year round. In summer they marched or travelled in whaleboats, bateaux or canoes; in winter they used sleighs, skates or snowshoes.[4]

On scouting missions rangers walked widely spread out to prevent more than one being a target for an enemy marksman. When crossing swampy ground, they marched abreast to confound trackers. They made camp after dark on a spot where sentries would have a clear view of the enemy and could not be surprised. When several hundred were out together, they marched in three columns, the outer ones some twenty yards from the middle one. Men so spread out were difficult to surround. They were adept at setting up an ambush — what Simcoe wrote as "ambuscade."[5]

Following the peace of 1763, Rogers entered into several enterprises that brought him into disrepute. He spent some time in England, where he was imprisoned for debt. After his debts had been paid by his brother James, Robert returned to North America in 1775. Viewed with suspicion by the rebels, he was confined in Philadelphia, from which he had escaped by 6 July. He made his way to Staten Island, where the British fleet had arrived, and General William Howe was about to land his army. From Howe, Rogers received a warrant, dated in August 1776, to raise a new regiment of Queen's Rangers.

The corps was enlarged when the Royal Governor of Virginia, Lord Dunmore, arrived at New York bringing with him the Queen's Loyal Virginia Regiment, which amalgamated with the Queen's Rangers. With the recruits Rogers's agents had found in New York and New Jersey and the Virginians, the regiment was close to full strength, 500 men. During the winter of 1776–77, Rogers relinquished command of the corps, possibly through loss of interest. The corps was employed on garrison duty in New York City, work that had scant appeal for this man of action.[6] Sent to guard the outpost at Maroneck, Connecticut, the Rangers were badly mauled on 21 October and forced to evacuate their position. An inspector general appointed to report on the Provincial units, found that the Queen's Rangers were in very poor condition.[7]

During the Seven Years' War, Rogers had treated his men as equals, but by 1776 he had undergone a personality change, possibly owing to alcoholism. Serving with the Rangers was William Jarvis. When his cousin, Stephen Jarvis, wished to transfer to the Rangers from the South Carolina Loyalists, Robert Rogers' behaviour gave him second thoughts:

> I set off to apply to Mr. [William] Jarvis to procure an exchange; when to my great surprise I saw the Lt. Col.

of this Regt., who was mounted, attack the Sentinel, at his Marquee, and beat him most unmercifully with his cane, over the head and shoulders. After viewing this transaction I wheeled about, took my knapsack, and marched off with my Regt., without even taking leave of my relations.[8]

After command of the corps passed to James Wemyss, who had come from Simcoe's own 40th Regiment, training began in earnest. In the previous autumn, the experienced Prussian officer, Baron Wilhelm von Knyphausen, had arrived from Europe with 4,500 German troops, and General Howe gave him the command of a division. After Major James Wemyss succeeded Robert Rogers, Howe assigned the Queen's Rangers to von Knyphausen's division. Howe's expedition reached Philadelphia via Chesapeake Bay in ships, and over land, by 26 September. Washington was to the north of the city. Howe left Henry Clinton in command and taking von Knyphausen's division, 9,000 strong, led an expedition to Germantown, seven miles off, to keep Washington's army at bay. On 4 October the two armies met. After heavy fighting Washington withdrew. At the Battle of Germantown, Major James Wemyss received the wound that opened the way for John Graves Simcoe. On 15 October, at Philadelphia, Howe gave him the command with the local (Provincial) rank of major, although he remained, for the time being a captain in the British Army. The Queen's Rangers were then encamped outside Germantown, and there Simcoe proceeded the next morning. Before long the army learned that both Howe and Clinton had been knighted, Howe for capturing New York, and Clinton as a peace offering because Burgoyne, not he, had been given command of the expedition from Canada.

SIMCOE'S REGIMENT

Meanwhile, since his wounding at Brandywine, Simcoe's health had improved. He now felt well able to assume the active command of the Queen's Rangers. With Howe secure in Philadelphia, Washington set up his winter quarters at Valley Forge, some twenty miles farther up the Schuylkill River. The stage was set for gruelling campaigns that were designed for ranger techniques. The North American colonies were thinly populated. Vast stretches of the seaboard colonies were still heavily wooded. Wagon roads were few, but the countryside was criss-crossed by forest trails bordered by suitable cover. Light troops, whether on foot or mounted, could avoid main roads, move along trails and launch surprise attacks or circle round to cut off the enemy or to attack flanks.

The Queen's Rangers had lost heavily, both at Brandywine and at Germantown. Simcoe's first task was to bring his corps up to strength again. While stationed in Philadelphia he acquired his company of thirty kilted Highlanders. From North Carolina, they had been captured at the fiasco at Moore's Creek Bridge in February 1776. An army of rebels had ambushed men belonging to the North Carolina Loyalists, killing many and sending more as prisoners to Philadelphia. Nearly all were Jacobites, but they nevertheless chose to serve "German Geordie." Early in 1778, Simcoe was able to form his first troop of thirty cavalrymen — the light cavalry he preferred to call Hussars. After a German Jaeger's "friendly fire" killed one of his riders because his cap resembled too closely those of the rebel cavalry, Simcoe selected a distinctive high cap so that his side would instantly recognise one of their own.[9]

He had a feel for the effective use of light infantry, and cavalry as well. He also formed a company of grenadiers who would be useful in following up where the lighter troops made openings. In his *Journal* Simcoe specified much that Robert Rogers had written for the first Queen's Rangers. The men must be very fit, and able to operate independently. When moving as a regiment, they to travel in three divisions, 100 yards apart. From Philadelphia, the Rangers were employed protecting local farmers who brought in supplies, and in attacking Washington's outposts, taking prisoners in many short skirmishes with rebel patrols. He claimed that his infantry could march ninety miles in a week, and the cavalry could cover more ground.[10]

He added some rifles as sharpshooters to his corps. Rifles had a longer range and were more accurate than muskets, but they also took longer to load. At that time riflemen were not equipped with bayonets, which prevented them joining other foot soldiers in a follow-up charge. Most of his light infantrymen carried muskets and socketed bayonets that they attached to their weapons. Discharging of muskets was usually the preliminary to charging with the bayonet, a technique that demanded considerable practice. When not on patrol, the Rangers trained constantly, not the parade-ground drill of the regular regiments but to operate in the fields or woods, learning the means of attack and defense, how to make use of cover, and to give support to one another. Rangers were also expected to behave well. Simcoe frequently cautioned them against mistreating prisoners or plundering, which would make them unpopular with the civilian population. He also kept a book on the conduct of the men, noting cases of drinking, which would also make Rangers offensive to the enemy. Guards, traditionally, were supervised by sergeants. Simcoe ordered commissioned officers to assume this duty, as the "Vigilance of Gentlemen" was superior to that of non-commissioned officers.[11]

In February 1778, word reached Howe that General "Mad Anthony" Wayne was out with a large force foraging for General Washington. Howe dispatched the Queen's Rangers and the 42nd Regiment to intercept Wayne. They first took up a position at Haddonfield, then fell back to Cooper's Ferry on the Delaware River, where under cover of thick woods they formed a defensive line. Some of Simcoe's Hussars went forward to lure the rebels towards the concealed British. The kilted 42nd attacked while the Rangers cut round the enemy left to hit them on the flank. The enemy were driven back in confusion. By then bad news arrived. France had formed an alliance with the Continental Congress, and in the spring would be sending a fleet carrying regular soldiers to come to Washington's aid.

Sir William Howe soon resigned, and Sir Henry Clinton became the new commander in chief. Clinton realised that he could not hold both Philadelphia and New York with the troops he had, and in June he began to evacuate the former. The withdrawal to New York would be by land, because he had not sufficient transports to carry some 20,000 troops. The army set out in two columns, the Queen's Rangers as the vanguard of the left column, skirmishing along the way. Washington followed after Clinton hoping for a chance to attack.

Near Allentown, about halfway, Lieutenant Wickham, of the Hussars, and Simcoe, while reconnoitering, encountered two men who approached, mistaking them for American officers. Wickham promptly introduced Simcoe as "Colonel Lee" — Henry Lee, Washington's cavalry commander. One said he had a son in Lee's corps, and the two proceeded to tell Simcoe just what he longed to know. Then, when one wondered aloud what Sir Henry Clinton was doing, Simcoe replied, as he took them prisoners: "You can ask him yourself, for we are British."[12]

Colonel Henry Lee, nicknamed "Light Horse Harry," was a true Virginia gentleman, whom Simcoe soon held in high regard. (He was also the father of another Virginia gentleman, Robert Edward Lee, who surrendered the Confederate Army to Ulysses Grant at Appomattox in 1865.)[13]

On 27 June the Queen's Rangers attacked a rebel patrol, then discovered 700 militia coming towards them. They attacked and the militia fled, but Simcoe was wounded. The wound was not life-threatening but the pain was "excruciating" and compelled him to retire. Captain Arthur Ross took temporary command. A heat wave struck and by the 28th when 6,000 of Washington's force attacked the British rear the heat had become horrendous. When more of Washington's forces arrived, the two armies joined at Monmouth. Simcoe was still off duty for the battle in which Washington had 142 killed and 300 wounded (37 dead of sunstroke). Of Clinton's troops 190 were killed, 390 wounded, and 57 died from sunstroke. The Queen's Rangers and other light infantry had penetrated so far into Washington's army that Clinton had to send two more battalions to extricate them all.[14]

On 5 July the Rangers, with Simcoe recovered and again in command, reached Sandy Hook, where they covered the army's embarkation for Staten Island. In the whole operation not one man had deserted or had fallen out, unfit to continue. From the safe Staten Island base, the Rangers continued skirmishing and reconnoitering. Sergeant Kelly, of the Hussar troop, was ambushed and captured by the enemy. Kelly had recently deserted the rebels to join Simcoe, who demanded an exchange. He threatened that if Kelly were executed he would execute six rebels in retaliation. Kelly was returned to him.

That summer of 1778, Banastre Tarleton, from the 79th Regiment, received the command of the British Legion. Often supporting each other's corps, Simcoe and Tarleton had much meeting of the minds. Simcoe acquired a three-pounder cannon, nicknamed a "grasshopper" because of its mobility, and three artillerymen to fire it. At this stage, the Queen's Rangers were considerably more than a conventional regiment. Before the weather had turned too harsh for campaigning, Simcoe had led his Rangers with the attacking forces at Quinton's Bridge, Hancock's Bridge, and Monmouth, all in New Jersey, and at East Chester, Valentine's Hill, and Tappan, in New York.[15]

The Quinton's and Hancock's encounters, which took place in March, were close together on the Alloway River. Judge William Hancock and his brother, both Loyalists, were killed accidentally when troops attacked the Hancock house. Simcoe was very upset because he understood that the judge was not living at home. No one told him that Hancock usually returned home for the night. American sources describe these actions as "massacres."[16]

For the cold season of 1778–79 the Rangers went into winter quarters at Oyster Bay, Long Island, but not for a restful time. Patrolling continued, and training when other duties did not interfere. Yet Simcoe found time to make more new friends. Major John André, of the 54th Regiment, was a deputy adjutant general to Sir Henry Clinton, who assisted in the gathering of intelligence. In André, Simcoe found another kindred spirit. The bond was similar to the one he had established with Edward Drewe before he was invalided home. Another new friend was Francis Lord Rawdon, heir to the Anglo-Irish Earl of Moira. Rawdon led the Volunteers of Ireland, a Provincial Corps nearly as active and effective as Simcoe's. Rawdon and Tarleton both came from wealthy families, an advantage that Simcoe did not share. The first two could call on private funds for equipment, while Simcoe was dependent on his own earnings or on the funds and equipment the army was willing to supply.

During the winter he was recruiting for his Hussars, whose ranks had been depleted in the field. At New York City he placed an advertisement in Rivington's *Royal Gazette*:

ALL ASPIRING HEROES
Have now an opportunity of distinguishing themselves by joining
THE QUEEN'S RANGERS
Commanded by
LIEUTENANT-COLONEL SIMCOE

> Every spirited young man will receive every encouragement, be immediately mounted on an elegant horse, and furnished with clothing, accoutrements &c, to the amount of FORTY GUINEAS, by applying to Cornet Spencer, at his quarters, No. 1033 Water Street, or his rendezvous, Hewitt's Tavern, near the Coffee House on Golden Hill.

> Whoever brings a recruit shall instantly receive TWO GUINEAS.

VIVANT REX ET REGINA

Simcoe may have been stretching things a bit. Forty guineas for each man's equipment was extravagant, and elegant horses were certainly in short supply, even at New York. Nor was he yet a lieutenant colonel, even in the field.

By the spring the Queen's Rangers were serving on the right flank of the army. Knowing that Howe was impressed with the corps, Simcoe wrote to his former commander in chief asking for "rank in the Army" for the Queen's Rangers.[17] Howe's response, which recognised the value of certain of his Provincial Corps, was not quite what Simcoe had in mind.

On 2 May, Howe arranged to have three of the corps placed on a special new American establishment, a higher status, but not for The Army List. The Queen's Rangers became the 1st American Regiment; the Volunteers of Ireland the 2nd, and the New York Volunteers the 3rd.[18] Simcoe now received local rank of lieutenant colonel. In late August, he led his Rangers back to Oyster Bay for a short break. Clinton, with Charles Lord Cornwallis as his second in command, set out for a second attempt to capture Charleston, South Carolina. This time they would be successful, although a long siege lay ahead of them. Left in command at New York was General von Knyphausen, a man Simcoe much respected.

When Simcoe learned of a "sinister event," he reported it to von Knyphausen. The rebels had assembled about fifty boats at Middlebrook, on the Rarita River, New Jersey, and Simcoe resolved on a raid to destroy the boats; otherwise, they might be used to transport a rebel force to attack New York. The operation was risky because militiamen and "Light Horse Harry" Lee's cavalry were thick on the ground. Washington himself was only twenty miles away, at Morristown.

With von Knyphausen's approval, Simcoe assembled his raiding party at Billop's Point, the southwest corner of Staten Island. He chose 300 Ranger infantrymen and Hussars, some mounted Loyalists from Colonel Christopher Billop's Staten Island Militia, and a troop of Bucks County Light Dragoons under a Captain Sandford. These dragoons had originally been raised near Philadelphia, and had come north with Clinton. The party crossed the short stretch of water in small boats, and captured the mainland village of Perth Amboy. Simcoe sent his infantry to South River Bridge and left them in command of his major, Richard Armstrong, to wait in ambush in the hope that some rebels would follow him there. And Simcoe set off with eighty of his cavalry and rode towards Middlebrook. At dawn militia were stirring, but most assumed that Simcoe's men were part of Henry Lee's cavalry.

Disappointment awaited. Simcoe found only eighteen boats at Middlebrook; the others had been moved elsewhere. After destroying the ones they found, they stopped at a rebel forage depot to feed their horses, still pretending to be Lee's men. To avoid returning to Perth Amboy, through an alarmed countryside, they went south to Hillsborough, released prisoners from the courthouse jail, burned the building and turned east. They intended to bypass an enemy post at Brunswick and meet up with the infantrymen Simcoe had left at South River Bridge.

A Loyalist serving as a guide accidentally led Simcoe into a large force of rebel militia. Riding with the advance guard of Hussars, Simcoe galloped forward hoping to break through the ambushing rebels, but his horse was shot dead under him and he fell, stunned. Captain Sandford took charge of the fierce fighting and rejoined the rest near South River Bridge. Major Armstrong led everyone to Perth Amboy and embarked. Henry Lee and Anthony Wayne attempted pursuit, but they were too late. Behind them the still barely conscious Simcoe was taken prisoner. One young rebel was about to plunge his bayonet into the prostrate Simcoe, but an older one called out, "Let him alone, the rascal is dead enough already!"[19]

NEW JERSEY 1776-1781

.

FOUR

Like a Common Criminal

Although the young rebel had decided against dispatching Simcoe with his bayonet, yet another militiaman claimed he would have shot him in the head, had he realised that he was looking at a colonel. "I thought all Colonels wore lace." A portrait of Simcoe as Colonel of the Queen's Rangers, 1790s era, shows him in an officer's coat, green with gold lace. Apparently, during the Revolutionary War, he wore a less ornate coat for service in the field so that he would not stand out from the other officers in the regiment.[1] Edward Drewe could be the man who influenced Simcoe to choose this form of camouflage.

Gradually, as Simcoe regained consciousness, he was appalled to find himself a prisoner of war. The rebels then removed him to the village of Brunswick and placed him in a tavern. The local people were ready for blood, because a popular Captain Vorhees, of the New Jersey Militia, had been killed during the raid. In his journal Simcoe sometimes wrote in the third person: "It was intended to bring Col. Simcoe to Capt. Vorhees's grave to shew him the cruelty of his people, but I could not answer it."[2]

The prisoners whom the rebels had captured "were with difficulty preserved by Mr. Clarkson, Mr. Morris (who bled Col. Simcoe) and another gentleman from assassination ..." The governor of New Jersey, William Livingston, after making:

> a little harangue ... to the populace, thought it necessary to give Lt. Col. Simcoe the following written protection. Tho the populace much angered, refrain from abusing a Br. officer & wounded — treat according to the rules of war as practised by all civilized nations.[3]

Mr. Alexander Kelloch, the Queen's Rangers' surgeon, soon arrived in Brunswick. He had come with a flag of truce to take care of his colonel. The flag was carried by a "Serjeant," bringing Edward Heifernon, Simcoe's servant, "to attend him unmolested." Some people recalled that Simcoe, as Captain of Grenadiers, had offered them his protection. They volunteered to help "preserve him from insults."[4] When word of his survival reached his regiment, the men shouted, "The father of the Rangers is alive!" This news arrived after Sir Henry Clinton had informed Lord George Germain, the Secretary of State for the Colonies, that Simcoe had been killed.

In due course Germain's reply reached New York:

> The loss of so gallant and able an officer as Colonel Simcoe is much to be lamented: but, I hope, his misfortune will not damp the spirit of the brave loyalists he so often led out with success. His last enterprise was certainly a very bold one; and I should be glad he had been in a situation to be informed, that his spirited conduct was approved by the King.[5]

On 28 October, Simcoe was removed on parole to Borden Town, and lodged in a tavern kept by one Colonel Hoogland "of the Jersey militia." Simcoe was "treated with great civility except by Messers Borden and Kirkbride who were especially violent." Simcoe and Surgeon Kelloch felt that only in the tavern were they safe. When they went out for a walk they were met with threats. Meanwhile, entirely false reports of Simcoe's cruelties were spreading, of which the rebel justices of the peace could not obtain any proof. Some people were even ready to testify to Simcoe's humanity.

When Colonel Henry Lee found out where Simcoe was, he wrote offering pecuniary assistance. A Lieutenant Campbell of the 74th Regiment, on parole at nearby Prince Town, offered Simcoe a loan. He chose to accept Campbell's offer rather than be beholden to an enemy, although he appreciated Lee's gentlemanly offer and sent him a polite reply. Writing on 6 November, Colonel Lee was pleased that Simcoe was comfortable, and he did not "credit reports of his cruelty." One of Lee's dragoons, captured and exchanged, informed his commander that he had been well treated by the British.

On 7 November, Governor Livingston himself came to Borden Town to confer with Simcoe for a speedy prisoner exchange. Fully expecting to be back on Staten Island almost immediately, Simcoe was disconcerted the next day when a rebel militia party arrived at the tavern, conducting Colonel Christopher Billop, the commander of the Staten Island loyal militia who had been taken prisoner. Both Billop and Simcoe were to be marched to the county jail in Burlington the following day. Colonel Hoogland intervened and put his "waggon" at their disposal. The regimental surgeon and the sergeant who had led the flag of truce would be allowed to return to Staten Island, but the servant Edward Heifernon — and perhaps Lieutenant John McGill of the Hussars — would be confined with Simcoe. No one was allowed to speak with Heifernon or McGill. Simcoe approved of the Scots-born McGill, because he had absorbed a certain Virginian veneer even though he retained a mild Scots accent. The Colonel was even more impressed when McGill told him that his grandfather had been a captain in the army of King William III.[6]

Simcoe did not explain how McGill came to be with him. He did not name him as being in the party that had come under the flag of truce. According to one source, McGill was captured during the same raid into New Jersey, but Simcoe did not suggest this. McGill had emigrated to Virginia when he was twenty-one years of age. He had been a lieutenant in the Loyal Virginia Regiment when that unit was absorbed into the Queen's Rangers.[7] McGill may have been captured. Equally well, he could have come with the flag, but Simcoe had perhaps forgotten to name this officer when he was turning his diaries into a military journal some years later. The answer could also have been sheer bravado; McGill decided on his own initiative to pay a private visit to his commanding officer. He may have assumed, as usually happened, that his green jacket would not identify him to the enemy as a Queen's Ranger.

Scarcely had the Simcoe party arrived at Burlington than a "mittimus" or warrant committing a person to prison arrived. It was dated 6 November 1779, and the sender was Elisha Boudinet, the Commissioner of Prisoners for New Jersey. The mittimus instructed the keeper of the common jail that Colonel Billop "was to have irons put on his hands and feet, and be chained to the floor in a close room in the said jail, to receive only bread and water till further orders." Billop received a letter from Commissioner Boudinet, also dated 6 November, informing him that he was being so treated as retaliation, to procure some relaxation of the sufferings of John Leshier and Captain Nathaniel Randal. Leshier was being held by the British for murdering a Loyalist; Randal, the commander of a vessel, was considered a militia private, who therefore was being denied release on parole.

From Burlington, Simcoe wrote to Governor Livingston, seeking his permission to go to Staten Island where he might negotiate his parole. Replying, Livingston refused his consent, but he hoped a prisoner exchange could be arranged while Simcoe remained confined in the jail. He retorted that if Simcoe was never released, it would be the fault of the British!

On 10 November, Simcoe again wrote Livingston, extremely perturbed. The treatment meted out to Billop was unprecedented, but he was learning first hand about the cruel fate that awaited Loyalists who openly embraced the King's cause. He had also heard that General Washington had refused to allow the men captured with General Burgoyne at Saratoga to be exchanged, which was further cause for concern. The Saratoga Convention, which both Burgoyne and rebel General Horatio Gates had signed, specified that his army would be repatriated. Simcoe was aware that before Burgoyne surrendered his army at Saratoga, he sent orders to his Provincial troops to escape in small groups and make their way north to Canada. He was afraid he could not protect them under the Saratoga Convention which specifically covered his regular troops.[8] Burgoyne, Simcoe thought, was a true gentleman, even though an inept commander.

Simcoe wrote again to Livingston, this time for permission to go to Staten Island to obtain winter clothing and wine. Livingston again refused. When Colonel Henry Lee heard of this downright rudeness, he personally sent some wine to the prisoner.

By then, the rebels were considering exchanging Simcoe for a Colonel Reynolds the British were holding, but they were thinking of exchanging Billop for an undecided number of rebel privates, which was also unprecedented. Simcoe then wrote to Sir Henry Clinton, informing him that Captain Vorhees was not killed until after Simcoe himself had been captured. Therefore he could not be held responsible for Vorhees's death. Colonel Billop, he assured Clinton, was a most respectable and amiable gentleman, suffering, according to the enclosed mittimus, by order of Elisha Boudinet.

Major John André replied on behalf of Sir Henry Clinton. He proposed to parole Simcoe to New York, in exchange for a Colonel

Baylor, who would be sent to Virginia. Clinton was astonished to learn that Simcoe was not free on parole, but was being treated as a criminal. If an officer's rights could be swept aside, the world was in a sad state indeed. The rebels were showing themselves, not officers of honour, but savage miscreants. Simcoe repeated that the exchange of a large number of privates for a colonel was unheard of. He wrote to General Washington, because Governor Livingston had claimed that Colonel Simcoe was a "prisoner of state" — also unheard of. Many letters passed back and forth concerning this matter, and Simcoe was growing ever more desperate. Meanwhile, Lieutenant John McGill and a prisoner named Bloxam had put their heads together.

They discovered that the militia arsenal was a locked room in the jail. Bloxam was a skilled armourer who had been serving on one of His Majesty's ships. One morning when the jailor was ill, all unwary, he entrusted McGill to undertake duties on his behalf in the jail office — a hint that McGill *was* just visiting. He quickly made a wax impression of the key to the arsenal, and Bloxam set to work on a pewter implement, most likely a spoon secreted from a meal. With this false key, Bloxam made ready to unlock the door. Meanwhile, Simcoe was a party to the plot whereby Bloxam and himself would appropriate arms and escape. McGill would sleep in Simcoe's bed so that his absence would not be discovered immediately. Here was another hint that McGill was not sleeping in the jail. If he had been, his own empty bed would have alerted the guards.

Simcoe panicked when Bloxam attempted to open the door, because the bottom of the pewter key broke inside the lock. What would the rebels do when they discovered that the lock would not open? Bloxam, however, managed to poke at the piece of key so that it dropped undiscovered into the bottom of the lock. When some of Colonel Henry Lee's men arrived, they had no difficulty opening it, and Simcoe heaved a sigh of relief. Bloxam by now had made a second key, and this time the scheme was to arm themselves, surprise Lee's party, steal their horses and ride for Sandy Hook. Simcoe disliked the entire plan and he worried over what John McGill's fate would be for his part in the business, but he was also more desperate than ever. He hesitated, which did not disappoint Bloxam, who thought the capture of Lee's horses could take place any time. On 23 December, to Simcoe's relief, Commissioner Boudinet wrote that he would be released very soon. He had been treated badly, the commissioner explained, because of like treatment by the British. Simcoe retorted that several unprincipled American militia officers, captured by his own side, had broken their paroles. Simcoe decided to postpone the jail break a few days to see whether Boudinet's word was worth anything. This time Boudinet was sincere. The date of release was 27 December, and Simcoe reached Staten Island on the 31st. There, he learned that forty "friends of government" had armed themselves and were near Burlington, planning to rescue him, when they heard he had been exchanged.

Not long afterwards, Bloxam escaped from Burlington jail and on reaching Staten Island he enlisted in the Queen's Rangers. He was killed later, while serving in "the Jersies." John McGill might have been exchanged at the same time, although Simcoe did not say so. For McGill's services, Simcoe offered him the choice of an annuity, or rank as the Quartermaster of Cavalry. McGill chose the latter. No man, Simcoe wrote, ever "executed that office with greater integrity, courage and conduct."[9] He made no mention of the long-suffering Colonel Billop, although he was eventually released. Along with his wife's father, Judge Benjamin Seaman, of Staten Island, and his brother-in-law, Richard Seaman, Billop became a founding settler in New Brunswick.[10]

John Graves Simcoe was a man of certain contradictions. He revealed his distaste for slavery in 1777 when he had recommended enlisting blacks, chiefly escaping slaves, into the Provincial Corps. After he assumed command of the Rangers he overlooked the possession of slaves by nearly all the fine gentlemen from Virginia who served as officers in his regiment or in other Provincial units.

Despite the weird and bizarre abuse meted out to him by the New Jersey and other American rebels, Simcoe did not lose his faith in the innate decency of the American people. Most resembled his Rangers more than they resembled the opposing rebels. In fact, some of his own men had deserted the rebel cause and joined the Rangers when they saw the light. Only the rebel leadership was misguided in this unholy fratricidal war.

During the year 1780, that dawned as he reached his regiment, Simcoe would be overwhelmed by the tragic fate of Major John André. Yet Simcoe would serve without apparent dislike or written word of complaint, Benedict Arnold, the man responsible for the loss of his very dear friend.

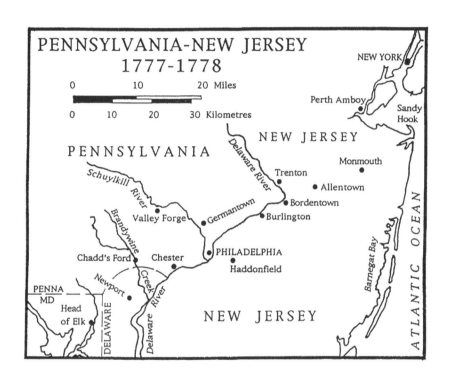

PENNSYLVANIA-NEW JERSEY
1777-1778

NEW YORK

0   10   20 Miles

0   10   20   30 Kilometres

Perth Amboy

Sandy
Hook

PENNSYLVANIA

NEW JERSEY

Schuylkill River

Delaware River

Trenton

Monmouth

Allentown

Brandywine

Valley Forge

Germantown

Bordentown

Burlington

Chadd's Ford

Chester

Creek

PHILADELPHIA

Haddonfield

PENNA
MD

Newport

Delaware River

Head
of Elk

DELAWARE

NEW JERSEY

Barnegat Bay

ATLANTIC OCEAN

FIVE

JOHN ANDRÉ, EDWARD DREWE, AND BENEDICT ARNOLD

By the time Simcoe had rejoined the British army, on 31 December 1779, his beloved friend, Major John André was already in secret correspondence with General Benedict Arnold, of Washington's Continental Army — the rebels' regular troops. Arnold had become disenchanted with the rebel cause, according to some sources owing to the influence of his "Tory" wife, to others because he was not receiving the recognition he thought he deserved. Carrying on his usual duties, Simcoe was unaware that André was treading on dangerous ground.

On his return to Staten Island, Simcoe learned of an expedition during the summer and autumn that had punished the warriors of the Six Nations, or Iroquois Confederacy, for being allies of Britain. An army 5,000 strong, commanded by rebel General John Sullivan, had marched through the natives' country, destroying villages and crops, chopping down orchards and driving off cattle through a scorched earth exercise that deprived these people of their winter stock of food. Now they were seeking shelter and sustenance from the officers of the stations of the Indian Department, chiefly from Major John Butler, at Fort Niagara.

Butler had formed a Provincial Corps of Rangers from among Loyalists whose homes were in the Mohawk Valley. Even before his capture, Simcoe had wondered about obtaining permission to join Butler and the natives in the frontier war they were waging against their rebel neighbours. Now, he was too late; the damage had been done. However, the coming summer would prove him wrong; Butler's Rangers, aided by Sir John Johnson and his Mohawk Valley Provincials of the King's Royal Regiment of New York, would stage retaliatory raids that would similarly affect the "breadbasket" of New York. Meanwhile, Simcoe was soon fully occupied with his usual duties.[1]

He was again operating out of Staten Island, and his Rangers were stationed in Richmond village, near the centre of the island. His active mind was conjuring up other schemes that he longed to carry out. He frequently sent notes to Colonel Thomas Stirling (sometimes spelled Sterling), the commander of the 1st Battalion, 42nd (Royal Highland) Regiment, with which his Rangers sometimes operated.[2] Stirling encouraged him, because the British Army stood in dire fear of a major attack. The winter of 1779–1780 was unusually harsh, and solid ice had formed between Staten Island and the New Jersey shore. The British garrison stood ready for an invasion over the ice, so much simpler than an amphibious operation.[3]

Simcoe proposed leading eighty of his infantrymen by little-used paths to the rear of Washington's encampment near Elizabethtown, New Jersey, in the hope of kidnapping the rebel commander in chief. Such an attack, even if Washington should elude them, would draw attention away from the British-controlled islands. If he felt overwhelmed, Simcoe could withdraw into the backwoods of Pennsylvania, ideal for guerrilla warfare. Captain George Beckwith, serving as an aide-de-camp, had placed his own plan before General von Knyphausen, which the northern commander preferred. The general would lead a main body of cavalry towards Elizabethtown, while Simcoe would stage a diversion by attacking some militia at Woodbridge, south of Washington's position and close to Perth Amboy.[4]

The Ranger infantry set out, and were skirmishing near Woodbridge when heavy rain fell. The snow on the roads turned to slippery ice that was impassable for horses. General von Knyphausen cancelled the operation and recalled Simcoe and his infantrymen. Meanwhile, Sir Henry Clinton was in South Carolina. By the end of March he was laying siege to Charleston. He sent orders for Simcoe to sail with other reinforcements, taking his infantry. The Hussars would remain behind with the garrison protecting New York. Only the few horses the officers needed would accompany the foot soldiers. Moving horses by sea was costly, and often a guarantee that some would not survive. The replacement for the mount killed when he was taken prisoner was Salem, a reliable, steady horse that Simcoe came to love.[5]

Simcoe and his infantrymen reached the waters off Charleston harbour in April. For the first time, four regiments of the American establishment would be represented in the same campaign. The 1st American was Simcoe's; the 2nd, Lord Rawdon's Volunteers of Ireland; the 3rd, Colonel George Turnbull's New York Volunteers; and 5th, newly honoured, was Banastre Tarleton's British Legion. The 2nd, 3rd and 5th had been in the south for some time. The 4th American was Colonel Edmund Fanning's King's American Regiment, which was at New York.

Charleston lay on a promontory between the Cooper and Ashley Rivers. Simcoe and his men circled inland and took up a position beside the Ashley River, blocking reinforcements reaching the town from that direction. Simcoe acquired two 6-pounder cannon and had them placed on the shore, sent an old sloop into the river to challenge rebel boats, and his men prepared fire rafts to provide light in the event of a night attack. They did not see action. Charleston surrendered on 12 May, and the Rangers were ordered back to Staten Island.

While awaiting the return of Sir Henry Clinton, General von Knyphausen planned a major diversion to prevent Washington moving part of his army to attack General Charles Cornwallis, who would remain in command of the south. By 21 June, Simcoe and his infantrymen had reached Staten Island. The Hussars had already crossed to Elizabethtown Point in New Jersey, serving as the vanguard of von Knyphausen's 5,000-man force, and part of the Rangers' infantry followed the next day. On the 23rd the Hussars drove the enemy out of Elizabethtown despite furious resistance. Then the army marched on to Springfield, but when heavy reinforcements reached Washington, von Knyphausen withdrew to Staten Island, the Rangers now in the rearguard.

In the skirmishing, a rebel officer named Fitzrandolph (or Randal) was killed. Simcoe identified him as one of the officers released through his own exchange. During the withdrawal they passed the home of Governor Livingston, where some "exasperated Loyalists" wanted to burn it down. Exhibiting very professional conduct, Simcoe stopped them, despite hurtful memories of how Livingston had treated him only a few months before.[6]

Lieutenant Aeneas Shaw, in command of Simcoe's riflemen, was among the wounded, but he recovered. The Rangers returned to their favourite camp, at Oyster Bay, on Long Island, for a well-earned rest. The officers, in particular, liked this posting. They could have billets in the fine houses in this long-settled area of the country where people prided themselves on their refinement. When Sir Henry Clinton arrived back in New York, he planned to capture West Point, a strong rebel fort fifty miles up the Hudson River. He chose Colonel Simcoe and his Hussars for the assault and added two more troops of dragoons attached to the Queen's Rangers.[7] The command at West Point passed to General Benedict Arnold in September.

Major John André

When word reached Long Island that Major André had been taken prisoner at Tappan by three rebel militiamen, Simcoe was devastated. He sought out Sir Henry Clinton and held confidential conversations over how he might effect a rescue, no matter how great the risk to himself and to any who joined him. André, he learned, had gone north, and attended a secret meeting with Arnold at West Point on 21 September. He was returning when he was captured, and incriminated by papers he was carrying in one of his boots. By order of General Washington he was to be tried by a specially appointed board of officers. Simcoe assumed that André would be sent to Philadelphia. If so, surely his escort could be intercepted along the route.[8] Clinton was less confident, and wary of finding the British in deeper trouble if Simcoe failed. Besides, he thought André's trial would be at Tappan to avoid the bother of moving him.

On 2 October, Simcoe received a letter from Light Horse Harry Lee, written from "Light Camp" in New Jersey. He was pleased that Simcoe had enjoyed the gift of his "best wines," but Lee had been thanked enough by his somewhat long-winded correspondent. Lee assured Simcoe that he expected André to be "restored to his country and the customs of war being fully satisfied." As officer and gentleman himself, Lee assumed that André would be exchanged for a major the British were holding. In Lee's view, and Simcoe's, André could not be treated as a spy because he had travelled north in his uniform. What Simcoe did not know at the time, was that Arnold had persuaded André to change to civilian clothing before he set out to return to New York.[9]

Washington demanded that Arnold, who had recently reached New York City, be exchanged for André, but Sir Henry Clinton decided he must refuse or the entire British administration would be discredited. Simcoe was furious. Clinton was permitting "a grave injustice." Washington found himself obliged to allow André's execution or face unpopularity from his own supporters. "Posterity will pass judgement on Washington over André," wrote Simcoe.[10]

On 2 October, the day Lee had written Simcoe, Major André was hanged, not even permitted a soldier's death by firing squad. Simcoe ordered the Queen's Rangers to add, in addition to green ones, black and white feathers to their caps in mourning for his murdered comrade.[11] Many in the crowd that watched the public execution wept. The handsome André had gone to the scaffold with courage and dignity, and during his imprisonment and trial at Tappan, he had acquired many admirers.

Simcoe continued thinking up plans and hoping for permission to carry them out. He recommended a raid on Burlington, to attack Light Horse Harry Lee's cavalry post. Clinton authorised such a raid but then cancelled it. The colonel then proposed capturing Billingsport, down the Delaware from Burlington, a scheme he thought superior to any others he had suggested. Success would give the British a port where an army could be landed. Again Clinton grew wary and refused his consent.[12]

Major Edward Drewe

From time to time, mail from home caught up with John Graves Simcoe. Jeremiah Milles had married an heiress, and seemed well pleased with himself. A wealthy wife, Simcoe had to admit, was just what an aspiring officer needed for faster promotions. Milles was lucky indeed. Distressing was word about Edward Drewe, now recovered from the wounds he had received at Boston, and promoted major of the 35th Regiment. He as now on duty in the West Indies, where his frankness, or just plain disobedience, had got him into deep trouble. Either way, he found scant sympathy among his fellow officers.

Drewe's satirical "Military Sketches" had so upset the establishment that he was court martialled, probably on a flimsy excuse. Among other sins, he had lampooned a uniform, that had a soldier

> screwed into a jacket of such excessive tightness that not a sinew had room to play, and the whole body resembled much the form of a rabbit; its legs were jammed into two long cases of black linen, so excessively strait as to vie with the French torture of Brodequin; its head was loaded with a quantity of flour, and dragged back upon its shoulders by the weight of an enormous queue made

of sheep's wool, and on the head was perched a hat
which seemed to be the manufacture of Lilliput.[13]

Verses published in Exeter in 1792 by Drewe and Simcoe's friend,
Richard Polwhele include "An Elegaic Epistle Addressed to a Friend, on
my leaving Boston in 1775, for the cure of my Wounds sustained at
Bunker's Hill." Polwhele concluded that Drewe referred to Simcoe, who
had been "reported killed in battle, and was much bewailed ..." and who
was now safe.

On learning of his friend's predicament, Simcoe wrote a character
reference for Drewe and sent it to be used in his defense. Drewe was
convicted at his court martial, and cashiered.[14] Of importance was
evidence that Drewe had influenced Simcoe to select practical clothing
for his Rangers, and for himself. The court martial took place at St. Lucia
in May 1780. Whether Simcoe sent his testimonial from New York, or
his next posting, is not clear.

With General Benedict Arnold to Virginia

Lord Cornwallis resolved to move his campaign northward, leaving a
garrison behind in Charleston. Both he and Clinton agreed that their
troops were spread too thin. If Cornwallis moved to Virginia, Clinton
could give him limited help, while still holding Washington at bay in
New Jersey. Clinton decided to make use of his new general, Benedict
Arnold, by sending him in command of troops to harass rebel strong
points, destroy supplies and buildings, and to follow Cornwallis's
orders on what else should be done. Clinton assigned a strong
detachment of Queen's Rangers infantry and Hussars to the
expedition. Arnold would take his new regiment, the Loyal American
Legion, while Simcoe would be his subordinate. Oddly enough,
neither in Simcoe's *Journal* nor in his more frank Appendix, did he
hint at any dislike of the man whose name would become synonymous
in American history with "traitor" and despite Arnold's hand in the
betrayal of Major André.

Cornwallis planned to leave the garrison at Charleston under Colonel
Nisbet Balfour, until Clinton could send more troops. The reinforcement
for Charleston, was 2,500 men under the command of General
Alexander Leslie. Part of Leslie's force would be Simcoe's captain, John
Saunders, and his troop of Hussars. Saunders was not pleased with the
posting; he preferred to operate in Virginia, his home territory. His

cornet was Thomas Merritt, of a New York family, who had served with Emmerich's Chasseurs before transferring to the Queen's Rangers.[15]

Arnold's expedition sailed from Sandy Hook on 21 December, a few days ahead of Leslie's, and reached Chesapeake Bay on the 30th, 1780. From there the transports sailed into the James River as far as Hood's Point, where an enemy gun battery barred further progress. Simcoe landed 130 Rangers and two companies from the 80th Regiment, circled round the enemy flank and forced them to abandon the gun battery. Thomas Jefferson, in command of Virginia militia, was a mere thirty miles away, in Richmond.

Arnold had only 800 men ashore; other transports were still on the way, but Simcoe persuaded him to attack Jefferson's force immediately. At the outskirts of Richmond, Simcoe's infantry dislodged the rebels from their strong position on a hill, and Captain David Shank and Lieutenant George Spencer led their Hussars in pursuit, driving them from the town. Returning to Richmond, to rejoin the rest of Arnold's force, they brought captured horses and prisoners.

From Richmond, the Rangers continued to Westham, to deal with a foundry and an arsenal of cannon, muskets and ammunition. Simcoe's men took what they could carry, set fire to the buildings, destroyed the remaining weapons and ammunition, and retired to Richmond. They celebrated on captured rum, and moved back to Westover for a rest. Simcoe's force had fought two battles and marched seventy-two miles in three days.

On 8 January 1781, Simcoe was patrolling with Captain Shank and some forty Ranger Hussars when they learned that 800 rebel militiamen were at Charles City Court House, only a few miles from Westover. A friendly black man led them by little-used roads. Near the court house, the Rangers dispersed the militiamen by their spirited, surprise attack.

> Simcoe could be alarmed, but rarely deterred: In saving three armed militia men from the fury of the soldiers, Lt. Col. Simcoe ran a great risque [sic] as their pieces were loaded, pointed at his breast, and in their timidity they might have discharged them.[16]

While the Rangers continued patrolling and skirmishing, the main army moved to Portsmouth, at the mouth of the James River, and commenced improving the defences. Portsmouth would be a strategic place for the receipt of supplies. There, Arnold was superceded as commander of the expedition by General William Phillips, an artillery officer who had served with Burgoyne. Following his parole and exchange Phillips had returned to duty. He proceeded to capture Williamsburg, and he sent Simcoe to secure Burrell's Landing, a defensive position on the James River.

Simcoe prepared a feint, a supposed frontal assault, while one company attacked the rebel flank. After a brief exchange of shots the enemy withdrew. With about forty of his Hussars, Simcoe continued on to Yorktown where he surprised and captured most of the rebel garrison, before rejoining Phillips at Williamsburg.

The army next attacked Petersburg, on the Appomattox River where it flows into the James. The Queen's Rangers, with other light troops, formed the vanguard. Two miles from Petersburg they confronted a rebel force led by Baron Friedrich von Steuben, a German who had done much to improve the training of the Continental Army. While the main army under Phillips planned a frontal attack, Simcoe and his Rangers rapidly flanked von Steuben. After a short exchange, the rebels fled across the Appomattox and withdrew to Chesterfield Court House.

On 25 April, Phillips moved on to Chesterfield. The Rangers, with detachments of the 76th and 80th Regiments, moved to Osborne's House, on the James River, where fifteen enemy armed ships were anchored. After firing 6-pounder guns from the shore and considerable musketry, the ships began to surrender, although some crews attempted escape in small boats. Two Ranger officers and a dozen men rowed out and seized one of the ships. Some of the Rangers remained while others rowed on and captured a second ship, turning its guns on ships still in rebel hands. They captured the entire fleet, except for some that were scuttled by their own crews. On 2 May when the British troops moved down the river, detachments of Rangers were manning the captured ships. Lord Cornwallis was steadily moving troops from the Carolinas into Virginia, and he sent an order to General Phillips to congregate his force at Petersburg. Phillips reached Petersburg in time to forestall the town being occupied by the Marquis de Lafayette, the young French aristocrat who had joined Washington's army. Lafayette who was in command of about 3,000 troops; a mixed force of Continental regulars and militia, retired to Osborne House, about twenty miles from Petersburg. Simcoe then received orders to take his cavalry, locate Cornwallis and lead him to Petersburg. He found the army thirty miles away, and Cornwallis reached the town on 20 May. Arnold had been in command before Cornwallis appeared. General Phillips had died of typhoid fever only a week before, on the 13th.

Cornwallis's first priority was the destruction of Lafayette's force, which had retreated, first to Richmond, then across the South Anna River. The timing was vital; General Anthony Wayne was en route with reinforcements from Pennsylvania. Unwilling to move his whole army too far from the supply base at Portsmouth, Cornwallis ordered Tarleton's Legion to attack Charlottesville, the state capital where the Virginia Assembly was sitting. Simcoe was to lead a force to Point of Forks, farther up the James River where Baron von Steuben, with about 400 troops, was guarding a depot of vital military stores.

Simcoe could muster at most 300 Rangers because so many were sick or recovering from wounds. Moreover, fifty were in effect barefoot, owing to the worn condition of their boots or shoes. Cornwallis added 200 men of the 71st Regiment Fraser Highlanders to join them. Knowing how poorly some of the men felt, Simcoe offered them the chance to stay with the main army, but "There was not a man who would remain behind the corps."[17]

Simcoe's men covered nearly sixty miles in two days, so that they were upon von Steuben's position before he was aware of their approach. Rangers who reconnoitred discovered that the enemy force was twice as large as intelligence had reported, and that the German officer was removing supplies from a depot and across the river. The Rangers and the others had been moving west, and Simcoe circled von Steuben's position and moved close to the river from the north. He found himself at Napier's Ford, over the South Anna River, north of the Forks. Lieutenant George Spencer went on patrol with two of his Hussars, proceeding cautiously to Napier's house, on high ground. He planned to spend the night and to recommend, at daybreak, an ambush of a ford below the house.

Spencer then approached a second house, that of a rebel Colonel Thompson, which was surrounded by very high fences. Dismounting, he faced Thompson, who had four militiamen with him. Spencer enquired the way to Baron von Steuben's camp. Suspicious, Thompson, although armed, ran with three of his men. The fourth, seeing that the two Hussars could not get over the fence or assist Spencer, "presented a double barrel piece within five yards of his breast":

> Lt. Spencer, with great presence of mind, immediately threatened to have him flogged on his arrival at the Baron's camp, and, pulling some papers from his packet, told him, that they were his despatches from M. Fayette: at the same time he moved gently towards him,

intending if possible, to seize the muzzle of his firelock, but, as the one advanced, the other retreated, keeping his piece still presented, until, getting over a fence at the back of the house, he ran towards the river.

Spencer could have shot him with a pocket pistol, but recalling that Simcoe thought the enemy had a post at Napier's Ford, two miles lower, "he prudently permitted him to escape, rather than make an alarm: these people left five good horses behind them."[18] Spencer investigated the ford, and met two mounted rebel militiamen who, unsuspecting, told him that von Steuben was at the Forks. Simcoe directed his force to proceed there.

Intending to convince the rebels he was Cornwallis's vanguard, Simcoe directed the red-coated men of the 71st to approach on a height, to suggest large numbers. A 3-pounder gun fired, denoting the threat of artillery. Ranger-style they spread out along the woods. Simcoe's men bivouacked for the night, and at dawn they found no sign of von Steuben. Deceived by Simcoe's ruse, von Steuben had evacuated his position and was marching his 900-strong force towards Cumberland Court House, thirty miles inland.

Simcoe's force secured a large haul of military stores, muskets, gunpowder, entrenching tools, sail cloth and several types of heavy guns. They ferried some of the loot by raft down the James River. Watchful for a counter attack, they destroyed on land or sank in the river everything they could not carry. The Rangers and the men of the 71st rejoined Cornwallis who, in their absence, had marched nearer to the Point of Forks, where Colonel Tarleton soon arrived. With 250 cavalry he had ridden to Charlottesville, but forewarned, the members of the Virginia Assembly had escaped. Tarleton had to make do by destroying all the stores he found there.

Cornwallis now ordered a withdrawal towards Richmond. During the march, the Queen's Rangers formed the rear guard Reaching Richmond on 16 June, Cornwallis ordered a few days rest, but the Rangers were as busy as ever, patrolling, trying to establish the exact location of Lafayette and Wayne. The French officer had moved south once he discovered that he was not being pursued, and Anthony Wayne arrived from Pennsylvania to reinforce him. As the British army was moving again, towards Williamsburg, Cornwallis instructed Simcoe and his Rangers, with a detachment of German riflemen — Jaegers under Captain Johann Ewald — to follow at a distance of two days march, as a rearguard to watch out for Lafayette and Wayne. Cornwallis intended to move his army close to Portsmouth, where he could not be cut off from Sir Henry Clinton and the

British garrison at New York, his source of fresh troops.

By 25 June, Simcoe was at Cooper's Mills, some twenty miles up the James River from Williamsburg. He did not know exactly where the enemy was, nor their strength, but he was determined not to be surprised. He promised a local man, known as a rebel sympathiser, a generous reward if he would go to Lafayette's camp and report back by seven o'clock the following morning, knowing full well that his "spy" would promptly spill everything he had heard to the French general. As soon as the man had departed, Simcoe's men set to work, and at two o'clock in the morning his infantry and baggage began to leave, while the Hussars prepared to follow. As Simcoe wrote in his *Journal*, "The next advantage to receiving good information is to deceive the enemy with that which is false." As expected, at dawn, General Wayne attacked the now vacant Ranger camp, and found no sign of life.

Simcoe, meanwhile, approached Spencer's Ordinary, closer to Williamsburg, for his first completely independent command.

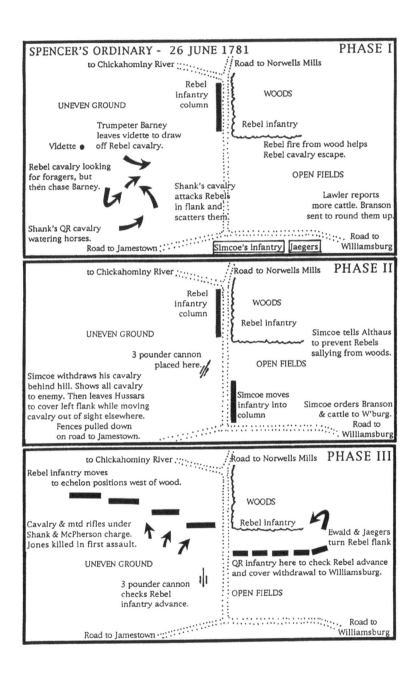

SPENCER'S ORDINARY - 26 JUNE 1781   PHASE I

to Chickahominy River

Road to Norwells Mills

Rebel infantry column

WOODS

UNEVEN GROUND

Trumpeter Barney leaves vidette to draw off Rebel cavalry.

Rebel infantry

Vidette ●

Rebel fire from wood helps Rebel cavalry escape.

Rebel cavalry looking for foragers, but then chase Barney.

OPEN FIELDS

Shank's cavalry attacks Rebels in flank and scatters them.

Lawler reports more cattle. Branson sent to round them up.

Shank's QR cavalry watering horses.

Road to Jamestown

Simcoe's infantry   Jaegers

Road to Williamsburg

PHASE II

to Chickahominy River

Road to Norwells Mills

Rebel infantry column

WOODS

Rebel infantry

UNEVEN GROUND

Simcoe tells Althaus to prevent Rebels sallying from woods.

3 pounder cannon placed here.

OPEN FIELDS

Simcoe withdraws his cavalry behind hill. Shows all cavalry to enemy. Then leaves Hussars to cover left flank while moving cavalry out of sight elsewhere. Fences pulled down on road to Jamestown.

Simcoe moves infantry into column

Simcoe orders Branson & cattle to W'burg.

Road to Williamsburg

PHASE III

to Chickahominy River

Road to Norwells Mills

Rebel infantry moves to echelon positions west of wood.

WOODS

Cavalry & mtd rifles under Shank & McPherson charge. Jones killed in first assault.

Rebel infantry

Ewald & Jaegers turn Rebel flank

QR infantry here to check Rebel advance and cover withdrawal to Williamsburg.

UNEVEN GROUND

3 pounder cannon checks Rebel infantry advance.

OPEN FIELDS

Road to Jamestown

Road to Williamsburg

SIX

SPENCER'S ORDINARY

The fight at Spencer's Ordinary was fairly minor, important mainly to John Graves Simcoe. His rebel opponent was Colonel Richard Butler, one of General Anthony Wayne's subordinates. Simcoe's force numbered little more than 400, Butler's some 570. The site for the encounter was a T junction. A road led south from Norwal's Mills and ended at an east-west road, which led east to Williamsburg, and west to Jamestown. Many hills offered concealment, as did woods, but part of the site was ploughed fields where either side would be vulnerable to attack from cover. Simcoe included a map in his *Journal,* with an attempt at showing sequence, but it does not enlighten exactly how the various positions changed.

Simcoe had been foraging for cattle and food, and making a reconnaissance towards the Chickahominy River. On 25 June, Lord Cornwallis's army was at Williamsburg. Simcoe's men had been subsisting on some Indian corn which an enemy commissary had left. The mission was disappointing because they found little to destroy. He was leading Rangers, some cavalry, some infantry, notably the Highland company under Captain John McKay. Also with him were two small detachments of German Jaegers, under Captains Ewald and Althaus[e]. (Althaus later transferred to the New York Volunteers as John Althouse and after the war he settled in New Brunswick.)

Jaegers had been recruited from among huntsmen, gamekeepers and foresters of Hesse-Cassel. Detachments from several companies served as sharpshooters with many units of the British Army. Like the Rangers, the Jaegers wore green. Their heavy rifles had short barrels, frequently octagonal, which could not take bayonets. Simcoe complained several times that his own rifle-equipped men, while useful as marksmen, could not partake in the bayonet charge so useful in dispersing an enemy.

When his little army arrived at Cooper's Mills, they were twenty miles from Williamsburg, where Cornwallis was halted temporarily. The Rangers found precious little to forage; Cornwallis's "waggons" had been at the mills the day before and had taken all the flour. Simcoe was feeling very insecure. He had not found any information on the enemy's movements, except that rebels were hurrying to General Wayne's standard, and clearly the enemy intended to follow Cornwallis "as far towards the neck of Williamsburg as with safety they could." He had not received any messages from Cornwallis, and he was certain that the commander's intelligence was very bad: "he [Simcoe] and Major Armstrong agreed with Capt. Ewald, that the slightest reliance was not to be placed on any patroles from His Lordship's Army."[1]

Major Armstrong, with Jaegers, infantry and their cannon, was approaching Spencer's Ordinary near dawn on 26 June. Simcoe followed with the cavalry, at a later hour. Spencer's Ordinary was little more than a tavern at the forks of the road between Williamsburg and Jamestown. Also with the expedition was a convoy of cattle, which a Captain Branson and some North Carolina Loyalists had collected. Near Spencer's Ordinary, Simcoe ordered fences to be torn down. He then rode into the open ground and inspected his surroundings, as was his custom. He remarked to his officers "that it was an admirable place for 'the chicanery of action.'" Lieutenant William Digby Lawler, sent to direct the infantry on to Williamsburg, returned and informed Simcoe that he had counted nearly 100 head of cattle in the neighbourhood. Captain Branson was detailed to round them up, and Captain Shank, commanding the cavalry, went to feed his horses at nearby Lee's farm.

Suddenly two shots rang out from the direction of the Highland company, which was posted as a "picquet" beside the road. Sentinels had given the alarm, and Simcoe saw Captain Shank galloping across the open field towards the woods, in pursuit of enemy cavalry. The rebels had passed through the downed fences and had arrived at Lee's farm in pursuit of the people collecting the cattle. Then Trumpeter Barney, stationed as a "vidette" (sentinel at an outpost) sounded the alarm and galloped off so as to lead the enemy away from the spot where the cavalry were watering their horses and collecting forage. He shouted, "Draw your swords Rangers, the rebels are coming."

Captain Shank now led a charge on the enemy flank and broke it up. Trumpeter Barney dismounted and took prisoner a French officer, who commanded one of the divisions. The enemy cavalry was totally scattered and they retired. Many were dismounted and would have been captured, but a blast of fire from the woods drove the Highland company from their cover. The same blast of fire protected the enemy cavalry and allowed them to escape. At the first shot, Simcoe ordered the infantry into column on the road towards the rebels, except for the light company and Captain Ewald's detachment. Those two were on the right, headed for the woods, ready to outflank the enemy by the length of their line.

Prisoners informed Simcoe that the rebels were coming in force, and that Lafayette, Wayne and von Steuben were not far behind the vanguard of riflemen. Simcoe employed his usual tactics against riflemen, by rushing them, and then:

> if each separate company kept itself compact, there was little danger, even should it be surrounded, from troops who were without bayonets, and whose object was to fire a single shot with effect: the position of an advancing soldier was calculated to lessen the true aim of the first shot, and rapidity to prevent the rifleman, who requires some time to load, from giving a second; or at least to render his aim uncertain, and his fire by no means formidable.[2]

Simcoe withdrew the cavalry from rebel range, and directed Captain Althaus, and his rifle company that was mounted, to dismount and check them if they sallied from the wood in pursuit of the Hussars. He ordered Captain Branson to go with the drivers and cattle to Williamsburg, because his red coat made him a target. He then ordered Lieutenant Adam Allen, acting as quartermaster, after he attended to the baggage, to have trees cut down for a barricade behind which the Rangers could rally.

The troops pulled down fences on the Jamestown road, in the rear of the cavalry, so that if retreat to Williamsburg were blocked, they could escape by that route. Next, Simcoe moved the cavalry down the hill towards the Jamestown road, and they reascended the hill at Lee's farm, "made a display of the whole force" then fell back behind the hill, leaving in front only a detachment of Hussars, both to prevent the left from being turned without notice, "and to deceive the enemy into a belief that the whole cavalry (whose force they had already felt) were behind the eminences, waiting for an opportunity to fall upon their right flank."

He directed the rest of the cavalry, undiscovered, to the road and formed them up out of sight and reach of the enemy, partly on the road and partly on its left. Beyond Captain Ewald's flank was open ground which Simcoe could see from the eminence. If the enemy appeared in the open, the cavalry could swoop down. The cavalry was also ready, in case the infantry gave way, to flank the enemy if they came in pursuit from the wood:

> the best substitute for want of reserve, which from the extent of the woods and the enemy's numbers, had been thrown into the line. Upon the left of the road the three pounder was placed, the amuzette [light rifled field piece] having broken down. There too the Highland company had retired.

The rebels now appeared in force, lining the fences on the edge of the wood, by echelons, but when a cannon shot sounded they did not advance. Simcoe did not think he could win a fight, but he was determined to try, by placing a line along the wood to check the enemy advance long enough to allow the convoy ahead of him on the road to reach Williamsburg in safety. Then he would withdraw after the convoy. He had great confidence in the men he led — "disciplined enthusiasts in the cause of their country, and who, having been ever victorious, thought it impossible to suffer defeat." He also admired the coolness and courage of Captain Ewald and his Jaegers. "I will take care of the left; while Ewald lives, the right flank will never be turned."[3]

"Fortune now decided in favour of the British troops": The road from Norwal's Mills was enclosed with high, strong fences. A body of enemy infantry was coming down the right of the road, and when Simcoe sent his infantry northward, the rebels clambered over the fences to save themselves. Once in the wood beyond the fences, Captain Ewald turned their left flank and his firing sent them fleeing in utmost confusion. Unfortunately, Ewald's riflemen were not supported by bayonetmen who could have dealt a more severe blow before the rebels could rally. Instead the Hussars had to charge. Cornet Jones, who led the first assault, was killed: "He was an active, sensible, promising officer."

> The mounted riflemen of the Queen's Rangers charged with Capt. Shank: the gallant Sergeant McPherson, who led them, was mortally wounded. Two of the men of this detachment were carried away by their impetuousity so far as to pass beyond the enemy, and their horses were killed: they, however, secreted themselves in the wood under some fallen logs, and when the enemy fled from the spot they returned in safety to the corps.[4]

Here is a rare instance where Simcoe mentioned having mounted riflemen. Usually they were on foot. Trumpeter Barney was wounded. "Captain [Francis] Stephenson was distinguished as usual: his chosen men and well trained light infantry were obstinately opposed: but they carried their point with the loss of a fourth of their numbers, killed and wounded." Captain John McGill was leading the grenadier company, who showed their gallantry. Captain Robert McCrea (M'Rae) reported that his subaltern, Lieutenant Charles Dunlop

> Who had served in the Queen's Rangers from thirteen years of age, led his division on horseback, without suffering a man to fire, watching the enemy, and giving a signal to his men to lay down whenever a party of their's was about to fire: he arrived at the fence where the enemy had been posted with his arms loaded, a conduct that might have been decisive of the action: fortunately he escaped unhurt.[5]

Simcoe's losses were ten killed and twenty-three wounded, among the latter Lieutenant Swift Armstrong and Ensign [Cornet] [William] Jarvis. The Jaegers' losses were one killed and two or three wounded. He noted that service with light troops "gives the greatest latitude for exertion of individual talents and of individual courage ... every officer, every soldier had his share in the merit of the action: mistake in the one might have brought on cowardice in the other ..."

> Lt. Col. Simcoe has ever considered this action as the climax of a campaign of five years, as the result of true discipline acquired in that space by unremitted

diligence, toil, and danger, as an honourable victory earned by veteran intrepidity.[6]

Simcoe never mentioned Colonel Richard Butler as the commander who opposed him. He must surely have known, but he saw no reason to dignify him by name. Rebel losses out of 570 engaged were calculated at nine killed, fourteen wounded, and thirty-two captured. Lafayette attributed rebel success to riflemen. Again, Simcoe repeated:

> The riflemen, however dexterous in the use of arms, were by no means the most formidable of the rebel troops; their not being armed with bayonets, permitted their opponents to take liberties with them which otherwise would have been highly improper.

Simcoe began to draw away and collect his force, informing Captain Ewald of his plan to retreat to Williamsburg. Examination of the prisoners taken indicated that Lafayette, von Steuben and Wayne, perhaps all three, were not far behind. Lacking wagons, he left the wounded at Spencer's Ordinary, with a surgeon's mate, under a flag of truce. The infantry filed off to the right and the cavalry closed the rear. The party reached a brook, where Lieutenant Allen, with the pioneers, had cut down some trees and was preparing defences. Fortunately, Lord Cornwallis met them less than two miles into their march. After examining the prisoners and his officers' intelligence, he concluded that the enemy, ready to act, were at least 1,200 strong, three times his strength — an overestimate of Colonel Richard Butler's numbers. At the same time, Lafayette's army was not far off.

Simcoe's detachment had marched twenty-eight miles without provisions. Fearful for the fate of his wounded, he galloped back to Spencer's Ordinary. He was in time; the rebels had not come and his wounded were where he had left them. He found a large foraging party with wagons in which he placed his wounded and dead. Simcoe observed that had it not been for the small battle at Spencer's Ordinary, this foraging party would have been mistaken for Cornwallis's advance guard, and most likely destroyed.

Cornet Jones and the other dead were buried with full military honours on 28 June at Williamsburg. That day, with public orders, Simcoe received a commendation:

> Lord Cornwallis desires Lieut. Col. Simcoe will accept

of his warmest acknowledgements for his spirited and judicious conduct in the action of the 26th instant, when he repulsed and defeated so superior a force of the enemy. He likewise desires that Lt. Col. Simcoe will communicate his thanks to the officers and soldiers of the Queen's Rangers, and to Captain Ewald and the detachment of Yagers.[7]

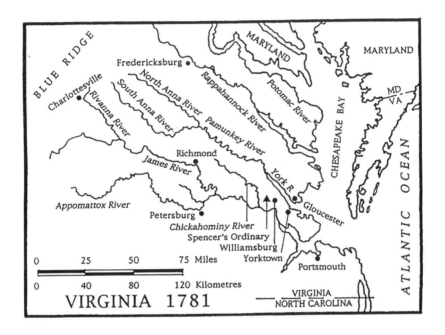

BLUE RIDGE

Fredericksburg •

MARYLAND

MARYLAND

Charlottesville •

Rivanna River

North Anna River

South Anna River

Rappahannock River

Pamunkey River

Potomac River

CHESAPEAKE BAY

MD
VA

Richmond •

James River

York R.

Appomattox River

Gloucester •

Petersburg •

Chickahominy River
Spencer's Ordinary
Williamsburg
Yorktown

Portsmouth •

ATLANTIC OCEAN

0	25	50	75 Miles

0	40	80	120 Kilometres

VIRGINIA   1781

VIRGINIA
NORTH CAROLINA

SEVEN

"THIS ILL-MANAGED WAR"

Soon after the fight at Spencer's Ordinary, Simcoe undoubtedly realised that the British Army would soon suffer another ignominious defeat similar to Burgoyne's disaster at Saratoga in October 1777. Cornwallis was withdrawing back to Portsmouth, expecting Sir Henry Clinton to send reinforcements from New York. The rebel campaign in the south was under overall command of General Nathaniel Greene; von Steuben, Lafayette and Wayne were his subordinates. Cornwallis knew he could not defeat the enemy if Washington moved south. French troops had arrived in Rhode Island, and Simcoe wondered whether, with French help, Washington would attack New York, or come to Chesapeake Bay to strike at Cornwallis. By 14 July most of the Cornwallis's army was at Portsmouth.

The Queen's Rangers embarked on ships to take part in an attack on Philadelphia. After Clinton countermanded the order, they were landed at Yorktown. Cornwallis was now asking to be allowed to return to South Carolina, to relieve Lord Rawdon, who was ill and had been ordered home to convalesce. Instead, Clinton ordered General Alexander Leslie, then in command at Portsmouth, to go to Charleston, taking with him two more troops of Queen's Rangers — Hussars under Captain Thomas Cooke and Lieutenant Adam Allan. Still at Charleston were the troopers under Captain John Saunders and Cornet Thomas Merritt. Clinton next ordered Cornwallis to detach part of his army to reinforce New York, on the assumption that Washington and his French allies would attack him. Cornwallis refused, because he was so short of able-bodied troops himself. Simcoe, too, was far from well. His Rangers were close to exhaustion, and still constantly on patrol out of Yorktown and conducting raids against the rebel outposts. The Colonel sent a request to Cornwallis, that if any troops were to be detached for New York, would he please send the Rangers. His corps badly needed a rest. Simcoe was feeling the effects of the long campaign personally, and wounds that had never fully healed were causing him considerable pain.

Cornwallis refused because he could not do without the constant patrols. To his distaste, he had already yielded to Benedict Arnold's demands to let him take his American Legion back to New York. [1] Looking about him at Yorktown, Simcoe saw it as a very poor defensive site. He recalled General Phillips, before his death, enquiring what strength of garrison would be required to hold Yorktown. Simcoe had replied that no less than 2,000 men might prevent it falling to the rebel force.

He recalled that Benedict Arnold, more pugnacious, had told Phillips that 4,000 would be required. [2] Whether Arnold made that recommendation on another occasion, or was present, is not clear. Simcoe had to agree that even 2,000 was too many, considering Phillips's other priorities. Yet probably not for the first time, and certainly not the last, Simcoe was recommending a strength far above what his superiors and the politicians in government were willing to contemplate.

In South Carolina, Captain John Saunders had been very active. He had tangled with, among others, Francis Marion, "the Swamp Fox." General Marion operated in the low-lying zones around Charleston with their pervading aura of methane gas. Cornet Merritt, out foraging, had been attacked by a superior force of rebels. Left for dead, recovering consciousness, Merritt managed to escape with the loss of his boots, helmet and arms. Later he was captured. Sent with a flag of truce to carry a letter from Colonel Nisbet Balfour to General Marion, Merritt was detained in retaliation for the detention of a rebel captain:

> They crammed Merrit [sic], with about twenty others, sergeants and privates of different British regiments, in

a small, nasty, dark place, made of logs, called a bull-pen; but he was not long here before he determined to extricate himself and his fellow prisoners, which he thus effected ...

Merritt saw his chance when the rebel guards became alarmed because they heard that a party of British had come near. He ordered the strongest of the prisoners to seize their sentry, who was posted at a small square hole cut through the logs, which served as both door and window. He pulled the astonished sentry through the hole with one hand, and threatened to cut his throat with a large knife, which he held in the other, if he made the smallest resistance or outcry. Merritt and the others crawled out of the hole, one by one, and the Cornet drew them into line. When challenged by the officer of the guard, Merritt threatened to cut the rebel guards to pieces if a single shot as fired. Although having only the sentry's weapons, and through intimidation, they marched to a nearby river. They found a rice boat which took them safely to George Town, a sub-headquarters on the coast some fifty miles north of Charleston.[3] The British were fairly secure in Charleston and Savannah, but the countryside around was dangerous as the rebels controlled more and more of the rural and unsettled areas.

By 2 June, Simcoe had a most unpleasant matter on his hands. While he had much cause to trust his Rangers, they were not perfect. From "Price Mile" Simcoe sent a letter to Lord Cornwallis, reporting on the appalling conduct of two of his men:

> My Lord,
> I have not the least doubt but that Jonathan Webster & Lewis Terrpan [sic] private Dragoons in Captain [Thomas Ivie] Cooke's troop of Queen's Rangers, were guilty of a rape on Jane Dickinson yesterday. I have the honor to be, My Lord, with great respect your most obdt & most humble servt.
> J. Graves Simcoe
> L. Coll. Commdr. Queen's Rangers.

Simcoe saw that the two culprits were executed for their crime. Of interest here is Simcoe's signature. On nearly all his letters he used J.G. Simcoe. Here he included Graves. This may be another indication that he was known as Graves to his intimates, rather than John.[4]

While Clinton stewed in New York about the danger of an attack by

Washington, he felt he could send little aid to Cornwallis. By 2 August 1781 the army in Virginia had pulled back to Yorktown. The Queen's Rangers and Tarleton's British Legion infantry were moved across the mouth of the York River to the Gloucester peninsula. Now Cornwallis awaited reinforcements from Clinton. His army was depleted to 7,400, many not remotely fit for duty. Clinton was slow to respond to rumours that Washington and his French ally, General Rochambeau, were marching for Virginia. At sea a large French fleet commanded by Admiral de Grasse was drawing close to the mouth of Chesapeake Bay, which would effectively bottle up Cornwallis's entire army.

Meanwhile, the badly weakened Rangers and Tarleton's infantry were holding back a force of 1,500 rebel militia on the Gloucester side of the York River. Finally, Clinton's intelligence informed him of the large scale move by Washington and General Rochambeau, his subordinate, and he prepared to set sail for Chesapeake Bay with 7,000 reinforcements. The British fleet was under the command of Admiral Thomas Graves, a cousin of Simcoe's godfather, Samuel, and his personal friend. Clinton was far too late. On 5 September De Grasse's fleet, well ahead of the British, had reached the entrance to the Chesapeake and was proceeding to establish a blockade.

The situation on Gloucester peninsula became more serious when French Lancers and Hussars joined the Virginia militiamen at worrying Simcoe's and Tarleton's much weakened garrison. French troops, ferried from De Grasse's ships, had been landing at Jamestown, while washington's army, more than 8,000 strong and the French force under Rochambeau, had marched overland. Washington, as the commander in chief, would soon have control of some 15,000 troops surrounding the British defences of Yorktown.

By early October the situation was truly hopeless. Admiral Thomas Graves's fleet was barred from landing Clinton and his 7,000 reinforcements which might have turned the tide. Helpless, Clinton ordered the fleet to return to New York, and Simcoe began working out a plan to escape while there might still be time. He would mount his entire regiment, break through the opposing militia and French, and drive straight north, to cross the Susquehanna and Delaware Rivers and continue along the best route he could find to Staten Island. With so much country wooded and peopled only by scattered, small settlements, he would have a good chance of success. He sent the plan to Cornwallis, who called him to a meeting and enquired whether Simcoe really thought he could escape with the cavalry. "Without the smallest doubt," the Colonel replied with a complete confidence that masked certain qualms.[5]

He was far from well, and he could not help wondering whether he would endure long days in the saddle, winter clearly not far off and ill supplied with whatever his foraging Rangers could find. Such winter clothing as the Rangers had possessed was threadbare or long lost. In fact, he was so ill that Tarleton, who had moved his cavalry to Gloucester, had taken over command of all their men. Cornwallis denied Simcoe permission to make his escape attempt. The entire army, he decreed, must share the same fate.[6] Simcoe could not help contrasting such a pig-headed outlook with that of Burgoyne, who had encouraged his Provincials to escape from Saratoga. Their Colonel was fearful that his loyal, hard working Rangers, and the other regiments of the American and Provincial establishments, faced punishment as traitors if they fell into the hands of their rebel enemies. By 1781 he had in his ranks some British regulars who had transferred to the Rangers, but the vast majority of his men were still colonials.

Now bedridden, Simcoe had Major Richard Armstrong compile a list of the Rangers who had originally enlisted with the rebel militia or the Continental Army, and who had deserted to enlist with the King. He stopped short of recommending outright desertion, but he suggested, where a Ranger thought he could get away with doing it, that he rejoin the rebel corps from which he had originally deserted, giving a plausible explanation for his absence. The best excuse would be a captive of the British, now so outnumbered in Virginia as to be unable to keep track of their prisoners. As days passed, some of these men disappeared, and Simcoe prayed for their safety.[7]

He continued examining ways of escape. He recalled that Benedict Arnold had had some boats built which he had left behind. They might be used to carry some Rangers and others away. He sent Lieutenant George Spencer to enquire whether Major Armstrong might have permission to try an evacuation across Chesapeake Bay into Maryland, where many inhabitants were still loyal, but this Cornwallis refused.

The formal surrender took place on 19 October, when the British marched out of the defences at Yorktown and grounded their arms before Washington, Rochambeau, and their subordinates. Cornwallis had wondered about moving all his troops to Gloucester, in the hope of escaping from there, but a shortage of boats and a severe storm interfered and the bulk of his army remained at Yorktown. Before the surrender ceremonies, Cornwallis received permission to send out the very ill aboard the sloop *Bonetta,* which, under the terms of capitulation would be allowed through the blockade with Cornwallis's dispatches for Sir Henry Clinton in New York. Because the physicians informed him that

Simcoe's only chance of survival lay in a sea voyage, Cornwallis agreed to let him go.[8] With Simcoe went as many of the most vulnerable of the Rangers and Tarleton's Legionaires as could be crammed on the ship. Because Simcoe was so ill, Major Richard Armstrong had already assumed command of the regiment.

Many Rangers and junior officers were marched to temporary prison camps. The higher ranking officers were allowed to keep their side arms and possessions. They expected to be allowed to go on parole to New York when ships were available. Some of the deserters who returned to their old units were executed, almost on the spot; their tales of being unable to return sooner were not taken seriously. Article 10 of the terms of capitulation which Cornwallis drafted stated:

> Natives or Inhabitants of different parts of this Country
> at present in York or Gloucester are not to be punished
> on Acc't of having joined the British Army —[9]

Just as Simcoe had feared, Provincials were not protected: Washington wrote, "This Article cannot be assented to — being altogether of civil Resort."

Landed at New York, Simcoe now lay in a military hospital, feeling somewhat stronger. He wrote Sir Henry Clinton concerning rank in the British Army for his Rangers, and half-pay for his officers. Clinton, about to be recalled, agreed to promote the suggestion with the War Office when he reached London. Simcoe, too, would soon be home, invalided aboard a ship shortly to sail.

Before he left, some of the officers had reached New York from Yorktown, among them Major Richard Armstrong, Captain John McGill, who brought Simcoe's horse, Salem, and Lieutenant George Spencer. Colonel Banastre Tarleton and a few of his officers had also returned. Simcoe discovered that a paymaster from the British Legion, whom he called only "Mr. H." had absconded to the rebels at Philadelphia, taking with him some of the Legion's trophies — regimental flags captured during clashes at such places in the Carolinas as Monck's Corner, Lenud's Ferry, Waxhaws, Camden, Fishing Creek, Blackstock's Plantation, even their disaster at Cowpens. Probably because George Spencer put the idea in Simcoe's head, he gave his permission for the lieutenant to rescue these standards. He felt he owed Colonel Tarleton a favour for assuming overall command of the troops at Gloucester.

Clad in his green Ranger uniform, Spencer set out on a round trip of 200 miles by direct routes, somewhat longer along less-travelled ones. He returned before Simcoe sailed, with a tale to tell. He had entered Philadelphia undetected, and a few enquiries directed him to the inn where Mr. H. was staying. Discovering him to be absent, Spencer found the room he was occupying and a hopeful-looking trunk. Inside were the precious colours. Spencer hurriedly removed his coat, waistcoat and pulled his linen shirt over his head. He wrapped the flags carefully around his bare torso, and replaced his shirt and waistcoat. Finding the jacket too tight now, he used a knife to split it up the back, and he put it on, buttoning it in front.

He set off for New York in a vehicle and delivered the "standards" to Major Armstrong. He reported that on the way he had been insulted at Brunswick (now New Brunswick, New Jersey) because of the anger of local people over incursions by the Queen's Rangers. The spectre of the dead Captain Vorhees, who was to have been married the next day, still haunted the Rangers. On one occasion Spencer was saved from attack during dinner by four American officers who were travelling in the same wagon. No one found the reclaimed colours he was carrying, or "an attack would have been a certainty."

Simcoe reached England in early December, about the same time as Sir Henry Clinton. He soon discovered that some of his officers had been ordered to surrender to the French, as a way of protecting them from irate rebels. Repatriating them promised to be complicated because some of them were on their way to France. While officially convalescing, Simcoe would be kept busy with letters to Dr. Benjamin Franklin, the American plenipotentiary in Paris, and with sending replies to requests for help. Apparently, Simcoe himself was on parole to the French, but he was safe at home. Franklin claimed to know nothing about British officers being held in France, but Simcoe had heard that the Americans had requested the French to detain them.[10]

The new commander at New York was General Sir Guy Carleton, a man experienced in dealing with Provincials in the Northern, or Canadian, Military Department. He had served at Quebec City as governor and commander in chief. From certain disenchanted individuals, Carleton heard charges of brutality perpetrated by the Queen's Rangers which he chose to believe. Although Carleton was competent, and he would deal well with the migration of Loyalists by sea to Nova Scotia, he was a man who held a grudge. He had formed a dislike of the Queen's Rangers and of their absent commander.

Unaware of Carleton's attitude, Simcoe would soon be on his way to Devonshire, to recuperate at Hembury Fort House, cradled in a valley in the Blackdown Hills. There his godfather, Admiral Samuel Graves, and his second wife, Margaret Spinckes Graves, had invited him to stay with them so that they could give him tender care. The one who took a particular interest in the well being of the veteran partisan was Miss Elizabeth Posthuma Gwillim, Mrs. Graves' niece.

With the evacuation of Charleston, in 1782, the four troops of Hussars reached New York and they were reunited with the rest of the Queen's Rangers under Major Armstrong. Later in the year the garrison at Savannah was withdrawn. In the colonies that had rebelled, only New York, the surrounding islands, and a chain of forts along the Canadian border, were still under British occupation. Benedict Arnold reached Britain not long after Simcoe himself. From the safety of New York, he had had no difficulty eluding any rebels who would cheerfully have hanged him.

John Graves Simcoe's contribution to the campaign in the rebelling colonies is best summarised in a letter Sir Henry Clinton wrote to Lord George Germain from Charleston, South Carolina, in May 1780:

> Lieut. Col. Simcoe has been at the head of a battalion since October 1777 and since that time has been in the perpetual advance of the army. The history of the Corps under his command is a series of gallant, skilful and successful enterprises against the enemy, without a single reverse The Queen's Rangers have killed or taken twice their own numbers. Col. Simcoe himself has been thrice wounded, and I do not scruple to assert that his successes have been no less the fruit of the most extensive knowledge of his profession which study and the experience within his reach could give him, than the most watchful attention and shining courage.[11]

Simcoe's decision as a teenager to "prefer the field to the forum" was more than justified.

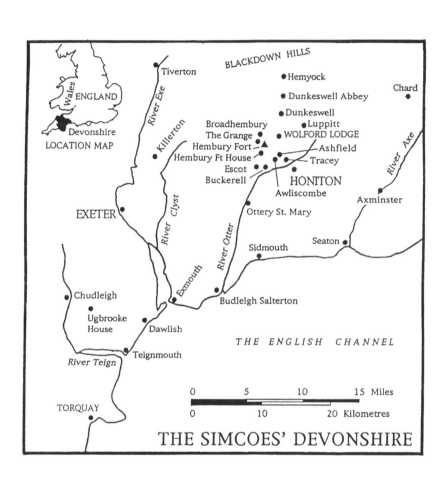

THE SIMCOES' DEVONSHIRE

PART III:
COUNTRY GENTLEMAN

From 1782 until 1791, Simcoe lived the life of a wealthy Devonshire landowner, although he remained deeply committed to outside events. The near-decade saw love, marriage, the purchase of properties, large and small, and a steadily arriving stream of children. Beyond Devonshire lay a turbulent Europe. The American Revolution was winding down, but British involvement with France, India and other trouble spots continued unabated.

In 1782, British Admiral George Rodney defeated a French fleet in the West Indies. Spain captured Minorca from Britain and laid siege to Gibraltar. Britain and France fought the naval battle of Cuddalore, off Madras. Admiral Richard Howe relieved Gibraltar. The Tipoo, ruler of Mysore, began a campaign that defeated the British in 1783.

The Peace of Versailles, signed 3 September 1783, between Britain, France, Spain and the United States, granted independence to the former British colonies. France recovered some West and East Indian possessions; Spain retained Minorca and regained Florida. By a separate peace, the Treaty of Fontainebleau, Britain and Holland settled their differences. Concerned that the private-enterprise East India Company was exploiting the peoples of India, the Pitt Ministry passed an act that placed the company under a government-appointed Board of Control that tried to forbid interference in the affairs of independent Indian states.

In 1785, Lord Cornwallis, of Yorktown, Virginia, fame, was appointed Governor General of India (which really meant mainly Bengal, then entirely under British control). Catherine the Great achieved an alliance with Russia and Austria in 1787. Britain and Holland formed their alliance in 1788, concerned over the future of the Austrian Netherlands (Belgium). The first British penal colony on the continent of Australia opened at Botany Bay. The British Parliament had a defeated vote to abolish the slave trade.

In France, the populace was stirring towards the outbreak that commenced in 1789. That August, French revolutionaries abolished the feudal system, and the National Assembly adopted the Declaration of the Rights of Man. Emigration of French Royalists began. The Netherlands rebelled against Austria. Owing to the first illness of King George III, Britain's Parliament passed a Regency Bill.

In May 1790, Britain and Spain were close to war, over the Spanish occupation of islands around Nootka Sound on the west coast of North America. That was settled when the Spanish agreed to withdraw. In July, Britain formed an alliance with the Nizam of Hyderabad. Power in France began to pass to the Jacobins. In July 1791, King Louis XVI was taken prisoner to prevent him leaving France.

EIGHT
LOVE IN THE BLACKDOWN HILLS

During the sea voyage, Simcoe's health improved as he had hoped, enough that he resolved to spend some time in London before accepting the hospitality of Admiral and Mrs. Graves. In London he could further his career and possibly benefit his regiment. He would do all in his power to have the Queen's Rangers placed on the British regular establishment, and numbered. Thus his officers would be eligible for half-pay and permanent rank in the army. He would need the support of highly placed friends. Burying himself in Devon would mean throwing away opportunities. He was well aware that competence counted for little in the unsavoury world of politics. What mattered most was having the right people speaking up for you. The most influential person he could approach was Francis Lord Rawdon, heir to the Earl of Moira, invalided home only a few months before Simcoe himself. Rawdon was now in London, and an aide-de-camp to the King.[1] He had been rewarded for his work in South Carolina, notably at the Battle of Hobkirk's Hill, near Camden, called by Lord Cornwallis "by far the most splendid of this war." When Cornwallis moved to

Virginia, Rawdon, commander in chief of the colony, was based at Charleston until he became too ill to continue.

His return to England had been more complicated than Simcoe's The ship carrying him had been captured by a French privateer and taken into Brest. Held as a prisoner of war, he was sent home through an exchange of prisoners. Rawdon was Anglo-Irish, born in County Down in December 1754, and he was less than two years younger than Simcoe. Educated at Harrow, Rawdon had been commissioned Ensign in the 15th Foot, but he had attended Oxford before joining his regiment. Like Simcoe, he did not stay for a degree. At Bunker/Breed's Hill he had taken two shots through his cap. He had been elected to the Irish Parliament while he was still in South Carolina.

On 24 December Rawdon wrote to Simcoe at his London address, inviting him to a dinner party at the St. James home of his uncle, Lord Huntingdon.[2] (Rawdon's mother was Lady Elizabeth Hastings, a daughter of the 9th Earl of Huntingdon.) The hour for the dinner was the then fashionable five o'clock in the afternoon. There Simcoe met several influential people who could help him further his ambitions. Rawdon was then working to have his Volunteers of Ireland, 2nd American Regiment put on the British establishment. In time he succeeded, and the regiment became the 105th. At the same time, Simcoe was confirmed as a brevet (rank without pay) Lieutenant Colonel of the Queen's Rangers.[3]

Satisfied with his progress to date, and very aware that he could no longer delay a complete rest, Simcoe set out by stagecoach for Honiton, and Hembury Fort House, the home of his godfather. This peaceful mansion, in its beautiful setting, was the ideal place to recuperate. Admiral Graves had built the house in 1765, high on a hillside with views towards the south coast and Sidmouth. Hembury Fort House, now a retirement home, stands amidst some of the finest scenery — the Blackdown Hills that extend along the Devon-Cornwall border. They form a land of lofty rises and plateaux, many extending 800 feet, cut by deep and mysterious coombes, the commons and heathland, watered by many streams that feed the Culm and Otter Rivers (the later immortalised by Samuel Taylor Coleridge in his "Ode to the Otter").

Human contact has shaped this landscape, long occupied by man. Close to Hembury Fort House is the Iron Age hill fort of Hembury, with earthwork fortifications. It was originally a Neolithic camp, and later used by the Romans. Nearby runs the Roman road west to Exeter (the Roman Isca Dumnoniorum). For some time Hembury Fort was thought to have been the "lost" Roman station of Moridunum, until 1991 when archaeologists from the Royal Albert Museum in Exeter identified the true site of Moridunum as Axminster, fifteen miles to the east. (The Roman station was uncovered during the course of the building of a modern bypass. Progress has some benefits for archaeology.)

The hills are dotted with sites of early "barrows" or burial mounds dating back thousands of years. In 1201, Cistercian monks founded Dunkeswell Abbey. The monks used the abbey, and outlying buildings they had erected, until 1539, the last year that Henry VIII was dissolving the monasteries. By the time Simcoe visited Hembury Fort House, local people had long been using stones from the Cistercian remains to build farmhouses, walls and cottages. One of Simcoe's interests was archaeology; he would find much to entertain him during his recovery.

By their nature the Blackdowns abound with legends of pixies and demons, smugglers, poachers, ghosts of Celtic and Saxon warriors, and ghosts of participants in the ill-fated Monmouth Rebellion of 1685 who were executed after Judge Jeffrey's "bloody Assizes." Such stories would also have intrigued the historian in Simcoe, and helped cultivate the romantic streak in his makeup.

Romance was also in the air. Waiting to greet him at Hembury Fort House were, not only Mrs. Margaret Graves and the Admiral, but her nineteen-year-old niece, Miss Elizabeth Posthuma Gwillim.

As her middle name hints, Elizabeth had been orphaned at birth, in September 1762. Her father, Thomas Gwillim, the lieutenant colonel of the 50th Foot, had died, probably in March, while serving with his regiment in Germany. Her mother, Elizabeth Spinckes Gwillim, had died in childbirth. She had been buried the following day in the family plot near All Saint's parish church, in the village of Aldwincle (now spelled Aldwinkle), Northamptonshire, not far from John Graves Simcoe's own birthplace.[4]

The Gwillims' only child, Elizabeth had spent her early years with her grandmother, Jemima Steward Spinckes, at her mother's home where she had been born.[5] She was the sole heir to Aldwinkle, the Spinckes estate, and to Old Court, the Gwillim manor at Whitchurch, Herefordshire. When she was fourteen, in 1776, her grandmother Spinckes died at Aldwinkle. Afterwards, a cousin, William Walcot of nearby Oundle — a good friend of John Graves Simcoe — took care of her interests at Aldwinkle, while her father's sister, also Elizabeth Gwillim, presided over Old Court. This aunt, as was the custom of the day, was called Mrs. Gwillim because she managed the family property, although she never married. After the death of her grandmother, Elizabeth divided her time between Whitchurch, Hembury Fort House, and the Graves's London town house.

In 1769, at age fifty-six, Admiral Graves had married Margaret Spinckes, who was forty-two. The admiral's first wife had been Elizabeth Sedgewick, of Staindrop, the birthplace of John Graves Simcoe's father. Samuel Graves may have met Miss Sedgewick through the Simcoe family. His godson could have met Miss Gwillim before he went to war when she was a mere child. At nineteen, she was petite, with dark hair and eyes that denoted her Welsh heritage. She was well schooled in the talents expected of a young woman of means. Although not as much an intellectual as Simcoe, she had been taught to draw and paint in water colours, to speak excellent French and some Spanish, and to be an "amiable companion." Typical of educated people of the time, both were writers of long letters and diaries.

She rode very well, and enjoyed jaunts into the Blackdown Hills. At first, Simcoe was content to take long walks, but as his strength returned he, too, loved to ride farther afield. Together they climbed to the top of Hembury Fort, in recent times overgrown, the top covered with brambles and bracken. The Romans had made use of it as a camp, but were thought to have abandoned it about 60 A.D. As the young couple came and went, Admiral Graves watched, satisfied, from the sidelines. Margaret was less enthusiastic about the growing relationship. She had made certain she had passed child-bearing age before marrying, and thought Elizabeth would do well to emulate her. Aunt Margaret had another complaint which no doubt Elizabeth often heard. With marriage, her fortune became the property of her husband. She had lost control of what was hers and she felt resentful of male dominance over women.[6] She also felt possessive towards her sole descendant. Gradually, however, her strongest opposition melted. Simcoe could charm her, and he knew he had to win her over. He had truly fallen in love.

Just how strongly Elizabeth reciprocated is difficult to assess. True to her time, she was what Jan Morris described as one of "the cool amusing ladies of the age of reason."[7] The admiral could see the virtue of marriage to his wife's niece. Simcoe had the talent to rise in the service, and the common sense to take care of Elizabeth's fortune. An admirable arrangement, he foresaw, a good husband for Elizabeth, and a responsible man who would use her fortune wisely. His godson was too honourable a man to marry her simply for her money.

As his energy revived, Simcoe occasionally rode into Exeter to see old friends, and to make new ones. In February 1782, he was made a Freeman of the City. Earlier, this honour had been bestowed on Edward Drewe, whose fortunes had not progressed much since his court martial back in 1780. He was still protesting his innocence. Another new friend, also named Edward Drewe, was a cousin of his old army friend. He was the son of Francis Drewe of The Grange, the manor house outside the thatched-roofed village of Broadhembury. This second Edward was studying for holy orders, and in a few years he would be ordained, a calling Simcoe thought was as worthy as the military.[8]

During the winter, Simcoe made a few more visits to London, in the hope of furthering his career. In 1782 the journey was not very comfortable — by stagecoach from Honiton, on the main coach route between London and Exeter. He had to stop overnight at a hostelry in or near the cathedral city of Salisbury. He must have found the travelling hard despite the improvement in his overall health.

He saw more of Lord Rawdon, and he made a useful new friend, James Bland Burges, an ambitious politician. Like Rawdon, Burges was better-born than Simcoe; his father, George, had a military career and was famous for capturing the standard carried by Bonnie Prince Charlie's body guard at Culloden in 1746. Later, George was comptroller-general of the Scottish customs. James Bland Burges's mother, Anne, was a daughter of the Scottish peer, Lord Somerville. Simcoe probably became acquainted with James through the latter's sister, Mary Anne Burges. Mary Anne, the same age and a very dear friend of Elizabeth Gwillim, was a regular visitor to Hembury Fort House, and for a time she had resided in Bath.[9]

Of the two young women, Mary Anne was the more intellectual, and the leader in their studies of Spanish. She was a competent botanist and fascinated by geology. She was also shy, but she entered heartily into discussions on the history and structure of the Blackdown Hills. Like Elizabeth she was a good rider. During her visits Simcoe often accompanied both girls to Hembury Fort and to other sites worth investigating. Still he was at a loose end and wondering when he might find new employment. Meanwhile, he was falling more in love with Elizabeth Gwillim. Elizabeth was his choice, although he found Mary Anne Burges a good companion. Whether Elizabeth's wealth made the difference is beyond contemplation. Mary Anne lived on a small allowance from her Somerville relations, and the earnings for articles she wrote for magazines and pamphlets.

Throughout the winter, responsibility for the welfare of the Queen's Rangers weighed heavily on Simcoe. Letters from Captain Stair Agnew particularly offended him. On 26 February, Agnew had written, from St. Malo's castle, reciting the hardships he had endured since before the surrender at Yorktown. Taken prisoner earlier in the campaign, he had been handed, as a prisoner, to the French, and with other officers, taken aboard the ship *Romulus*. Agnew was moved, with others, to the *Hermione* for transport to France, but the ship was rerouted to Boston. There he was put on *La Concorde* bound for "St. Domingo," where he arrived on 6 July. He would have been sent to the common prison except for the humanity of the captain of *La Concorde*. He was kept in a hospital for four months, where the "cells were very hot." At that time the French and the American rebels were operating in Virginia. On 23 October, which was after the surrender at Yorktown, the officer-prisoners were put on ships "armed en Flute" (at the time a term applying to naval transport vessels) for France. The passage had been dismal.

Here, Agnew stated that his father had been among the prisoners. One ship foundered, while the one carrying Agnew and his father lost its rudder in a storm. They escaped from the endangered ship, only to be treated more barbarously in France. On 6 December they reached Brest, and were confined in Dinant Castle, possibly as hostages for French officers held captive by Admiral Arbuthnot. (Marriot Arbuthnot had a reputation as a bungler.) The Agnews were placed in the castle dungeon, and Stair suspected "a secret reason for such treatment." He had written to Lord George Germain before he had been denied pen, ink and paper. He hoped that Simcoe would inform his friends of their miserable situation in case his own letter should not reach Germain.

Captain Agnew wrote again, on 20 August 1782. He had not heard from Simcoe, but was now on parole, by order of the Duke of Harcourt, the governor of Normandy. The American minister (Benjamin Franklin) had sent word that the Americans wanted captured officers detained in France, probably until they had negotiated a peace with Great Britain. Agnew enclosed a letter from Franklin to Germain, disclaiming all knowledge of prisoners detained in France. In the next breath Franklin agreed that prisoners could reside in Caen. "Such are the misfortunes attendant on civil war," Agnew concluded. "Are we not British officers? Are we not French prisoners?" Simcoe was aware that Germain had been negotiating for the release of prisoners before he himself had returned to England, thus far to no avail.[10]

After he had done what he felt he could for the unfortunate Agnews, Simcoe thought of making a visit to the Newcastle area in the hope of tracing his father's relations, people named Blackett, although he wondered whether they were "extinct." During his mother's lifetime, she might have told him something, but typical of youth, his curiosity had not yet been aroused. From London on 1 July 1782, he wrote to Admiral Graves thanking him for a letter of credit.[11] At that time his social life would have been rather expensive. His calendar included a visit to

Strawberry Hill in Middlesex, then a delightful village on the Thames River not far from London. Apparently William Pitfield of Exeter had "ordered" him to visit the place. Simcoe was travelling at that time with his old friend, William Walcot, who was visiting from Northamptonshire. In closing his letter, Simcoe sent his respects to Miss Gwillim and Miss Graves. The latter was probably Mary Graves, the only daughter of naval Captain Thomas Graves, a nephew of the admiral.[12]

While he was in London, Simcoe endeavoured to have his promotion to brevet colonel backdated to the date of his Provincial promotion during his active command of the Queen's Rangers. He was also concerned about his seniority in the British Army, which would affect his pension. He travelled back to Devonshire in late summer, looking forward to the company of Miss Gwillim. Whether an understanding existed before his return is unknown, but soon after he arrived at Hembury Fort House he began looking for an estate that would make a suitable home for his bride to be. It would, of course, be purchased mainly from Elizabeth's fortune, but Simcoe was determined to make a wise choice.

A good-sized property known as "Woolford Church" caught his eye. It lay above the valley through which flowed the tiny River Wolf. The land was situated in the parish of Dunkeswell, high in the Blackdowns, north of Honiton, and only a short way from Hembury Fort House, as the crow flew. He employed Robert Gidley, a Honiton agent, to explore the estate's potential. The old single-storeyed manor house, which he thought would have to be replaced, was situated with a view down towards the sea at Sidmouth. The site was admirable, the dwelling impossible.

Author J.A. Sparks thought that Wolford (or Woolford) took its name from a 7th century Mercian king, Wulfer, and that a church may have stood there, named in his honour — thus "Wulferchurche." It may have been presented to the Cistercian monks of Dunkeswell Abbey, which had been founded in 1201 A.D. In 1496 the name changed to "Wullforde Churche" and by 1782 to "Woolford Church." On the other hand, the name may derive from a church that Cistercian monks built on the River Wolf as an adjunct to their abbey. Perhaps the interesting background of the property held a strong attraction for a man much fascinated by history.[13]

On 9 November 1782, Robert Gidley wrote to Simcoe supplying him with information about the "Wolford Church Estate," owned at that time by a Mr. Peter Genest. Wolford Church was let to a farmer named John Marks for a term of seven years from Lady Day 1778 at an annual rent of £128 "tithe free." The best part of the house, Gidley reported, was preserved. Mr. Genest discharged the Land Tax (a form of taxation introduced in 1762 and destined to remain in force until 1832. The usual rate was four shillings in the pound. Records from 1780 to 1832 list individuals paying the tax in each county.) Gidley had arranged for the property to be surveyed and he informed Simcoe that Genest had fixed a price of £2,730. Tithes, theoretically a tenth of the income of the estate from its various sources, went to the upkeep of the incumbent of the local parish church.

Gidley wrote again on 26 November, enclosing a comprehensive history of the parish of Dunkeswell together with details of transactions involving Wolford in 1632. The individuals concerned were Theophilis Marwood and Hannibal Rowe. Gidley confirmed that he had instructed Mr. Townsend, Mr. Genest's lawyer, that Simcoe was also interested in acquiring an additional property named "Little Wolford Church."

Meanwhile, preparations were well in hand for the wedding of Colonel Simcoe and Miss Gwillim. The ceremony would take place at the parish church of St. Mary and St. Giles, Buckerell, situated about a mile from Hembury Fort House. Still, Simcoe found time for another visit to London, and was there when Gidley wrote to him on 21 December:

> I have received the favour of your letter and will do the best in my power for your service but apprehend from it you do not mean for an absolute bargain until you return into the country [Devon] nor does there appear to me any necessity for it as you will be here again so soon and there is no present appearance of another purchaser. If I mistake you please set me right. I have writ Mr. Townsend and by the same note have asked the price of the other estates and titles as you desire.

> As to the right of enclosing the common from all other proprietors I think it cannot be done, at least without their full consent, which will be difficult to obtain [,] great parts of the land being under settlement — several parts of it have been inclosed, from time to time by several of the proprietors for which small acknowledgements are paid by them at the court but this cannot give any permanent right to such [letter torn] ... made several inclosures on the Common which the first Mr. Genest disputed with him, at great expence, succeeded, and threw all the hedges down again. The

banks are still to be seen there.

Mr. Genest's covenant to produce the Title Deeds to protect your title to the premises if his title is approved of and you become the purchaser effectually answer your purpose, it is everyday done and when Gentlemen dismember their estates it must, of necessity be done this way, especially when a Gentleman reserves any part of the estate to himself as in the present case; an attested copy of the original conveyance of Mr. Genest's Estates from Marwood and Rowe to go with the conveyances. The Rights and Immunities belonging to the premises being very particularly granted by those conveyances which will be proper for you to have by you to refer to on all occasions.

I am, Sir, your &c
Robt. Gidley.[14]

Enclosure of common land was one method of enlarging an estate. Much has been written about the evils of the system which deprived the poor of free grazing. In fact, enclosure was part of the agricultural revolution. Open fields, and leaving potentially arable land for common grazing, were inefficient. If land was to become more productive, the old system required reform. Rather than depriving the poor of their livelihood, Simcoe as showing foresight that was characteristic of the man.

He was back at Hembury Fort House by 30 December, and he probably found Gidley's letter waiting for him. On the 25th, the Queen's Rangers were officially put on the British establishment, and all the commissions bore this date. The officers would receive the benefits as regulars, no longer second-rate Provincials. Simcoe himself was now the lieutenant colonel commandant of the "Queen's American Rangers." Thus they ware described on The Army List, but unlike Lord Rawdon's Irishmen, Simcoe's regiment was never numbered.[15]

On the 30th the party left Hembury Fort House and drove by carriage to the peaceful and pretty village of Buckerell, to the fifteenth century parish church. Ancient yew trees shade many of the graves of past parishioners, a spot reminiscent of part of Thomas Grey's "Elegy":

> Beneath those rugged elm, that Yew-tree's shade,
> Where heaves the turf in many a mouldring heap,
> Each in his narrow cell for ever laid,
> The rude Forefathers of the hamlet sleep.

Buckerell lay in the "Hundred" of Hemyock. A "hundred" was an administrative division of a shire, introduced into England in the tenth century. The name is now historic. A parish is still of considerable importance in the county structure and has its own council of elected representatives. Like others, the church of St. Mary and St. Giles is usually locked. The church can be visited by arrangement with the incumbent or churchwarden, to view a memorial to Admiral Samuel Graves, and an 18th-century plan of the church showing the location of the Graves' family pew.

Lieutenant Colonel John Graves Simcoe and Miss Elizabeth Posthuma Gwillim were married by licence, more costly than having the banns read and customary among the wealthy members. The local curate, Thomas Roskilly, officiated. His surname signified West Country origin, but Cornish rather than Devonian. The witnesses were Admiral and Mrs. Graves. Most likely, the church was filled to capacity by the local gentry and by friends who had come from Exeter, London, from the bride's family in the Welsh borderlands, Northamptonshire and elsewhere. Some of the guests would have stayed with the Graves, other members of the gentry, or at coaching inns such as the Dolphin in Honiton. Military uniforms lent a note of colour, in addition to the ladies' gowns. One man who was certainly invited was the local Member of Parliament, Sir George Yonge, whose country seat was Escot, near Honiton. John Graves and Elizabeth were now Colonel and Mrs. Simcoe. Still unsettled was a place to live.

NINE
WOLFORD LODGE 1783–1787

The war was as much as over. Preliminary articles of peace had been signed in Paris. The Queen's Rangers, in limbo on Long Island, would be taken by sea to Nova Scotia for resettlement. Some of the officers would prefer England, but the majority were to be settled in the landward portion of the colony that would be separated the following year as the Province of New Brunswick. Two who would be coming to England were Captain David Shank and Lieutenant George Spencer. Major Richard Armstrong was in command until the Rangers would be disbanded on British territory. Captain Stair Agnew was able to leave France and settle at Nashwaak (north of Fredericton), an area allocated to the Queen's Rangers and their dependents. John Agnew, the regimental chaplain, also settled there. John may be the father Stair did not mention by name in his letters to Simcoe. Many Ranger officers would be leaders in the civil and military life of New Brunswick.[1]

In his account of the war years, Simcoe revealed nothing of his religious views. That he was a devout Anglican emerges as he settled into civilian life in Devonshire. He did not refer to the work his chaplain did during the arduous campaigns, but it must have been significant. As his circle of friends in Devon increased, many were members of the Church of England clergy.

In April 1783, Robert Gidley, the agent, informed Simcoe that acquiring "Little Woolford Church Estate" posed no problem, but he had had no word from Peter Genest, the owner of "Woolford Church Estate." Simcoe's new legal adviser, Christopher Flood, helped with the final details, and by 15 June, Simcoe was sending his letters showing his address as "Wolford Lodge" (his spelling). He had had work started demolishing the manor house, to make way for a fine new mansion suitable for a well-to-do county family. Some time would pass before the house was ready for its occupants. In the meantime the Simcoes rented a place in Exeter. Sir George Yonge offered them part of Escot, but Simcoe preferred to make his own arrangements.[2]

Meanwhile, many letters had flowed to and from Long Island, where the Queen's Rangers were packing to leave. One, dated 10 July 1783, was from Captain John McGill. Simcoe had requested the Quartermaster to send his horse, Salem, to England. He longed to care for the horse through his final years. McGill wrote that Salem would embark on "the good ship *Nancy* " on 15 July. The vessel was bound for Liverpool. McGill had arranged for one Thomas (likely his surname) to travel with the horse to Liverpool, and then ride him the 240 miles to Honiton. Thomas was probably a Ranger who needed a cheap way to reach England. McGill had paid Thomas to 24 October. During the ride to Honiton, estimated to take fifteen days, Thomas would require two shillings a day. McGill added, "I hope to preserve Salem for a milder fate than that mentioned by you." McGill had drawn £40 from Captain James Kerr, acting paymaster for the Rangers, to cover Salem's expenses, a tidy sum to save the beloved quadruped.[3]

Although his letter to McGill has not been found, Simcoe revealed his motive in a letter to William Walcot:

> I have a poney [sic] come fr. America, an old servant. I ordered it to be led to a grave with all its trappings & then shot rather than the American Chiefs, the miscreants of the Earth, should ride him OR that it should be sent home for when I allotted £40 the latter was effected to my joy. He is not worth 10 — but I love an old servant.[4]

The Simcoes continued enlarging their domain. When Christopher Flood discovered that the "Percy Estate" was for sale at £1,670, Simcoe purchased it.[5] He still sought advancement in the military field — and in politics. The best way to achieve the first was to become involved in the second. On 1 January 1784, the Exeter *Flying Post* published his letter "To the GENTLEMEN, CLERGY, FREEMEN and FREEHOLDERS of the City of EXETER." He claimed to have left retirement owing to the "alarming Situation of Public Affairs" and he would offer himself as a candidate to represent them, should Parliament suddenly be dissolved. On the 8th the *Flying Post* published a second letter. When he learned that the present Member, John Baring, would seek re-election, Simcoe withdrew his offer, ... "for the tranquility of the City." This last was perhaps an excuse; as a relatively new figure in the district, he risked a humiliating defeat by the well-known Baring. Coincidentally, on the very day of Simcoe's "withdrawal" he was apparently enjoying a drink or two with friends in the Globe Tavern. An Exeter gentleman named Samuel Poole was in the habit of recording what he described as "Remarkable Occurrences" that took place in Exeter. Poole noted an incident:

> 1784 8th Jany Died Mr. John Rice Fuller of this City he was making merry with Lieut Colonel Simcoe and some other Gentlemen at the Globe Tavern he fell down dead & never spoke again.

Was Simcoe drowning his sorrows with supporters of his candidacy, or simply attending a meeting of his Masonic Lodge? Perhaps he was merely enjoying a quiet pint of ale with friends.[6]

On the domestic front, Simcoe was a worried man, anxiously awaiting the birth of a child. Elizabeth was in good health, but he could not forget how her mother had died.[7] On 28 January 1784, a daughter, the first of their eleven children was born. She was baptized on 1 September by Reverend John Land, at the parish church of St. Nicholas, the event set down in the Dunkeswell Parish Register: "Eliza, Daughter of Lt. Col. John Graves Simcoe and Elizabeth Posthuma, his Wife, born at Exeter January 28th 1784, baptized at Dunkeswell."

Work on Wolford Lodge continued. When finished it would have two storeys and forty rooms. It was set on a knoll, about 800 feet (250 metres) above sea level, with superb views across the Vale of Honiton towards the south coast at the Sidmouth Gap. On either side of the valley, below the house, wooded hills framed a view that has altered very little with time.

Simcoe embarked on a large-scale landscaping project. As well, the Simcoes were establishing relationships with the local gentry, farmers and villagers in Dunkeswell and the surrounding parishes. They continued their fascination with prehistoric sites. During this period, the Scadding family became involved with the Colonel and his lady. The Scaddings were a local family who had been living in southeast Devon for generations. One branch had been at the village of Hemyock since the early 17th century. They were of good yeoman stock, the backbone of agricultural England. Although mainly farming folk, some in Hemyock worked in the cloth making industry. In the 1780s two Scadding brothers, John and Thomas, lived in the Dunkeswell area. John became estate manager for the Simcoes, and in ensuing years he was as close to them as any man in his position could be. He played a vital part in helping the Simcoes create their estate, making it one of the most delightful in the area. Simcoe introduced species of trees and shrubs alien to the neighbourhood, a practice popular in the 1780s, but now out of favour as a threat to native flora.

On 18 August 1785, a second daughter was born, and she was baptized Charlotte at St. Nicholas, Dunkeswell, on 3 September. When Charlotte was a few months old, both girls contracted smallpox. This was no accident. Eliza and Charlotte had been inoculated.[8] Each girl was given material from someone suffering a mild form of the disease. As a result, most children so inoculated developed a mild form of smallpox and were immune thereafter. The parents had taken a calculated risk. Occasionally a child would develop a severe form, and would die or be badly scarred for life. Already the English physician, Edward Jenner, had begun his experiments with a vaccine made from cowpox material, but he did not inoculate his first patient, an eight-year-old boy, until 1796. Both girls made a good recovery, to the satisfaction of their relatives.

Mary Anne Burges, living in Bath in 1786, had become a close neighbour. She had leased Tracey, a large country house in the parish of Awliscombe, adjacent to Dunkeswell and only three miles from Wolford Lodge. Mary Anne and Elizabeth were now seeing each other almost daily. The distance made a pleasant walk or ride either way. The two young women pursued their interests in sketching, improving their Spanish, studying botany, and playing with the little girls when it suited them. At Wolford Lodge an army of servants obeyed the instructions of a nursemaid in the remote part of the upper floor that was reserved for the children. Elizabeth enjoyed doing embroidery, but Mary Anne, who had to watch her pennies, used her needle to repair mundane items such as gowns and bedsheets.

Among the Simcoes' dearest friends were the Hunts. Mrs. Mary Ann Hunt was the widow of a naval captain who had served with Admiral

Graves. She had three children, Mary, Caroline and Edward, the latter a future curate of Benefield, near Oundle, the home of William Walcot.[9]

Mary was probably the elder daughter, because she was addressed as Miss Hunt; Caroline was referred to as Miss Caroline. Mother and daughters had been frequent guests of Mrs. Graves at Hembury Fort House. They lived in lodgings in Exeter, and Mary worked as a tutor to well-to-do families.

Following the birth of Charlotte, Simcoe had written to Miss Hunt, who was with the Graves at the time:

> I return your book. We are delighted with the sweet lines you have sent Charlotte and as she cannot at present express her approbation and thanks gives me leave to do it for her and when you favour us with a visit she should give you some kisses extraordinary. It's with great pleasure we expect you here and hope Mrs. Hunt will give us as much time as she can with convenience to herself. I am
> Yours affectionately
> J. Simcoe[10]

Towards the children Simcoe was playful, especially when they were very young. He possessed a light touch, which children adored. In contrast, Elizabeth, the orphaned only child, was often puzzled by their actions and reactions. She loved them, but she was more reserved in responding to them.

Letter writing was ingrained. Miss Hunt was only five minutes away, at Hembury Fort House, yet etiquette demanded the Colonel's charming letter. Farther away was Admiral Elliot[t], who lived with his wife and daughters near Colchester in the eastern county of Essex. Elliott was probably another old friend of Captain John Simcoe. In a letter to Admiral Elliott, Simcoe said he hoped they would soon have the opportunity of meeting Mrs. Simcoe for the first time. The Colonel also issued an invitation to the Admiral's son:

> I would be happy if you could spare Luther to visit Devonshire on his approaching Holy Days; the coach is no longer in coming from Colchester to Honiton than it is to Colchester and I apprehend you are not, in the least fearful of his travelling. We should be most happy in his company.

Before closing he had a request of one of Elliott's daughters, either Frances Anne or Mary:

> I beg my kindest comps to Miss Elliot and that you will tell her if she will send me a few lines which when I was a good little boy, I wrote to my mother; my wife is an admirable copyist will send her some others which I edited when I left all childish things.[11]

Simcoe was still making frequent visits to London, to maintain contacts with influential people. Lord Rawdon, now elevated to Baron Rawdon of Rawdon, was still his principal social contact as he sought a military appointment. William Pitfield was a regular visitor to Wolford Lodge and Hembury Fort House. When too busy with his duties at Exeter Hospital, Pitfield turned to letters. On one occasion he wrote, "Be pleased to send the boy to me on Thursday next before eleven and trust me for his admission to hospital."[12] The unidentified boy would have been a village lad or a son of a family friend who was in need of special attention.

Among the more impressive visitors to Wolford Lodge was the Reverend Samuel Badcock, who "attended on" the Simcoes in the autumn of 1786. Born in South Molton, Devon, to dissenting parents, Badcock had been sent to a school at Ottery St. Mary (about six miles south of Wolford Lodge) for the sons of people opposed to the Church of England. He was educated for the dissenting ministry, but about the time of his visit to Wolford Lodge, Badcock was seeking service within the established church. In 1787 he was ordained as a curate by the Bishop of Exeter and sent to serve at Broadclyst near the cathedral city.[13]

The word "Dissenter" is revealing. Evangelicals such as the Wesleys were still within the Anglican Church; Methodism as a separate denomination lay in the future. Although Badcock gives no hint, here may have been the influence that turned Simcoe into an Evangelical Anglican. Methodism would find fertile ground in the West Country. Simcoe's motive could have been to counter any movement that might interfere with the unity of the church.

Reverend Badcock was a theological and literary critic, and a prolific writer who contributed to many journals, including the very popular *Gentleman's Magazine*. In the latter, in 1788, Badcock described his visit to Wolford Lodge two years before:

> I have spent a fortnight with my old friend Col. S. at his charming retreat near Honiton, and there truly

enjoyed the feast of reason and the flow of souls. The Colonel divides his time between his studies and the improving of his estate. His studies are also divided between tactics and antiquities, Arrian and Dugdale. The former he was about to give a new translation of, illustrated with remarks founded on the examples of modern heros, particularly the Duke of Marlborough and the King of Prussia.

If Simcoe ever completed his translation of Arrian, his work has not been found. Sir William Dugdale (1605-1687) prepared, in liaison with Roger Dodsworth, "Monastican Anglicum" (a compilation of records of monastic property) and he wrote two classical works of historical importance, *The Baronetage of England* and *Antiquities of Warwickshire*. Badcock's journal continues:

> He is also engaged in tracing out the Roman Camps in the West of England; and is exploring, with great zeal, the remains of Monastic antiquity. He hath promised to communicate his collection ... The Colonel's house lies in the Parish of Dunkeswell; and near it are the remains of the ancient abbey of that name. We went one morning to visit it, and my mind was much impressed with the recollection of that period when monastic institutions flourished in this kingdom.

He was very taken with a young lady also staying at Wolford Lodge, who wrote lovely poetry. This same young lady had been for some months at Hembury Fort House. "The Colonel proposed a trial of poetic skill: I wisely declined the contest with superior genius."[14]

The lady, never mentioned by name, could be Mary Hunt, who wrote a poem about Dunkeswell Abbey that was published some years later.[15] Among Simcoe's own poems was a long one about the Earl of Essex's raid on Cadiz for good Queen Bess:

> Essex! ye Muse bless his name! thy flight
> Nor shall mischance nor envious clouds obscure
> Thou the bold Eaglet, whose superior height,
> While Cadiz towers, forever shall endure.
> O, if again Hope prompts the daring song,
> And Fancy stamps it with the mark of truth,

O, if again Brittania's [sic] coasts should throng
With such determined and heroic youth,
Be mine to raise her standards on that height,
While thou, great Chief! thy envied trophies bore!
Be mine to snatch from abject Spain the state,
Which in her mid-day pride, thy valour tore!
And oh! to crown my triumph, tho no Queen,
Cold politician, frown on my return,
Sweetly adorning the domestic scene,
Shall my Eliza with true passion burn,
Or smile amid her grief, at fame, who hovers o'er my urn.[16]

Was Simcoe taking liberty with the name of the Virgin Queen, or did he really mean his own wife or small daughter?

By October he was again negotiating to increase his holdings. Agent Robert Gidley advised him that Lawyer Christopher Flood found that Mr. Harrison expected £1,100 for his estate, which he could acquire by "Lady Day next" — 25 March, Annunciation Day. Whether Simcoe bought at that time is uncertain.

A third daughter, Henrietta Maria, nicknamed Harriet, was baptized at St. Nicholas Church on 24 April 1787. Like her older sisters, Harriet would be inoculated early, and again the Simcoes were lucky. By the time she arrived, the family was settled into Wolford Lodge. On 8 March 1787, Admiral Graves died at Hembury Fort House. Aunt Margaret then moved into Wolford Lodge. The Admiral had left his own house to his nephew, Richard Graves, a Captain in the Royal Navy.[17] About the same time, Simcoe became one of the twenty-six original subscribers to the formation of the Exeter Free Grammar School Old Boys' Society. In time he would become one of the society's four Stewards. Both events were published in the Exeter *Flying Post*.[18]

The Simcoes followed a set routine. "The Colonel," as Elizabeth and most others called him, rose early and rode over the estate, often in the company of John Scadding. He conducted prayers for the family, guests and staff, morning and evening in the new drawing room. That the house was so large was a blessing. Aunt Margaret was a spoiled old lady, accustomed to having her own way, and Elizabeth had to become adroit at coping with her.[19] In the meantime, Simcoe was pursuing some literary efforts. As a result he published two books, both printed in Exeter, before the end of the year.

The first, rather trivial, was *Remarks on the Travels of the Marquis de Castellux in North America*. It was a short critique of the Marquis's own book and the anti-British comments it contained. The second and by far the more significant was Simcoe's record of his time with his Rangers, *A Journal of the Operations of the Queen's Rangers from the end of 1777 to the conclusion of the late American War.* Using his own records, he wrote this work to counter charges of his conduct during the war, and that of his regiment. The main body of the journal is impersonal, but he added an appendix where he displayed more of his own feelings.[20] He incorporated plans for many of the encounters with the rebels. Lieutenant George Spencer, rescuer of the British Legion's trophies and other exploits, was the mapmaker who supplied some of them.[21]

As Simcoe was enjoying the comforts of home and family life, he remained concerned about events in the triumphant colonies that had been granted their independence. Through the Treaty of Separation of September 1783, the tie that bound the Americans to Britain was broken. The war had been successful, partly through French aid, and partly because Britons themselves had no stomach for continuing after Yorktown. At New York, Sir Guy Carleton, Sir Henry Clinton's successor, had sent some 40,000 Loyalists to the Maritimes.

By September 1787, a Constitutional Congress meeting in Philadelphia had resolved to create one country, the United States of America. The Continental Congress that had directed George Washington's Continental Army, had been a loose coalition to conduct the war. Following the peace treaty, thirteen vulnerable independent little republics went their various ways. As time passed, states' rights remained an issue, but strength through union was obvious. The congress passed a constitution, and the federation was born.

What, Simcoe pondered, would be the fate of the remaining provinces of British North America? Might the victorious Americans cast eyes on Canada, Nova Scotia, New Brunswick (established in 1784), Cape Breton Island, Isle Saint John (Prince Edward Island) or Newfoundland? Canada, he recognised, would be the most vulnerable because it was the most accessible overland. Loyalist troops who had served in the Northern Department had been resettled, with their dependents, along the shores of the upper St. Lawrence and the Great Lakes, places easy to attack. Thirteen republics had united, but not the little Republic of Vermont that had been neutral territory since 1781. Then legally part of New York, the people of the Green Mountains had declared their independence and set up their own government. Simcoe had never been in Vermont, but during the war he had envisaged those Green Mountains as a fine place to have a home.

In 1788 he sent a copy of his military journal to Sir Henry Clinton, who was preparing his own memoirs of the history of the American war, although they were never published. By that time Elizabeth had presented the Colonel with a fourth daughter, who was baptized Caroline at St. Nicholas, Dunkeswell, on 27 November.[22]

Clinton was feeling neglected since his return to England, and because of his many fruitless trips to London in search of a job, Simcoe was haunted by thoughts of Vermont:

> I wonder not at the sensibility you shew at the unworthy treatment you have met with; yet I doubt not but in the course of events, ample reparation awaits you, & you will be universally justified; for me the cold neglect even I humble as I am, have met with, weighs so strongly on my mind, that were my Four Girls Boys, I have little doubt but I should adjure England & become a citizen of Vermont; and this Idea has gained force since my last residence in London. Eton, Oxford & the Army has almost furnished me with the measurement of the Capacities of most of our Rulers & I fear their Hearts are not much better than I believe their heads to be, there is scarce a Statesman among them, trifling politicks and low pursuits govern all their Ideas — nor is our military Line much better; had I been Aid de Camp to the Prince, I heard resignations were threatened by men who could not prove one Enterprize & who would have it difficult to say where they were ever in the personal hazard of a musket ball.[23]

Maybe some day, he might achieve that dream. Joining Canada would benefit Vermont. Her best resources were timber, from which rafts could be built and floated down Lake Champlain and the Richelieu River to the St. Lawrence. Simcoe knew of negotiations whereby Vermont might be persuaded to become a British province, and he hoped they would succeed.

Ambitious though he was for a military appointment, he never felt entirely in good health. Elizabeth's aunt, Mrs. Gwillim, had once written from Whitchurch, enquiring about " ... the Colonel's bilious problem."[24] People knew very little about what caused digestive upsets and the true sources of most ailments. Certain herbal and metallic medicines were in use, but bacteria and their antidotes had yet to be discovered. Elizabeth liked to have her home kept clean, which helped, but not every illness could be prevented by a standard of hygiene that was high for the time.

TEN

INTO PARLIAMENT

Over time, the friendship between the Simcoes and the Drewes of Broadhembury and The Grange strengthened. A little background on the Drewes reveals how the county families were interconnected, and how the name Edward extended into the past. The story begins with a tablet erected in St. Andrew's Church, Broadhembury, to the memory of Francis Drewe (1712-1773):

> He was lineally descended from Edward Drewe Esq., Sergeant-at-law to Queen Elizabeth and Recorded of the city of London in that reign. Tho he moved in a less conspicuous sphere of life than his ancestors, He contented himself with living to establish the character of a diligent and upright magistrate, a valuable neighbour, a faithful friend and one of the best of parents.

In his will, dated 5 September 1771, he mentions his two wives, his surviving children and his brother Edward, who, with Francis's son

105

Thomas Rose Drewe and his nephew James Bernard Esq., proved his will in April 1773. This Edward was the father of Simcoe's friend and cashiered officer, Major Edward Drewe. Francis's seventh son, Herman, three years older than Simcoe and another dear friend, was in holy orders. Francis's eighth son (this one by his second wife) also Edward, was baptized on 27 September 1756 at the church in Broadhembury. He was four years younger than Simcoe, and was also a valued friend. While Simcoe was becoming a warrior, this Edward was destined for the church. His mother, Mary Johnson, was a cousin of Elizabeth Sedgwick, Admiral Graves's first wife, whom he probably met through Captain John Simcoe or his wife Katherine.

In the churchyard that surrounds St. Andrew's are many Drewe graves. Broadhembury has changed very little since the days when Colonel and Mrs. Simcoe paid social calls on the Drewe family. Every property is thatched. The male line of the family at The Grange died out in 1903 and the properties were sold. Yet every effort has continued to ensure that Broadhembury retains its original appearance. Francis Drewe, who was born there in 1919, recorded that his grandfather purchased the village, but not The Grange. They took up residence in Broadhembury House. Although the present Drewe family that owns Broadhembury can not prove direct descent, there must be a connection.[1]

Noteworthy is the link to the time-honoured hymn "Rock of Ages." The vicar of St. Andrew's from 1768 to 1788 was Reverend Augustus Toplady, who wrote the words — sung to three different tunes, at least. A popular pub is the Drewe Arms. Passing through its stout wooden door is like stepping back several centuries — but mind your head, the beams are low; watch how you step on that uneven flagged floor!

Although the Drewes were such dear friends, they were not people of great influence. Simcoe placed greater hope in Mary Anne's brother, James Bland Burges, Member of Parliament for Helston, Cornwall, 1787-1790. He was a supporter of William Wilberforce, the leader of the movement to abolish the slave trade, a cause Simcoe lauded. All the while he was constantly trying to settle the matter of his seniority as a lieutenant colonel. He continually badgered the authorities, in particular the Secretary at War, Sir George Yonge. He complained that Banastre Tarleton had been given preference by the King for the rank of full colonel. In November 1788 Sir George tried to appease Simcoe by offering him the Lieutenant Colonelcy of the 14th Regiment of Foot. This would bring Simcoe back into active service, but John Graves was not impressed and declined the offer as an "inferior position."

Yonge made his offer shortly after Simcoe had returned from St.

Omer, where he submitted a plan to the Duke of York, Commander in Chief of the Army. The plan, dated 28 November 1788, drawn by Lieutenant George Spencer, on half-pay from the Queen's Rangers, was sent to the Duke through Yonge:

> On my return from St. Omer I desired Major Hazer respectfully to offer your Royal Highness, in my name, a plan of the manoeuvers [sic] on which his troops were exercised. [2]

The Colonel did not indicate whether his visit to St. Omer was on his own initiative or some sort of official expedition. The name "Hazer" does not appear on The Army List for that era, which suggests that he belonged to an ally. At the time, the Triple Alliance, of Britain, Holland and Prussia, had been formed to preserve peace in Europe. Making the others nervous was France, suspected of threatening that peace.

At home, Simcoe's right hand-man on the estate, John Scadding, was playing his own part in local life by accepting a public duty. In August 1788 he became responsible for repairs to part of the Honiton Turnpike. On the 18th, at a meeting of the Honiton Turnpike Trust, Scadding was made a surveyor of a section of the local road. The meeting took place in the still extant Dolphin Inn. Records designating Scadding were signed by Robert Gidley, Simcoe's agent. Gidley supplied Simcoe with a copy of the section of the minutes relating to Scadding's appointment:

> This appointee John Scadding of Dunkeswell, Yeoman, to be responsible for repairs for the road commencing at Clapper Land within the Borough of Honiton, home to the four mile stone on the Taunton Road, at £9-8s a year.[3]

The meeting stipulated that Scadding would be supplied with statute labour from affected parishes — workers who gave their time in lieu of taxes. Turnpike Trusts had begun in 1706, owing to the appalling condition of the roads. With the increase in wheeled traffic, the trusts were to extract tolls to pay for improvements. Trusts were set up somewhat later in Devon, because the increase in wheel traffic came later than in more heavily populated counties. In *From Trackway to Turnpike,* published in 1928, Gilbert Sheldon wrote:

> The lanes and pack horse tracks of the eighteenth century were completely ruined by these cumbrous

vehicles as were the droving roads at the beginning of the twentieth century by the invasion of the motor lorry.[4]

Sheldon quoted from C. Vancouver's *A General Survey of the County of Devon*:

> These narrow ways ... are by traffic of carts bulged and forced out upon their sides, when the only passage remaining is a narrow ridge on top of the road, but which, from excessive coarseness of the materials of which it is made, is soon broken into so many holes and uneveness as much to endanger the knees of the horse and neck of the rider.[5]

John Scadding would need plenty of statute labour. Even today in Devon many of the minor roads and lanes are very narrow and steep; a few are green and would not appear to have changed much since 1788. Honiton was in a somewhat better situation than other towns. Of Honiton, Sheldon commented:

> The trimness and beauty of its broad, handsome, well paved street, well shouldered up to each side with pebbles and green turf, which holds a stream of clear water with a square dipping place opposite each door, were extolled by eighteenth century travellers.

Much has changed, but Honiton still has its broad attractive street where markets are held twice a week.

On the whole, the year 1789 was uneventful in the lives of the Simcoes, except for the arrival of a fifth daughter. Sophia Jemima was baptized at St. Nicholas, Dunkeswell, on 25 October. Simcoe spent some time in Leicestershire and Northamptonshire. In the latter, he visited Elizabeth's cousin, William Walcot, who owned estates and stayed most of the time at his house in Oundle. Elizabeth still owned All Saints manor, Aldwinkle. The Colonel went to confer with Walcot over the administration of these lands. In Leicestershire he visited with Francis Rawdon Hastings; with the death of his father, Francis was now the 2nd Earl of Moira. After yet another fruitless visit to London, Simcoe went off to Whitchurch to assure himself that his wife's aunt, Mrs. Gwillim, had no need of advice. On 2 August, Elizabeth had written her Colchester friend, Miss Elliott, that the Colonel was away a lot that year on his "little trips."[6]

He was again preoccupied with the future of Canada, and of Vermont. Preserved is a very long letter dated 3 December 1789, that he wrote to Evan Nepean, since 1783 Under Secretary of State. To show his understanding of the situation, he was sending Nepean a copy of his military journal, a "trifling return for the many favours for which I am indebted to you, and in this spirit I hope you will receive it with a kindness which the nature of the subject has no claim to expect."

First, he advocated "annihilating every vestige of the present military government," and "undermining by degrees the miserable feudal system of the old Canada" which should not be difficult in an area where "liberty universally ranges abroad ... I should be happy to consecrate myself to the Service of Great Britain in that Country in preference to any situation of whatever emolument or dignity."

> The minds of thinking men are anxiously turned towards America. Mine naturally must be so from the part I bore in the War, and from belief my Father to have been the principal means of the Attack on Quebec having taken place, and the recent embassy I apprehend Washington has sent by Captain Guion to demand the Forts of Lord Dorchester, deserves the utmost attention. I hope therefore a few remarks which I take the liberty of offering to you will meet with your pardon and favourable acceptance.

He referred to the chain of forts along the Canadian border that were still garrisoned by British troops. Lord Dorchester was Guy Carleton, honoured with a barony for his withdrawal of the Loyalists and the British soldiers from New York. He was now Canada's governor. Canada, Simcoe maintained, would not keep the forts "without an alliance with Vermont, and should they be given up, the loss of Canada ultimately and not very remotely must follow."

> The inhabitants of Vermont are a brave, virtuous and English Race of People, descendants of the best Families in the Country: the Pierponts, Seymours, Stanleys &c., Episcopalians and Enemies of New Yorkers and Congress. They claim the territories on which Michilimackinac and Detroit now stand, and are disgusted with the United States, whose policy has allotted them to Connecticut.

An Alliance, defensive and commercial, with this State, is a matter of great facility. They are anxious for it because all the waters of their Country fall into the St. Lawrence and they can from thence receive salt and rum at a much cheaper rate than from the Southern Coasts and Rivers.

Simcoe foresaw a canal cut from St. Jean to La Prairie, sixteen miles, to bypass rapids in the Richelieu River, at a cost of £10,000. The canal could become "the key to that Country, the Inhabitants of which are estimated already at 250,000." If they were permitted to pay for it in raw materials, "Every individual would consume five pounds in English goods ... and we should not have the precarious Trade of the Baltic to depend upon for our Naval Stores ... this Country would be like another Switzerland between Canada and the United States. Mr. Chittenden the Governor is a fast friend of Great Britain."

My information is principally derived from a respectable Loyalist, in correspondence with him, whom I never saw, but who has sent to me the outline of a treaty of Commerce between Canada and Vermont, as he believes I have the Interest of my Country at heart and more Influence with the Government than it is reasonable to suppose that a person in my secluded situation can possibly expect.

Vermont, in short, had much to gain through alliance with Canada, and the erection of two new governments:

with perfect English constitutions, one at Montreal and one on the Upper Lakes will secure our American Colonies for ages, not as the poor Canadians are held, in frigid neutrality thro' dread of purgatory, but in active friendship and willing obedience: for my Father in a Momoir [sic] dated in 1755, many years before the conquest of Canada says: "Such is the happy situation of Quebec, or rather of Montreal, to which Quebec is the Citadel, that with the assistance of a few Sluices it will become the centre of Communication between the Gulf of Mexico and Hudson's Bay, by an interior navigation; formed by drawing to itself a wealth and strength ... to

lay the foundation of the most potent and best
connected Empire that ever awed the World.[7]

Just who this Loyalist was is a mystery. However, further on in his
letter, Simcoe mentions a "Mr. Smith commonly called Billy Smith who I
believe to be in Office in Canada whose opinions should be examined
with caution on any point in which Vermont or New York interfere with
Canada." William Smith, a Loyalist from New York, was the Chief Justice
of Canada at that time. Simcoe viewed Vermont through rose-tinted
spectacles. He did not mention the real ringleaders of Vermont secession,
Ethan and Ira Allen, Joseph and Jonas Fay, backed by an army of Green
Mountain Boys. Few would have called the governor, "One-eyed Tom"
Chittenden "a fast friend of Great Britain"! Rough-necks all. If Simcoe,
admittedly a snob, thought he might meet gentleman in Vermont, he
would have had a rude shock. Aristocracy was the furthest thought from
the aspirations of Vermonters, but:

> I am clearly of the Opinion that Government should act
> by America as it has done in the past, and appoint to its
> Superintendency one of the most respectable of our
> Nobility.I trust to your goodness that you will excuse
> these thoughts thrown together "Currente Calamo."[8]

Amidst his concern with problems in North America, his future as a
soldier or public servant, and the Wolford Estate, an old thought
returned. His best chance of obtaining a public appointment was through
active participation in politics. He had acquired a new friend of
influence, George Grenville, 1st Marquis of Buckingham, whose younger
brother, William Grenville, was in the government. The Grenvilles were
cousins of William Pitt the Younger. Another friend of value was Henry
Addington, Member of Parliament for Devizes, in Wiltshire, some sixty
miles east of Honiton. Addington had been the Speaker of the House of
Commons since 1789, a useful person to know. However, mainly
through Buckingham, Simcoe stood for "St. Maws" (Mawes), in
Cornwall, and he won. St. Mawes "belonged" to Buckingham. By June,
Simcoe was in the House. When he rose to speak, he addressed himself
mainly to matters concerning Canada, probably his main reason for
entering into politics.

Colonel Banastre Tarleton was elected the same year as Simcoe,
representing Liverpool, where his father, a wealthy merchant, had also
been the mayor.[9] Tarleton represented the interests of the textile

manufacturers who depended on raw cotton from the southern United States. He rose to speak forcefully against abolishing the slave trade; reduction in the supply of slaves would mean economic disaster for his constituents. Simcoe, the man who had wanted to recruit blacks, naturally supported William Wilberforce, the evangelical Christian and member of the house since 1780 who was prominent in the fight to rid the Empire of such a vile practice.

Even though Simcoe was more involved than ever in his own interests, with Elizabeth he continued exploring the countryside in Devon and Somerset. Of one of their excursions, Elizabeth wrote a long account to Miss Elliott, at Copford, near Colchester, Essex, on 10 October 1790. Miss Elliott had only recently left Wolford Lodge after visiting the Simcoes. The cover of the letter was stamped "Honiton October 12th 1790" and marked "Free J.G. Simcoe." Being a Member of Parliament had its privileges; franking — free post — was one of them.

On the journey Elizabeth described so vividly, they had gone into the more unsettled parts of the counties. Accompanied by Mary Anne Burges for the first few miles they set out on horseback without servants. "My dear Friend," Elizabeth began:

> I hope you had as good weather for your journey, as we were fortunate enough to meet with on our expedition, how many times did I wish for you to have engaged with the noble charming scenes I saw; Hembury Fort and Tracey Hill are mole hills compared with the grand scale of country I had passed.

They had left "soon after you, in a very wetting fog which continued all the way up the hill, at the end of which we parted with Miss Burges, who I believe was all the time wishing herself in your little trunk, for she certainly would not have encountered the wet ..." Here the Simcoes displayed qualities, when travelling, that became their trademark in later letters. They were undeterred by foul weather. In any case the weather soon turned fine. They went to Huntsham Castle and the Roman Camp, visited some fine woods, traced Roman roads, amusing themselves with their discoveries until they reached Dulverton (famous for its association with R.D. Blackmore's novel *Lorna Doone*). Elizabeth did not specify how they spent that night, but in the morning they were on their way again into Exmoor, the vast expanse of moorland (now a National Park). The next day, which was fine, "we undertook, trusting in our abilities and our little map to cross Exmoor without a guide."

After going some little distance out of our way by wrong directions we soon got going again into a right path crossing a most grand and noble scale of country, crossing mountains torrents and such steep paths that were frequently obliged to dismount and walk down them, we continued our road from Hawkridge guided by Tumuli to Withpole [Withypool], the capital of the Moor ...

It consisted of five wretched cottages. On they went to "Simmons Bath" (Simonsbath), a single cottage or ale house "just fit for the execution of Count Fathom's horrid story; but as I had not heard that read the other night my mind was not oppressed by it." She may have been thinking of Captain Fantom, a mercenary mentioned in John Aubrey's *Brief Lives*, an unscrupulous murderer and ravisher of women. She continued:

> I very contentedly eat my dinner of the (I believe stolen) mutton of the forest. We were there told we could not go on to Linton [sic] without a guide owing to the dangerous bogs; a man of the name of Lock who was going home to Linmouth [sic] offered to guide us if we could wait until 4 o'clock, but being not willing to wait until that time we boldly set out alone and in a mile or two found ourselves involved in a bog where our horses sunk so deep were obliged to get off in the middle of it, that they might extricate their legs.

At that point they saw Mr. Lock riding towards them. He guided them safely to Lynton on the north coast of Devon, "tho thro' many unpleasant, but not dangerous bogs." That they should ignore advice and set out without the recommended guide was typical of both John Graves and Elizabeth Simcoe. (On Exmoor the danger was quicksand — sloughs; in Upper Canada they would not be deterred by heavy snow or rotting ice.)

Earlier during their explorations of Exmoor, Elizabeth told Miss Elliott that they had steered clear of Mole's Chamber, a famous bog called after a man named Mole who had been "lost" in it. In his book *An Exploration of Exmoor*, John Page explained the source of the name. Exmoor did not furnish as exciting if sometimes apocryphal stories "supplied by the more grim neighbour Dartmoor":

> The only loss of life recorded — save for Lorna Doone and there are doubts even about that, is placed to the

credit of Moles Chamber, in which a farmer is said to have perished many years since, on his way home from Barnstable market. The unbelieving, however, trace the name to the River Mole, a tributary of the Taw, which takes its source hereabouts.

The slough, Page added, was no longer a menace to the traveller because it had been drained[10]

At Lynton they could not find decent accommodation. The hospitable Mr. Lock offered to give them a bed at his house. They went to the Lock house after supping at a Lynton ale house. The proprietor had nothing but bread, butter and herrings, "but they were so excellent that an epicure might well go a hundred miles" for the delight of enjoying such fare.

Elizabeth observed that the herrings had only a back bone, a discovery in "natural history which I have made ..." She was delighted with Lynton and with "Linmouth" (Lynmouth). The latter was "the most romantic and charming situated village" she had ever seen. It stood close to the sea at the foot of high cliffs, some bare, others covered with woods, and with "two mountain torrents pouring over vast stones with a prodigious noise" as they ran into the sea. Lynton Church, also "romantically placed," overlooked the sea from one of those immense cliffs. "I could have stayed there a month, I never took sketches so ill, being on so much a larger scale that I was accustomed to."

> You may travel for miles on Exmoor without seeing a man, house or tree, but the vast falls and precipitous risings of the mountains together with the unity and simplicity of colouring give a grandeur which is very fine, we returned next day thro' Countesbury, to Porlock and Minehead sleep there and then passed to Dunkery Beacon [also made famous by R.D. Blackmore].

They rode to Winsford on the Ex, and saw Bampton Castle and some ruins of an abbey at Cannon's Lee as they turned their horses towards home. "If you have a map of Somersetshire" she advised Miss Elliott, her friend could trace their excursion. She found a book in "Exmore dialect" which she found perfectly horrible and unintelligible, although three inhabitants of the moor spoke better English than any common people she had met in Devonshire.

> The Sheep on the Moor are perfect beauties, white as
> driven snow their wool very silky; they are very small,
> there are likewise numbers of ponies like Mrs. Graves'
> quite wild, who inhabit the Moor.

A friend, Mr. Leman, who was in Honiton when they returned home, told them that Lynmouth was nothing compared to Ilfracombe, but Elizabeth was skeptical because they had not gone that far and could not judge for themselves. She was pleased that she had not caught cold, although her feet were wet through ten times a day, while dismounting on the hills. She was miserably fatigued the first day, but the stiffness wore off with continued riding. They had gone thirty miles a day for the first two days, very demanding rides indeed.

At Wolford Lodge a letter from Mary Anne Burges awaited Elizabeth. Her friend was then visiting her uncle, Colonel Hugh Somerville, at Fitzhead Court, his home near Taunton in Somerset. Elizabeth hoped that Miss Elliott had had a comfortable journey home to Copford, and had found Admiral and Mrs. Elliott well and in good spirits. Miss Elliott's elder brother, Elizabeth finished her letter, had sent the Simcoes a brace of very fine pheasants, for which they were grateful.[11]

Many a modern tourist would envy the Simcoes' opportunity to see the moor and the north coast while the land was so primitive, the tracks ancient or non-existent, and hardly any bridle paths. The countryside, as Elizabeth found, is in mountainous contrast to Tracey (now St. Cyres) Hill or Hembury Fort. Dunkery Beacon is twice their height. The Blackdown Hill region is much gentler than the high windswept wild moor, with its deep coombes and high coastal cliffs. A valley such as Blackmore conceived, concealing the outlaw Doones' habitation, would be impossible in the Blackdowns. (In later life, a friendship developed between the Simcoe family and author Blackmore's father, who in the 1820s was curate in the parish of Culmstock, only five miles from Wolford Lodge.)

Over the years, John Graves Simcoe saw the hand of the Romans in virtually all buildings and sites of any antiquity. He was often mistaken, but he did not have the benefit of knowledge gained from later years of archaeological excavation and research that would have proved or disproved his "theories." At Huntsham Castle there never was a Roman camp; the castle is, in fact, like Hembury Fort, a fine example of an Iron Age hill fort, predating the Romans by several hundred years.

By 1790, Simcoe found new hope, but also new setbacks. Among the members of parliament and friends, the future of Canada was an important issue. Something had to be done about the 8,000 or more Loyalists who had been resettled to the west of the French seigneuries of the lower St. Lawrence River. Under the terms of the Quebec Act of 1774, Canada had French civil law and feudal land tenure, and Roman Catholicism as the established religion. The Loyalists were petitioning for a separate colony, where they could have English civil law and freehold land tenure — their rights as British subjects. They resented being forced to fit into a foreign system. To Simcoe, a separate province held out hope for a new British Empire in the interior of North America.

On 3 June, William Wyndham Grenville, brother of the Marquis of Buckingham, President of the Board of Trade and cousin of then Prime Minister William Pitt (the younger) wrote to Lord Dorchester. Formerly Sir Guy Carleton, Dorchester was now the governor in chief of Canada, His Lordship had requested, when the province was partitioned, that the lieutenant governor of the upper (western) portion be Sir John Johnson. Sir John was the son and heir of Sir William Johnson, the 1st Baronet of New York and the influential Superintendent of Indian Affairs in the northern colonies until his death in 1774. Sir John, the 2nd Baronet, had commanded the largest Provincial Corps that had served in the Northern Department, the King's Royal Regiment of New York, which consisted of two battalions. The other Provincial Corps of the Northern Department had only one each. Dorchester was certain that the choice of Sir John would find favour with the Loyalist settlers he would govern.

Grenville informed Dorchester that he had recommended John Graves Simcoe for this important post, rather than Johnson.[12] Although never spelled out, opinion favoured an outsider over a man who might have too many vested interests in the new province. As the only Brigadier General of Provincials in Canada, Sir John Johnson was entitled to vast acreages in the new province and he might not make an impartial ruler. Dorchester, who had already formed a poor opinion of Simcoe as leader of the now demobilised Queen's Rangers, was far from pleased when his recommendation was refused.

ELEVEN

THE GREAT EMPIRE BUILDER

On 22 June 1790, Mrs. Simcoe wrote to Mrs. Hunt informing her of recent events in the lives of her family. Although the Colonel's appointment as the lieutenant governor of the new province, to be named Upper Canada, had not been officially confirmed, everyone knew that the job was his. Elizabeth expressed doubts about going owing to the unsettled nature of conditions on the European continent, especially the situation in revolutionary France:

> I am under great uneasiness about the war. If that does not take place I shall go to Canada with Coll. Simcoe next Spring. He has had a very desirable civil government ... in that country offered to him which he accepted but if the war happens it will certainly prevent my quitting England & everybody says a war is inevitable. Our children are quite well. I am glad to have the small pox over. I was much alarmed in the coming out of that disorder but they had it very favourably.

The younger girls had been inoculated, and again the Simcoes had been lucky that they suffered only mild cases. Elizabeth also recounted the visit to Wolford Lodge of the famous historian/antiquarian Richard Polwhele. That guest had been most interested in the poem about Dunkeswell Abbey by Miss Mary Hunt. Polwhele, a man of the cloth, wrote a history of Devonshire, and edited a work entitled *Poems Chiefly by Gentlemen of Devon and Cornwall* (in two volumes, published in 1792). Among these poems were some of Polwhele's own, Major Edward Drewe's that he dedicated to John Graves Simcoe, and Mary Hunt's on Dunkeswell Abbey. Apparently Polwhele rated Miss Hunt as a "Gentleman" or was she covered by "*Chiefly*"?

Richard Polwhele was a significant figure in the West Country, especially Devon and Cornwall. As well as a theologian, he was a topographer and writer, a man very much after John Graves Simcoe's heart. A native of Truro in Cornwall, Richard matriculated as a "Commoner" at Christ Church, Oxford, in 1782. That same year he was ordained as a curate at Lamoran, Cornwall, and accepted a curacy at Powderham Castle, Devon, the seat of the Earls of Devon, whose family name was Courtnay. In 1793 he became a curate at Exmouth, Devon, and was vicar of Manaccan in Cornwall and later at Newlyn, Cornwall.

He was a member of a literary society that met every three weeks in the Globe Inn, Exeter. The members recited prose and verse and "dined at three." The efforts of these gentlemen led to the publication of the collection of poetry which Polwhele edited. Among his other literary works were a history of Cornwall and contributions to *Gentleman's Magazine*, the *Anti-Jacobin Review* and other journals.

Like earlier enthusiasts, Polwhele was impressed with the magnificence of the Simcoes' "Wolford Church" estate, which he described in great detail. New was his mention of shells, by which he clearly meant fossils: "The hills rise boldly — having been former cliffs, out of which hath been dug a great variety of shells never before found in the county." He was referring to the Greensand limestone of the Cretacious geological era, especially noted for well-preserved fossils. The Upper Greensand was overlain by clay containing flints and chert so useful to early man.[1]

Simcoe was still scribbling his own poems, and searching for opportunities to enlarge his estates. Because his interest was widely known, a prominent landowner, Mr. W. Hawker of Poundisford, near Taunton, wrote offering to sell Simcoe an estate named Dunkeswell Grange, which adjoined the Wolford land. Hawker wanted to free some capital in order to purchase Cothelston Estate in the Quantock Hills of

Somerset. However, the purchase of Dunkeswell Grange was not completed for some years.[2] Simcoe was more preoccupied with plans to leave for Upper Canada.

Certain of his friends and advisers regarded Simcoe's enthusiasm for an outpost of empire in the wilds of Canada as bordering on insanity. With the danger of war so great, by staying home he would soon be sent to the Continent where promotions in the field would be quick. James Bland Burges, now under secretary of state in the foreign department, wondered why Simcoe would bury himself at the end of the earth when he could further his military career with a more convenient active command.[3]

Simcoe, meanwhile, was busy making more plans for Upper Canada. First came the question of defense. He would need a strong garrison to keep the new province safe from American intruders. That peninsula lying north of the Great Lakes was vulnerable to attack by land along several narrow spots, and more so by water. He wrote to Henry Dundas, the home secretary, on 12 November 1790, recommending raising a corps of "twelve companies, each company to consist of a Captain, 2 Lieutenants and one hundred rank and file with two troops [of cavalry] of similar numbers, the whole forming 1200 rank and file with two Majors."[4] This regiment would be the third Queen's Rangers. Most of the men would be recruited in the West Country, but Simcoe hoped that some of his favourite officers, now on half-pay in New Brunswick, would elect to serve again under him. The sole reply for months was word that Simcoe had finally been promoted full Colonel in the British Army on 18 November.[5] The promotion let him feel optimistic. Now he hoped for a knighthood, so appropriate for a future lieutenant governor of a British province.

He revealed much of his imperialistic ambitions for Upper Canada in a letter he wrote to Joseph Banks, the botanist who had sailed with Captain James Cook, onetime navigator aboard Captain John Simcoe's ship *Pembroke*. In 1778, Banks was appointed President of the Royal Society, and he was well known as a liberal patron of science and literature. Because he was a man of influence in society, Simcoe resolved to court him as a useful ally. His letter, a very long one, is dated 8 January 1791:

> Sir,
>
> I was much disappointed that the variety of business in which my good friend Sir George Yonge was engaged, and by my own avocations, prevented me from having

the honour of being introduced to you, as soon as it was generally made known that I was to be appointed to the Government in Upper Canada.

Fearful that he would not have the time for an introduction, Simcoe had resolved to put his thoughts in writing. He wanted to procure advantages for the community he was to govern, and to encourage in "this Nation [Upper Canada] those Arts and Sciences which at once support and embellish our Country..." He asked Banks for his assistance and hoped to be in frequent communication with him. He was willing to undertake "this species of banishment" because the new province could become such a valuable asset to the Empire.

As one who saw the consequences of the loss of "our late American Dominions" Simcoe feared calamity in case of war. He longed to restore his King and family "to their just inheritance" and to form a new union that would be permanent. A renewal of Empire would be desirable to His Majesty, and the sooner this task was begun the better:

> I mean to prepare for whatever Convulsions may happen in the United States, the Method I propose is by establishing a free, honourable British Government, and a pure Administration of its Laws which shall hold out to the solitary Emigrant, and to the several States, advantages that the present form of Government doth not and cannot permit them to enjoy.

Of the inherent defects in the congressional form of government, "the absolute prohibition of an order of Nobility is a glaring one." The true New England Americans, he claimed, had as strong an "Aristocratical spirit" as that to be found in Great Britain, nor were they "Anti-Monarchial." Simcoe hoped to have an hereditary council at the core of the nobility. For commerce, union and power, he proposed to site the colony "in that Great Peninsula between Lakes Huron, Erie and Ontario, a Spot destined by Nature sooner or later, to govern the interior World."

His capital would be in the very heart of this country, upon the River LaTranche (the Thames), navigable by bateaux for 150 miles. He would lure Loyalists still in Connecticut to settle, if the home government approved. He would have a bishop, an English chief justice, among other appointed officers. He meant an established church and English civil law. Narrow-thinking individuals and self-interested "monopolists" might find his plan ahead of its time, "not what this Country is yet prepared for" though he expected that the New England provinces might be receptive.

He would seek to demonstrate that Upper Canada, having all the advantages of British protection, would have a better government than the United States could ever attain. Important to achieving the kind of civilised society he envisaged, there must be a place for the arts and sciences and like embellishments, to make the statement that his form of government would be more polished. "I would not in its infancy have a Hut, nor in its Maturity, a palace built without this Design."

The Marquis of Buckingham had suggested a sum of money for a pubic library, and had donated an encyclopedia, extracts from which might be published in newspapers. With respect to "Botanical Arrangements" Simcoe suggested introducing plants into Upper Canada, hemp and flax, for example, which Great Britain then bought from other nations. Education was so far shamefully neglected. The province would need schools, and a "College of a higher Class would be eminently useful ..."[6]

Simcoe knew nothing about the traditions of Connecticut, the most democratic of any American state. It was founded as a charter province; under the terms of the charter, all officials were elected, even the governor. Although the franchise was restricted to males who met a stiff property qualification, nevertheless Simcoe's notion of a nobility and appointed officers would have been repugnant to such highly individualistic folk as Connecticut Yankees. Whether Joseph Banks gave Simcoe any assistance is unknown. When he began his letter to Banks he was feeling let down by Sir George Yonge, who had been less helpful than Simcoe felt he had a right to expect.

Simcoe also turned his attention to acquiring accommodation. Since he had no hope of finding a suitable government house, on 24 December 1790 he told William, now Lord Grenville, that he intended taking a portable house with him:

> My Lord,
> Having in a former conversation mentioned to Your Lordship that a CANVASS HOUSE similar to that sent with the Governor of Botany Bay, might be highly convenient if not necessary, in the various expeditions t'will be proper that I should make in order to be an eye witness to the situation of the new proposed Government & a faithful reporter of your Lordship

thereon ... I shall be obliged to you to give instructions accordingly to Mr. Nepean, as the advancing Season admits of little delay.[7]

Simcoe was able to purchase a "Canvas House" in London that had once belonged to his father's one-time subordinate, the navigator and explorer Captain James Cook. Whether Grenville was of any help is not known. In fact, the Simcoes acquired two canvas houses — glorified tents but with wooden floors and frames, and walls that were papered. Elizabeth, too, was busy with plans to go to Upper Canada, deciding what they would take with them for her role as the mistress of government house, even though it might be of canvas. She would need ball gowns, and her Nankin china, a few servants, linens and some furniture. The Marquis of Buckingham had presented them with a tapestry from Stowe, his country house in Buckinghamshire. It could be used as a wall hanging to add warmth during the severe Canadian winters. Elizabeth, Marchioness of Buckingham sent her friend Mrs. Simcoe a spinning wheel that had been a gift for her from Queen Charlotte.[8]

The most serious matter concerned the children. The Colonel believed that they should leave all but Sophia, the youngest daughter, at home with a governess, supervised by their Great Aunt Margaret Graves. Elizabeth was appalled at the idea of abandoning Eliza, Charlotte, Harriet and Caroline. By early 1791 she knew she was expecting their sixth child, who would certainly accompany them, and surely they could find a way to take all their daughters. Simcoe was adamant; he had seen enough of the North American wilderness to know that a comfortable home for so large a family would be impossible to find. Besides, they would meet very few people of education, and certainly not anyone who could be employed as a tutor. The older girls must stay home at Wolford Lodge to receive the education that would make them amiable companions in later life. Elizabeth elected to remain behind, but Simcoe felt he could not possibly manage without her, and for more than moral support. She could take many vital tasks out of his hands, and she had the ability to sketch with as much skill as any officer of the Royal Engineers.

The difference between them as parents is striking. Simcoe, the affectionate, demonstrative father, would leave four vulnerable children for many years with hardly a qualm. Patriot and imperialist, nothing must interfere with his duty to King and Empire. Elizabeth, less at ease with the girls, was torn by the prospect of leaving them, and fearful she might never see some of them again. They had been fortunate thus far not to have lost a child; so many ailments threatened children especially in their most tender years.

Mary Anne Burges rose to the occasion. She promised to see the girls frequently, to watch over their studies, to sketch with them — and to be entirely frank with their mother about their welfare. Elizabeth pleaded to be told the bad, as well as the good, and this Mary Anne agreed to do, in packets of letters that could go in her brother James's government "bag" more securely and at less cost than in the regular mail.[9] There remained the choice of a suitable person to oversee the nursery staff at Wolford Lodge, and to take responsibility for the girls. When Aunt Margaret suggested Mrs. Mary Ann Hunt, Elizabeth knew she was right. Miss Mary Hunt agreed to live in Wolford Lodge, too, as governess and tutor, and Elizabeth's mind was even more relieved. Both the Hunts knew Aunt Margaret so well that they would not be disconcerted by mood swings or unreasonable demands. Elizabeth had told Mrs. Hunt that they would be setting out in the spring of 1791, but they changed their plans when they found that the next little Simcoe would arrive in June. They would not be leaving until the autumn.

In March 1791, Simcoe's illusions over Vermont were shattered. On the 4th, that republic became the fourteenth member of the United States of America. Despite all the advantages of rejoining the British Empire, those scoundrel leaders had probably been holding out hopes to the British and American governments to avoid being coerced by either side. The Vermont leaders were not gentlemen after all. Simcoe would show the way, set the example; he would govern Upper Canada guided by the finest principles of Great Britain.

He made frequent trips to London, working on final details. He was still waiting for a reply to his request for a new regiment of Queen's Rangers. He was also calling for reinforcements of regular troops for the forts along the Canadian border. Technically, these forts were on United States soil, but the government felt justified in retaining them. One excuse was protection of Britain's native allies, and of Loyalists still resident near the forts. Stronger garrisons would dissuade the former colonists from attacking them. Policy on the aboriginal allies was foggy; there was a hope that an Indian state would be a buffer zone between the American states and British North America. On one hand, war-weary Britain did not want to provoke a war with the United States; on the other hand, allowing land-hungry Americans to drive the natives from their tribal lands, as a part of national expansion, was equally unpalatable. Whatever the future, Simcoe was convinced that a strong army was absolutely necessary to ensure the safety of Upper Canada.

He attended the House of Commons during the spring. A new friend and fellow member was a Devon neighbour, John Pollexfen Bastard (the accent on the *second* syllable). The Bastard country seat was Kitley. (In Upper Canada, Simcoe would name two rural townships: one after John P. and the other after his Devon home.)

On 28 March, Simcoe addressed the House of Commons on the subject of army recruiting. His most relevant, if limited, contribution was his words on the Canada, or Constitutional Act of 1791. According to the *Parliament Register*:

> [on] 12 May Colonel Simcoe read an extract from an American paper to prove that the Congress thought a very small number sufficient for the members forming the House of Assembly for the Western Province, and that two or four would be enough to represent Montreal and Quebec.

The newspaper seemed to imply that in the event of annexation of Canada, this would be the distribution of representatives. On 16 May:

> [the] Colonel spoke in favour of the Bill and having pronounced a Panegyric on the British Constitution, wished it to be adopted in the present instance as far as circumstances would permit.[10]

The Canada Act divided the old Province of Canada into Lower — the French seigneuries along the lower St. Lawrence, and Upper — the land along the upper St. Lawrence and the Great Lakes. Each part would have a legislative assembly. The established church in Lower Canada would be Roman Catholic, and in Upper Canada, or so Simcoe fervently hoped, Church of England. The lieutenant governor of Lower Canada would be Major General Alured Clarke, like Simcoe a veteran of the American War of Independence. Clarke's Devonian connection was strong; he was related to Dr. Alured Clarke, a Dean of Exeter. Superior to both lieutenant governors was Lord Dorchester, a situation Simcoe mistrusted, not so much because he was aware of Dorchester's prejudice against him, but out of a wish to be in full control of his territory. Dorchester, as Captain General and Governor in Chief of Upper and Lower Canada, would be in command of the armed forces in both provinces, and in a position to interfere with Simcoe's administration.

On 6 June 1791, the Simcoes' sixth child was born, and on 17 July he was baptized Francis Gwillim at St. Nicholas, Dunkeswell.[11] Gwillim came from his mother, but the choice of Francis allows speculation. Did Simcoe honour his old colleague, Francis Lord Rawdon, rather than his own father, John, or Elizabeth's father, Thomas? Elizabeth was no doubt relieved that she had given the Colonel his male heir. Simcoe himself may have been overjoyed, yet his great love of his daughters shines through his own letters, and in those the girls wrote throughout their lives. Clearly he admired and loved the boy, but equally well he seemed to have adored his girls. As with his sisters, Elizabeth hired a wet nurse to feed Francis. Women of wealth did not suckle their own babies, although most recognised that mother's milk was the best food for a newborn.

When Simcoe received a letter from the War Office, dated 29 August 1791, he felt that his wings had been clipped. Henry Dundas informed him that no regular troops would be available to reinforce the border forts. He had permission to raise a corps of two companies, each of 200 men. On 20 December Sir George Yonge wrote him further details. Each company would have a captain, captain-lieutenant, two lieutenants, two ensigns, six sergeants, six corporals and a drummer, as well as staff officers. Simcoe would serve as colonel commandant without pay.

Writing to Miss Elliott about the plans for Canada, Elizabeth admitted that Simcoe was not without concern for the horse, Salem. The Colonel had made arrangements for a Mrs. Bowman, of Exeter, to look after the now elderly "old servant."[12] He would need a horse in Upper Canada, but he could not put Salem through a second Atlantic crossing.

The new Queen's Rangers would not be primarily a fighting force. Even Simcoe expected them to serve as artificers, on construction of houses and barracks, and to help build roads. They were expected to remain in the province after their enlistments were ended, as capable settlers and experienced pioneers. The truncated Queen's Rangers would, however, have a "Band of Music." The drummers, and fifers as well, were signalers and part of each infantry battalion. The band of music consisted of brass and woodwind instruments. The musicians were paid by the officers, chiefly the Colonel, and they played during marches and at concerts. The Marquis of Buckingham donated the instruments for the Queen's Rangers band.[13]

By September the Simcoes' plans were nearly complete. The reliable John Scadding would be in charge of the estates during their absence. On the 15th Colonel and Mrs. Simcoe, with Sophia and Francis and their nurses, set out by carriage for Weymouth, where they would board the 28-gun frigate *Triton*. Behind followed the baggage in wagons, accompanied by the few servants who would travel with them. During the farewells everyone was smiling. As soon as the departing loved ones were out of sight, Miss Burges and Miss Hunt took the four girls for a walk. When Caroline complained of weariness one of the women carried her while the other three capered about. The axe fell when they returned home and faced a tea table no longer presided over by their parents but by Mrs. Graves. That selfish old lady, rather than comfort her great nieces, launched forth with a tirade about being left with so much responsibility. Beside Miss Burges, Eliza began to weep softly. When Aunt Margaret noticed she demanded to know what ailed her.

"I can't help crying when you are so cross with my dear Mama and Papa," Eliza managed through her tears. "Oh, if only they would turn back and stay with us."

The sensitive Eliza mourned for months. Charlotte and Harriet, more boisterous, fared better, while three-year-old Caroline was still young enough to be comforted by the Hunts, especially Mary. Those who needed their parents most had been left behind, while the two who could have been cared for by any kind person were on their way to Canada.

After tea the day the Simcoes left for Weymouth, Mary Anne Burges walked home to Tracey and in the early evening she began to write the first of nearly 900 pages she would send to Elizabeth Simcoe over the next five years. She described Mrs. Graves's pique and Eliza's tears. Farther on in the letter she wrote that Eliza's sobs would have a "happy effect," for Mrs. Graves would be more careful in future over what she said in front of the children.[14]

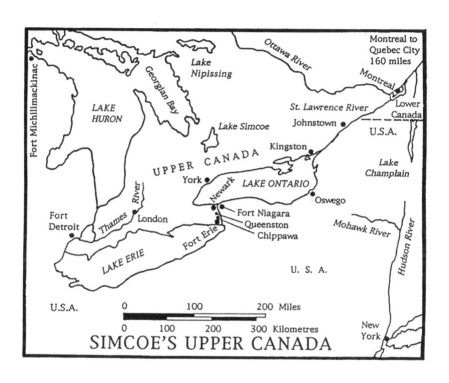

SIMCOE'S UPPER CANADA

PART IV
ACHIEVEMENT AND FRUSTRATION

In recounting John Graves Simcoe's years in Canada, the diary of his wife claims a wider attention than the governor's voluminous correspondence. Whereas an overview of his administration can be assembled quickly from his many letters and reports, revelations on the day-to-day occurrences are found in the writings of Mrs. Simcoe. She exposes as much of her husband's feelings as she does of her own. The events in their lives were closely interwound.

In February 1792, while the Simcoes were waiting out the winter in Quebec City, the soldiers of Britain and Hyderabad defeated the Tippoo, who parted with half of Mysore. Slowly, Britain was gaining a larger hold on the Indian sub-continent, through conquest and alliance.

At the time, Austria and Prussia were allied against France, where Jacobins had wrested power from the less-zealous Girondins. In 1793, the French guillotined Louis XVI, established committees of public safety, and the Reign of Terror commenced. Russia and Prussia partitioned Poland. In September, France launched a new offensive against the Netherlands, during which an army led by the Duke of York was defeated at Hondschoote and in the Rhineland. French troops reached Rome. In November the United States ordered an embargo on British shipping. That December, France invaded Holland, and abolished slavery in all the French colonies.

Russia and Austria partitioned Poland in 1795. The Dutch surrendered Ceylon to Britain. Spain signed a treaty with France, and ceded to that country the Spanish part of San Domingo. The French suppressed a revolt in Brittany in 1796. That July, Britain captured Elba. Meanwhile, the Dutch ruler, Prince William V of Orange, had come to England. The British seized the Cape of Good Hope in September, as a place of refuge for William. In October, Spain declared war on Britain while the Simcoes were en route home from Upper Canada.

TWELVE
WINTER AT QUEBEC

Mary Anne Burges began her letters to Mrs. Simcoe immediately after her friends had left home on 15 September for Weymouth. Just days later, Elizabeth began writing a diary or journal for the residents of Wolford Lodge and more personal letters to Miss Burges, Mrs. Hunt and other close friends and relatives. Her letters to Mary Anne interconnect with her friend's. Most of Elizabeth's letters from Canada have vanished. However, much can be deduced from Mary Anne's replies and comments. Information on the loved ones back home comes from Mary Anne's letters. Elizabeth's are less personal, and in her diary she gives almost no detail about the children who were with them. Well aware of how much the four little girls at Wolford Lodge were missing them, Elizabeth felt constrained. In contrast, Mary Anne wrote at length about Eliza, Charlotte, Harriet and Caroline, asking for reports on Francis and giving advice on how to manage a defiant Sophia.

Two versions of Mrs. Simcoe's diary have been published, the first by the Toronto newspaperman John Ross Robertson in 1911, the second by Mary Quayle Innis in 1965. More revealing are the many watercolour sketches Elizabeth made during her years in the province. Her representations of trees in the valley of the Don River evoke foliage of today, even though modern motorways have so altered the appearance of the land along the river.

John Graves Simcoe left extensive correspondence about Upper Canada. Five thick volumes were edited by Brigadier Ernest A. Cruikshank, a man who compiled considerable information on the history of Ontario from manuscript sources. Simcoe's writing is serious, detailed and repetitious. Elizabeth revealed the lighter side of life in the Canadas. Simcoe had a fine sense of humour, but he found little to laugh at during the Canada years. If he viewed Upper Canada as the hub of a new British Empire, to which the United States could be attached, the home government and Lord Dorchester did not. A Loyalist province was a fine objective, but expenses were to be kept to a minimum, as in the case of the reduced size of the Queen's Rangers.

The regiment, like its predecessor, would have green jackets.[1] For himself, Simcoe was bringing two dress regimental coats. One was green, which he would wear when he was appearing as the Colonel Commandant of the Queen's Rangers. The other was red, correct for a Colonel in the British Army. This he would wear at functions which he attended as the lieutenant governor.[2]

Simcoe had already selected some of his officers. The commissions were dated 1 September 1791, although he did not then know for certain which of them would accept a place in the new regiment. His captains would be David Shank, who had settled in England, and Samuel Smith, then in New Brunswick. His choices for "Captain Lieutenant and Captain" were Aeneas Shaw, in New Brunswick, and George Spencer, who had drawn maps for his former commander. John McGill, also in New Brunswick, would be the adjutant, with the humble rank of ensign. Simcoe probably regretted not having enough captaincies to allow him a higher rank.[3] Two of his former cornets would be coming to Upper Canada. William Jarvis would be the Provincial Secretary. He had moved to England, and married Hannah, a daughter of the Reverend Samuel Peters, who had left Connecticut for England after threats from his rebel neighbours. Cornet Thomas Merritt wanted to leave New Brunswick, as did Ensign Christopher Robinson.[4] Coming from Ireland was Captain Edward Littlehales, heir to a baronetcy, as Simcoe's brigade major and military secretary.[5]

For Deputy Quartermaster General, Simcoe chose Captain Charles Stephenson, 5th Regiment. He appointed the Reverend Edward Drewe, son of Francis Drewe of The Grange and Broadhembury, chaplain to the garrison of Upper Canada, at a stipend of £100 per annum.[6] Simcoe suspected that Drewe, the first cousin of his old comrade, cashiered Major Edward Drewe, might elect to remain in England, merely using the position as a sinecure. Generally, Simcoe disapproved of handing out appointments to men who would not take them up actively, but his fondness for the clergyman and his family overcame any scruples. He was especially pleased with commissions to men in New Brunswick. After pioneering there, they would give leadership to the officers from Britain, and to the rank and file, expected in the spring, who would be unfamiliar with life in an unsettled land. Most were recruited in the West Country, but the regimental depot was at Chatham in Kent.

Upper Canada was a forested wilderness, best penetrated by the rivers, and with a barebones administration. When Lord Dorchester arrived as governor in chief in 1786, Canada was divided into two administrative districts — Quebec and Montreal. The Loyalist townships were part of the latter. In preparation for separation, Dorchester had divided Upper Canada into four such districts, each with a court and a board to grant tracts of land to Loyalists and other settlers. He named the most easterly district Luneburg. Mecklenburg lay west of the Cataraqui River. Nassau was the Niagara peninsula, while Hesse extended beyond Detroit. Dorchester chose German names to please King George III. Within each district lay settlements of Loyalists — disbanded soldiers and their families — and a few civilians. While the population of Lower Canada was about 150,000, that of Upper Canada was estimated at approaching 10,000.

Eight rectangular townships, each of 100 square miles, had been surveyed along the upper St. Lawrence, leaving a space between the last French seigneury to be filled in later by Roman Catholic settlers, adjacent to their co-religionists in Lower Canada. The lower five townships were for Sir John Johnson's 1st Battalion, King's Royal Regiment of New York. The upper three were for Major Edward Jessup's Loyal Rangers. Five townships on the Bay of Quinte were for Sir John Johnson's 2nd Battalion, more Loyal Rangers, some King's Rangers led by Major James Rogers (brother of Robert), a few German regulars who elected to remain, and some of the 1st Battalion, Royal Highland Emigrants. At Niagara were two townships being settled by John Butler's Rangers, their commandant now a lieutenant colonel. Along the Detroit River were more Butler's Rangers, and some Royal Highland Emigrants who were disbanded there in 1784.

Native tribes in the province spoke an Algonkian language and were locally called Ojibway, Mississauga or Chippawa. Refugee warriors of the

Six Nations, or Iroquois Confederacy, had come from northern New York. Ousted from their tribal lands, they had been resettled along the Grand River by Dorchester's predecessor, General Frederick Haldimand. A splinter group of Mohawks led by John Deserontyn had elected to reside in Tyendinaga Township, west of the five allocated on the Bay of Quinte to disbanded Provincials. Suspicious of all Americans, the Mohawks wanted to be able to keep watch over Lake Ontario to be forewarned of attack. Inland along the Grand River they might be taken by surprise. Leader among the Mohawk and other Six Nations refugees was Captain Joseph Brant (Mohawk name Tyendinaga), a war chief during the Revolution.

Residing in a house at Kingston was Joseph Brant's sister, Molly, widow of Sir William Johnson and step mother of Sir John. Molly had retained her maiden name, Brant, so that she would not lose status among her own matriarchal people. As a matron, Molly had used her influence to keep the Mohawk warriors loyal to Great Britain. Four of the members of the Iroquois Confederacy — Mohawk, Onondaga, Cayuga and Seneca — had allied themselves with the British. Most of the Oneida and Tuscarora Nations had chosen the American side, although many would move later to Grand River. In time they found that their former rebel allies would not respect their claims to the lands that had been theirs for centuries.

Delayed Departure

When Simcoe's carriage reached Weymouth on 17 September, the Colonel discovered that his commission as lieutenant governor had not been sent from London, and they would have to wait for it. During the delay, while Simcoe fretted, Elizabeth enjoyed a busy social life. Among the visitors were Lord Grenville, Lady de la Pole, and members of the Poulett and Rolle families. Lord Poulett, from Somerset, and Lord Rolle, from Devon, were on friendly terms with the Simcoes.[7] Weymouth was a popular resort for the gentry, mainly because it was a favourite with King George, who loved going into the sea in a new invention called a bathing machine. The Simcoes were introduced to the King during their stay at Weymouth.

Meanwhile, Colonel Simcoe fumed. Not only was his commission overdue, but no word came that a knighthood was in the wind. At the docks the *Triton*, with Captain George Murray, waited. Travelling by the armed frigate was necessary because no one knew at what moment the

French might declare war. Being caught on the high seas thus carried some risk of capture. Another danger was bad weather as the season advanced. With each day's delay, the possibility of icebergs in the Gulf of St. Lawrence, and a frozen port of Quebec loomed larger. The commission, but no honour, arrived on the 26th and the *Triton* set sail on the six-week voyage. Travelling with them was Captain Charles Stephenson, the Deputy Quartermaster General. As storm after storm passed, Captain Murray warned the Simcoes that they might have to run south for the Barbados and try again to reach Quebec in the spring, a thought distressing to both.[8] The Colonel could have used the winter persuading friends to help him get better terms as lieutenant governor, while Elizabeth could have been with their older daughters. Elizabeth recorded on 15 October:

> Wind N.W. hard gale, cold. This hard gale did not cool the Cabbins which had been so extremely heated; I was therefore glad to be on Deck to get rid of the headache not withstanding the weather was so rough that I was obliged to hold fast by a Cannon. The waves rising like mountains, has the grandest and most terrific appearance & when the Ship dashes with violence into the Sea & seems to lose her balance as much as a Chaise in the act of overturning, it is surprizing that she rights again. I viewed this tempestuous scene with astonishment.[9]

Below decks everything was wet and dirty "besides being bruised by sudden motions of the Ship & half drowned by Leaks in the Cabbin." Both the children's nurses were seasick. Francis fared well, but Elizabeth felt that the only safe place for Sophia, who had her second birthday at sea, was in her bed. A young midshipman was kind enough to take her for walks when the weather was not too frightful. Nevertheless the wild life fascinated Elizabeth — whales, dolphins and the many sea birds. They were still worried about finding Quebec iced in. They were sailing south of Newfoundland, which meant that Simcoe might not see the waters off Anticosti Island, where his father had been buried at sea. More than likely, he carried a copy of Captain John Simcoe's journal, leaving the original safe at Wolford Lodge. The Colonel longed to sail through the Strait of Canso, described in his father's journal, but Captain Murray thought that narrow route too dangerous so late in the season. Off Louisbourg a sea fog closed in, which prevented them seeing the old fortress. In the Gulf of St. Lawrence they encountered outward bound ships. Off the Magdalen Islands, the *Liberty* hove to and a ship's boat brought newspapers and took mail for England. Elizabeth sent off the next installment of her diary. Down below, Simcoe threw aside a newspaper he had been reading in disgust. Lord Dorchester would not be in Quebec to receive them. His Lordship, he read, was then sailing home, on a leave of absence.

Dorchester had waited until the arrival of Prince Edward Duke of Kent, in command of the 7th Fusiliers, which had come as the replacement garrison at Quebec. Before his promotion to Colonel of the 50th Regiment, Elizabeth's father, Thomas Gwillim, had been a major in the 7th, and had served at Quebec under General Wolfe. In addition to his own commission, Simcoe had been entrusted with those for Lord Dorchester and Major General Alured Clarke. Dorchester's absence meant that no important decisions could be made until he returned.

On 7 November they did sight Anticosti in the far distance, to Simcoe's satisfaction. On the 9th they were able to get a pilot at "Bique" — Bic — on the south shore a few miles west of present day Rimouski. The pilot appeared promptly after Captain Murray fired a gun to signal for him. Simcoe had been worried that all the pilots who knew the safe passage into the harbour at Quebec would have left for the winter. The pilot told them he had just returned downstream, to attend a dance, before retiring upstream to his winter home on Ile aux Coudres.[10]

On the 11th the *Triton* dropped anchor at Quebec, in a grey drizzle. Simcoe left immediately in a ship's boat to call on General Clarke at government house, the Château St. Louis in the Upper Town. Captain Murray soon called upon Elizabeth to ask her to vacate their cabins as quickly as possible. He had passengers waiting for them, and he wanted to clear Quebec by the 13th, to give the ship a better chance of escaping the ice. Lieutenant Edward Talbot, of the 7th Fusiliers, brought a party aboard and helped her move their belongings to an inn on the waterfront.

There an angry Simcoe found them. Under the terms of the Canada Act, he could not be sworn in as the lieutenant governor until three members selected for his executive council were present. The only one close by was Alexander Grant, who had served as commodore on Lakes Erie and Huron during the Revolution. Expected from England in the spring were Lawyer William Osgoode, the chief justice, and the receiver general, Peter Russell, who had served in America during the Seven Years (French and Indian) War and the Revolution. William Robertson, with mercantile interests in Detroit, was temporarily in England. Others expected from England in the spring were John White, the attorney general, and Provincial Secretary William Jarvis.[11]

Resigned to winter in Quebec, the Colonel rented a house in Rue St. Jean, in the fashionable Upper Town. Simcoe's frustrations at not being able to get on with his work continued. In a letter he had written to Secretary Dundas in August 1791, he showed his awareness of the actions of the native tribes in what was then the northwest, in the Ohio Valley:

> The neighbours of the Colony are the Indians & the United States.
>
> The Indians are individually as eminent for that neglect of being and passion [sic] for Glory which when duly regulated renders Armies invincible, as any Europeans of the best principles whatsoever & far excell all mankind in their patience of fatigue and tolerance of Hunger. They are all at present confederated in a War against the United States.

How the war would end was not easy to foresee, but probably neither disaster nor victory would "disunite the Confederacy," for "while these people remain Hunters they must remain Warriors." The warriors were the terror of any infant colony "as their warfare is by surprize, devastation, torture & destruction."

The native tribes, Simcoe affirmed, must be contented with whatever boundary the United States would allow them. He could see a role for Great Britain as mediator. If a satisfactory boundary settlement could not be met, the warriors would turn on the colonists of Upper Canada. The only way to prevent attack would be the assurance that a formidable garrison awaited them. For this reason Simcoe had demanded reinforcements of regular troops for the border forts, and a much stronger battalion of Queen's Rangers.

Another matter preoccupying Simcoe and some of his friends was the effect Sir John Johnson might have on the running of Upper Canada. On 3 June 1790, Lord Grenville had written Lord Dorchester assuring him that whatever Sir John's personal thoughts, he would never be disloyal. Simcoe himself requested promotion to the rank of major general, for two reasons. Alured Clarke was already a major general, although Simcoe was senior to him. Sir John Johnson was a brigadier general on the American establishment. As a colonel, Simcoe could be overruled by either officer. He would have to wait a while for a reply to the latter concern.[12]

Stuck in Quebec, the Simcoes attended many functions, although only Elizabeth enjoyed plays put on by the garrison. The Colonel thought them too frivolous, and beneath the dignity of British officers. Walking was dangerous on the icy, steep streets of Quebec. They found that they had more traction if they put socks over their shoes.

The proclamation of the division of Canada into two provinces was duly read on 26 December, amidst celebrations, illuminations, balls and dinners. Of note was a ball at the Château St. Louis on the 28th, where Elizabeth danced with Prince Edward. Meanwhile, they were making many friends. Elizabeth was delighted with Mme Dell Marie-Anne, wife of François Baby, an executive councillor for Lower Canada, and Mme de Salaberry, of a distinguished family. Elizabeth's French allowed her to mix comfortably with the old Quebec elite. Among new English friends were Colonel Henry and Ann Caldwell, who had a house at Belmont, a short distance west of the city. Caldwell had commanded the "English Militia" at the siege of Quebec in 1775–76 (the Canadian Militia was entirely French-speaking). Caldwell had served in the Seven Years' War, and had met Colonel Thomas Gwillim in Quebec. although at that time neither he, nor Elizabeth, made the connection.

Late in January, accompanied by Captain Stephenson, Simcoe set out in a sleigh for Montreal, warmly covered with bear and buffalo skins, hot bricks at their feet. While in Montreal, Simcoe had a meeting with Sir John Johnson. The baronet, unexpectedly cordial, raised only one issue. Sir John had prepared, for Lord Dorchester, a list of half-pay officers he thought worthy of being legislative councillors. Left off His Lordship's published list was Sir John's half-pay captain, Richard Duncan, who lived at Rapid Plat, in Augusta Township on the St. Lawrence. Simcoe promised to reinstate Duncan, and the two parted amicably. When Simcoe and Stephenson returned, with them was Lieutenant Thomas Talbot, stationed with his 24th Regiment in Montreal. Talbot, a relative of the Marquis of Buckingham who had recommended him to Simcoe, had received a leave of absence to act at the Colonel's private secretary and aide de camp.[13] On 7 February, Elizabeth reported an incident at the house in Rue St. Jean:

> At two o'clock the kitchen Chimney was on fire. It was soon extinguished as the people here are expert in using fire Engines. The house being covered in shingles (wood in the shape of tiles) fires spread rapidly if not immediately put out. The Prince, General Clarke etc dined with Coll. Simcoe & this accident retarded the dinner, so that I went to bed before dinner.[14]

On the 15th, Elizabeth and the Colonel were out for a walk "on the Pont." A plank had been laid down to bridge some open water between the shore of the St. Lawrence and the ice, which Simcoe crossed:

> & stepping back to give me his hand he slipped into the water, but luckily caught hold of the plank which supported him until the Canadians who were near & on my screaming out "Au secours" assisted him out. We walked to Monsr. Baby's, & I ran home to order dry clothes to be brought there.[15]

The Baby house, in Rue Sous-le-Fort, was closer to the shore than the Simcoe dwelling Rue St. Jean.[16] Fortunately, Simcoe was rescued quickly enough from the icy water to avoid too much loss of body heat, and, to Elizabeth's relief, he suffered no ill effects. The memory of his drowned brother taken from the River Exe must have haunted Simcoe before he was pulled out safely.

By this time the Colonel was thoroughly frustrated. He longed to make his way to Upper Canada during the winter, when travel was by sleigh and much more comfortable. Sleighs slid smoothly over the packed down trails, and over ice where rivers had to be crossed. Keeping warm was not difficult in "carioles" deep with blankets and robes, so long as they could find shelter from high winds and blizzards. By the time they could leave, they would have to go by boat, or over roads clogged by stumps that had not had time to rot away. Few streams were bridged, which meant long detours to fordable spots. Simcoe was aware of the poor road conditions during spring and summer, without even thinking of the hot, humid weather so prevalent along the St. Lawrence, the black flies and mosquitos.

On Sunday 4 March, a commotion in the hallway attracted Elizabeth's notice. Being greeted boisterously by Simcoe were five bearded men in greatcoats and moccasins, muffled against the outdoor cold. Their leader was Aeneas Shaw, a captain in the old Queen's Rangers, now captain-lieutenant in the new regiment. They had come on snowshoes from Fredericton, New Brunswick, 260 miles in nineteen days, by way of the Saint John River and a chain of small lakes:

> Their mode of travelling was to set out at daybreak, walk till twelve when they stood ten minutes (not longer because of the cold) to eat. They then resumed walking till past four when they chose a spot where there was

good firewood to Encamp. Half the party (which consisted of twelve) began felling wood, the rest dug away the snow till they had made a pit many feet in circumference in which the fire was to be made. They cut the Cedar & Pine branches, laid a blanket on them, & wrapping themselves in another found it sufficiently warm with their feet close to a large fire which was kept up all night.[17]

John McGill, captain in the old Rangers, ensign in the new, who had set out with them, had cut his knee while felling wood. He had been left at Madawaska, a settlement on the Madawaska River, and would join the others when he was fit again. One of the party, a "frenchman used to the mode of travelling" carried a sixty-pound pack, but walked faster than the rest. They were guided by the sun, a river and a pocket compass. "Capt. Shaw is a very sensible pleasant Scotchman, a highlander. His family [a wife and seven children] are to come from N. Brunswick to U. Canada next summer."[18]

With the arrival of spring, Elizabeth felt cooped up in the house. The streets were soaking with water flowing over the melting ice, dangerous for horses and people alike. The social whirl of the winter came to a halt because visiting was so hazardous. However, the arrival of spring meant new adventures, as they began to plan their journey to reach Simcoe's province. At the same time, as she wrote Mrs. Hunt:

> I assure you that this Winter has been a very bad prelude in going into the Upper country if I am to find it a solitary scene as people say. I should have been fitter a great deal for solitude & enjoyed it more, coming from Black Down than after spending six months in the midst of Balls, concerts, assemblies & Card parties every night.[19]

They had Francis inoculated, to have that illness out of the way before they had to begin travelling. Elizabeth wrote to Mrs. Hunt on 26 April: "I am so happy that the little Boy has got over the small pox before he sets out."[19]

The first contingent of Queen's Rangers arrived, and Captains Shank and Smith were expected shortly with the rest. Simcoe soon arranged for the Rangers to be sent up the St. Lawrence to begin erecting huts at Kingston, to serve as a temporary barracks. Captain-Lieutenant Shaw would be leaving, too. The second captain-lieutenant, the enterprising George Spencer, who had retrieved the trophies of the British Legion and later drawn maps for Simcoe, was delayed in England by illness.

The new Queen's Rangers, which when he first proposed raising them — as a regiment independent of the rest of the regular army — would be more a work force than a fighting unit. Simcoe wanted them to train for two days a week, and the rest of their time would be spent building strategic roads, working on public buildings, and clearing land for settlers to purchase. That would help cover the cost of the corps. After their enlistments were over, they would remain as settlers, a "vital principle of the Colony":

> Following the great Masters of the World, the Romans
> of old, I propose to consider the Winter Stations of
> these Companies as the Germs of so many well affected
> Colonial Cities.[20]

On 1 June the ship *Henneken* arrived bringing Provincial Secretary Jarvis and his family. The following day another ship landed Chief Justice William Osgoode, Attorney General John White, and Receiver General Peter Russell. The latter brought his sister, Elizabeth, to be his hostess and housekeeper. With Alexander Grant, four members of Simcoe's executive council were on the scene and he now had the quorum he needed to govern Upper Canada. He hired three bateaux to take his own party up the St. Lawrence as far as Kingston, at the foot of Lake Ontario, a booming village, which many people hoped would be the new provincial capital.

A bateau was a flat-bottomed, oared boat with an awning to shelter passengers from the sun, and a lateen sail. It was about twenty-four feet long, rowed by a crew of eight. Supervising the bateaumen was the pilot, making in all twenty-five in the crew. One bateau was for Mrs. Simcoe, the Colonel, and his two aides. Lieutenant Thomas Talbot had been joined by Lieutenant Thomas Grey of the 7th Fusiliers. Like Talbot, Grey had left his regiment to serve Simcoe. In the second bateau were the two children, their nurses and other servants. Francis's wet nurse had returned home, and Elizabeth had hired a new nurse for him, an American girl named Collins. The third bateau carried the baggage and some substantial furniture, but not the two canvas houses, which would be sent after them.[21]

The Simcoes left Quebec City on 8 June. Each night the men slept in the boats, but the Colonel tried to make arrangements for the women and children to sleep under cover. They stayed in houses or inns, and on one occasion with the wife of a local seigneur. At Trois Rivières Elizabeth was annoyed when a landlord overcharged them for their breakfast. Simcoe left such trivia to his wife, his mind absorbed with the task that awaited him when they passed the last seigneury. They reached Pointe aux Trembles, on the Island of Montreal, on the 13th.[22]

THIRTEEN
A Vice-Regal Progress and a Royal Visit

In Montreal, they stayed at the Château de Ramezay, an old stone building that was the local government house. The heat and humidity were oppressive, although the château was cooler than outdoors and spacious. They were joined here by Captain Charles Stephenson, confirmed as quartermaster general, and Captain Edward Littlehales, newly appointed major of brigade for Upper Canada and Simcoe's military secretary. Joseph Frobisher, the wealthy fur trader, entertained the Simcoes at Beaver Hall, and the Baronne de Longueuil, wife of William Grant, the Baron, who received them at their home on St. Helen's Island.

The governor and Mrs. Simcoe drove up Mount Royal, with its splendid view over the little city, but they found the road appallingly rough. On 17 June, Simcoe reported to Sir George Yonge that Captain-Lieutenant Shaw had reached Kingston with the first contingent of the Queen's Rangers. The Simcoes left on the 22nd, by road, for Lachine, while the bateaux were drawn upriver through the rapids. They passed a country house belonging to Sir John Johnson, who was not in residence.

He had obtained an extended leave of absence, and by that time he was nearing Trois Rivières with his family, waiting for a ship to take them to England.[1] Some of his children travelled back and forth, but Sir John did not return to Canada until the autumn of 1796.

The Simcoes rejoined the bateaux on the 23rd, at 6.00 a.m. Elizabeth remarked on the dirty-looking water as the Ottawa River emptied into the sparkling clear St. Lawrence. The men walked to lighten the boat at the Cascades Rapids. On the 24th they rode through the tiny shallow locks on the eighteen-inch deep canal at Coteau du Lac that bypassed the Cedars Rapids. At Pointe au Baudet, Simcoe announced that they were now in Upper Canada. When they reached the main settlement in Glengarry, a boat arrived from John Macdonell, a half-pay captain from Butler's Rangers, whose home was Glengarry House. By the time Simcoe crossed into Upper Canada, officers of Provincial Corps were permitted half-pay when their regiments were disbanded. Aboard Macdonell's boat were kilted Highlanders come to escort the governor and his three aides ashore. Elizabeth planned to rejoin them when the bateaux reached the Macdonell house.

Scarcely moments later, and with awesome speed, the sky blackened, billowing clouds of a threatening grey-blue filled the heavens. Great flashes of lightning, the like of which she had never before beheld, bombarded her senses. When the wooden awning on the bateau tore, and the boat rocked fiercely, she demanded that the crew land. She spent the night in a farmhouse, and early the next morning she breakfasted with the governor and Macdonell at Glengarry House.

Farther on they spent a night with James Gray, a half-pay major from Sir John Johnson's regiment. From there Simcoe went to St. Regis, a Mohawk village on an island, to greet those loyal friends of Great Britain. Waiting at the foot of the spectacular Long Sault Rapids was John Munro, one of Sir John's half-pay captains and a legislative councillor. Munro, of Augusta Township, had brought horses to carry them along the rough track that bypassed the dangerous stretch of water. Richard Duncan, now a legislative councillor, as Simcoe had promised, had loaned the horses, a generous gesture because the province was very short of livestock of all kinds. Footing for the horses was treacherous, the track was so rutted, and bridges were mere logs laid side by side where a horse might easily break a bone. They sampled fresh-caught bass, and wild strawberries tastier than those grown at Wolford Lodge.

Off Johnstown, a tiny hamlet in the forest, a group of half-pay officers in their old uniforms met them in a boat. They took the governor to inspect Chimney Island, where the French had built Fort

The Manor House, Cotterstock, Northamptonshire, generally accepted as the birthplace of John Graves Simcoe. Photo by Paul Dixon of Cotterstock.

Two re-enactors at Fort York, Toronto. On Victoria Day in May, green jacketed "Queen's Rangers" join in a military review with other period troops. Photo by M.B. Fryer.

John Graves Simcoe (1752–1806). Painting by George T. Berthon, photo by Tom Moore. Ontario Government Art Collection.

Elizabeth Gwillim Simcoe (1762–1850). From a miniature drawn by her friend, Mary Anne ("Mrs.") Burges. National Archives of Canada, C 81931.

The Simcoe Vase. John Graves Simcoe presented this silver vase to the Coleridge family. Simcoe's sons, Francis and Henry, were pupils of the Reverend George Coleridge at The King's School, Ottery St. Mary. Photo by Shirley Dracott, permission of Lord Coleridge.

The Drewe Arms, Broadhembury. Photo by M.B. Fryer.

The John Graves Simcoe Memorial on the South Choir Wall, Exeter Cathedral, by the sculptor Flaxman. Exeter was severely bombed during the Second World War and the stained-glass windows were destroyed. They have been replaced by plain glass. Photo by M.B. Fryer.

The Simcoe Window, St. George's Church,
Sibbald Point, Lake Simcoe, Ontario. Made by
the Simcoe daughters. Photo by M.B. Fryer.

The rededication of Wolford Chapel. The Very Reverend Patrick Mitchell, KCVO, was until recently the Dean of Windsor. He is shown conducting the service. Photo by George Hutchison. Government of Ontario.

Lévis, and they fired off one of the old cannons. Simcoe took note of several guns, in case they should be useful to protect Kingston. As he was returning to the bateau, the officers saluted him with shouted huzzahs, to his delight. Old soldiers were special men, a breed apart. At an inn at Johnstown, Simcoe held his first levée. The officers, still in uniform, spoke to many toasts. Dr. Solomon Jones, surgeon's mate in the Loyal Rangers, responding to a toast, recounted some of the exploits of the new governor during the late war. Elijah Bottum (or Bothum) in the green coat of a Loyal Ranger, sporting "a formidable basket-hilted claymore, then addressed them in brief, military phrase and gave one of the old war slogans."[2]

Simcoe was pleased. He would enjoy governing such men, although he was sensing how different was reality from his thoughts before leaving England. Very few of the settlers were Anglicans, which might bode ill for establishing the Church of England. As far as possible, the Loyalists had been settled according to their denominations. Highlanders living closest to the last seigneury were mainly Roman Catholics. At nearby St. Regis, Simcoe had met Father Alexander Macdonell, their Highland-born priest. West of the Highlanders were Lutherans, mainly Germans, while in the upper townships, he heard, many were New England "sectaries," not the loyal Anglicans he had hoped to attract from Connecticut. (Reverend Samuel Peters, who had fled from Connecticut, was an Anglican, but the Congregational Church was the established one.)

In the townships were at least as high a proportion of followers of John Wesley as could be found in his own West Country. Badly educated but bewitching saddlebag preachers from the United States regularly toured the settlements, "Thunderers at our doors!" enlisting many converts.[3] (Simcoe or no Simcoe, within less than a century, Methodism would grow into the strongest Protestant denomination in Canada.)

Also worrying was the presence of Moravian missionaries on the River La Tranche, who had come with refugees of the Delaware nation after the Revolution. He feared they, too, might be spreading their non-conformist notions in what he hoped would be the heartland of the province. He must ask for Anglican missionaries from home to counter such influences.

At Gananoque they met militia Colonel Joel Stone, who had built a mill on the river of the same name. Elizabeth sketched the mill, and the governor added a dog in the water below it, and some notes (now too faded to be read) which amused her. The bateaux were now in the heart of what the French had named *Les Milles Iles*, the Thousand Islands. The natives, more poetic, had called the area "The Garden of the Great

Spirit," pretty lumps of black-streaked pink granite with patches of broad-leafed or coniferous trees. Again, Elizabeth was busy with sketch book and pencil. They followed the bateau channel westwards, more protected than the wider channel near the south shore of the St. Lawrence. There, sailing vessels tacked back and forth against the strong east-flowing current.

By the morning of 1 July they were off Kingston harbour, before which were a number of large, flatter islands. As the bateaux moved towards the mouth of the Cataraqui River, they could feel the strength of the wind that whipped up whitecaps on the crests of the waves on Lake Ontario. Kingston was the naval base, but Simcoe resolved to find a better site because this harbour offered so little shelter against the prevailing southwest wind. Carleton Island had a superior harbour, but the international boundary might run north of it necessitating its evacuation. On the island, Fort Haldimand, so busy during the late war, now had only a small caretaker garrison.

A warm welcome awaited them ashore. Again half-pay officers were in their old uniforms. Cannons boomed, joined by musket volleys fired by Mohawks who had come from their village of Deseronto, a few miles west in Tyendinaga Township. Drawn up in their ranks were the Queen's Rangers, whose rows of small white tents were visible in the background. Here lay the military, naval and commercial heartland of the province, yet it consisted of about fifty wooden houses, interspersed with stumps and muddy tracks. Close to the water lay the old French Fort Frontenac, recently rebuilt, and alongside were merchants' storehouses. Simcoe's practised eye noted that a gun placed on some heights across the Cataraqui River could easily destroy the low-lying old fort and most of the town. At the very least, a blockhouse must be erected there. Elizabeth was delighted to find, on a knoll, a small but cool and airy house that had been prepared for them.

The honeymoon was soon over, as far as the Kingstonians were concerned. As the foremost community in Upper Canada, they assumed that Simcoe would choose Kingston as his capital, especially since Lord Dorchester had more or less promised them. They were dismayed when, at the outset, Simcoe announced that he would be moving on to Niagara, which was more central although in the long term no safer from attack. For the present, Niagara suited Simcoe, and it was defensible as long as Fort Niagara, across the narrow Niagara river, was in British hands. Although the land was legally part of New York State, it had been garrisoned by regular troops. The 5th (Northumberland) Regiment had been rotated there from Detroit only in June. Simcoe assumed that

Britain had no intention of withdrawing the troops as long as the Loyalists and native peoples needed protection.

Especially indignant was Kingston's leading merchant, Richard Cartwright, a Loyalist who had served at Fort Niagara during the Revolution. Cartwright's house, visible from the water, was the only one of stone in the settlement. The logical place for the capital was here, where, incidentally, Cartwright owned many of the mills and whose bateaux had almost a monopoly over the carrying trade.

Elizabeth joined the governor on many of his tours of inspection. At other times she was accompanied by Lieutenant Thomas Talbot. She, who had always loved nature, was disillusioned with how untidy it was in this near-wilderness, so untamed by the hand of man.

A mosquito had bitten her so severely through a leather glove that she felt faint. Her "Musquito" was more likely a hornet or a ground wasp. A boat was more satisfactory than trying to go anywhere by land. The exception was an evening when the woods caught fire, and the smoke drove the mosquitos away. Besides, the woods were so "picturesque" as flames illuminated the dark trees. "Perhaps you have no idea of the pleasure of walking in a burning wood, but I found it so great that I think I shall have some woods set on fire for my evening walks," she wrote Mary Anne Burges.

John Scadding, she put in her diary for the girls at Wolford Lodge, had found a small green grass snake that he showed her. He kept it a few hours then let it escape. He had come, at the request of Simcoe, who needed his expertise to evaluate agricultural land. Scadding had left Wolford and the other Devon lands in the hands of his capable brother, Thomas.[4]

For Sunday 8 July, Simcoe prepared to take his oath of office, surrounded by every bit of pomp and pageantry the tiny community of Kingston would allow. With his officers in dress uniform, Simcoe in the red of a colonel in the army, they set off in solemn procession, the drummer marking the beat, bound for St. George's Church (now the Anglican cathedral). Government was about to commence. Present were Receiver General Peter Russell and Jacques Duperon Baby of Detroit, newly appointed to the Executive Council. (The other two members of the council were Alexander Grant and William Robertson, neither of whom was present.) Standing by in knee breeches and silk stockings were Richard Cartwright of Kingston and Robert Hamilton, who had come from Niagara. Chief Justice William Osgoode administered the oath, and Russell and Baby signed as witnesses. Afterwards, Elizabeth joined the governor for the swearing-in ceremony, where Reverend John Stuart gave the blessing. Stuart had been the Anglican missionary to the Mohawks at Fort Hunter, in New York's Mohawk Valley, before the Revolution. He had been held under house arrest until permitted to leave for British territory. He was the first clergyman in Upper Canada, after serving as chaplain to the 2nd Battalion King's Royal Regiment of New York.

Simcoe met on the 9th, with the Executive Council, the date of the members' appointments. With them he discussed the composition of the Legislative Council or upper house, of which the executive was a sort of cabinet. In addition to Osgoode, Russell, Grant, Robertson and Baby, Simcoe approved Richard Cartwright, Richard Duncan from Augusta Township, Robert Hamilton from Niagara, and John Munro of Matilda Township, who had brought Duncan's horses to the Simcoes. The Legislative Council thus had nine members, including the members of the Executive Council. Chosen as speaker was Chief Justice Osgoode.

One man who was not appointed must have felt affronted. Captain Justus Sherwood of the Loyal Rangers, now resident in Augusta, had been of great value to Dorchester's predecessor General Frederick Haldimand. Sherwood had been head of Haldimand's secret service, a commissioner of prisoners and refugees, and negotiator with Governor Chittenden and the Allens and Fays, for Vermont to reunite with Great Britain. Reunion failed, but Sherwood had kept Vermont neutral from July 1781 until after the Treaty of Separation, no mean achievement. Sherwood, a justice of the peace, had been appointed to the Legislative Council in May 1784, to represent the District of Montreal.[5] Since such appointments were for life, Sherwood had the right to expect that transfer to the Legislative Council of Upper Canada would be automatic. Later, Simcoe wrote Dorchester that he knew that Sherwood had been employed by Haldimand in "intercourse he held with the inhabitants of Vermont," but he gave no opinion on the man's merits.[6] Sherwood appeared to be just the sort of man Simcoe needed. Something had gone wrong. Perhaps General Clarke had warned Simcoe that Sherwood was outspoken, and a democratic Connecticut Yankee who was a potential troublemaker.

While Simcoe was busy with his council and certain proclamations, Elizabeth was making friends with the young wife of the surgeon to the garrison, James Macaulay. They had named their newborn son John Simcoe Macaulay. To Elizabeth's delight, they would soon be following the Simcoes to Niagara. The government ship, H.M.S. *Onondaga*, an armed 80-ton topsail schooner, was standing by. Simcoe wanted to go to Niagara by small boat, to evaluate harbours and townsites, but he decided to go on the schooner and get his family settled first. On 23 July they boarded the *Onondaga*. Two days later Lieutenant Talbot pointed out the spray rising above the great Falls of Niagara, forty miles in the distance. Elizabeth could hardly wait to sketch them.

Niagara, which Simcoe renamed Newark (to dispose of an uncivilised word) had scarcely a dozen houses — really mere cabins. Butler's Rangers, a very active Provincial Corps, had operated out of Fort Niagara. The fort, dating from the French regime, stood across the river where heavy guns and the British garrison could protect the settlement. Disbanded Rangers who had received grants of land along the west bank of the river had been establishing farms for the past ten years. Their commanding officer, Colonel John Butler, the man Simcoe had once thought of joining, was one of the leading settlers, and a deputy superintendent in the Indian Department.[7] (In fact, many disbanded Rangers had named their settlement Butlersburg, in honour of their colonel, and were hardly pleased with Simcoe's choice of Newark.)

The British Indian Department had been established mainly to control trade with the tribes, and to forge alliances, first, in the tug-of-war between the interests of Britain and France, and later to retain the loyalty, particularly of the Iroquois nations, during the Revolution. The department had a military function, and the subordinates to the superintendents held officer ranks. Thus Alexander McKee, deputy at Detroit, was a colonel; Matthew Elliott, whose home overlooked the Detroit River, was a captain. Among the more intriguing residents was Simon Girty, an interpreter who had been the brains behind important Ranger and native successes during the late war, a man the "Kentuckers" hated. The absent Sir John Johnson was the superintendent, but Colonel Butler was in charge of the department at Niagara. Simcoe would have much to do with the department during his years in Upper Canada.[8]

When the Simcoes reached Newark, no house such as they had found at Kingston awaited them. They had to make do with four rundown wooden government buildings called Navy Hall, once the headquarters for the navy on Lake Ontario. These were being prepared for occupancy, although they would not make a proper, even comfortable, dwelling. As a temporary shelter, Simcoe had three large tents erected on the hillside overlooking the Niagara River. One would be for themselves, one for the children and their nurses, and the other for the servants. The site was high enough to catch the cool breezes, much less stifling than Navy Hall, which stood on low ground beside the water. Elizabeth Russell was particularly distressed to find only a two-room cabin for herself and the receiver general, her brother Peter. Simcoe was unperturbed. His councillors and civil servants would build houses and a lovely town would spring up almost overnight. Nevertheless he was not enchanted by Navy Hall. He wrote to James Bland Burges:

> I am fitting up an old hovel, that will look exactly like a carrier's ale-house in England when properly decorated and ornamented; but I please myself with the hopes that some future "Gentleman's Magazine" will obtain drawings of the first Government House, the first House of Assembly, etc., and decorate it with the "Aude, Hospes, Contemnere opes" of old Evander.[9]

He was planning a journey to Detroit without delay, and he wanted Elizabeth to accompany him. She would sketch the countryside while he inspected the post's defences. Afterwards they would follow the La Tranche River to its forks, where he hoped to find a site for the future capital of Upper Canada, central and at a safe distance from attack. On their return he would establish his provincial government. Thus far the only form of government was the district court where appointed magistrates presided. He would also get rid of the German names Dorchester had imposed on them. Luneburg would become the Eastern District, Mecklenburg the Midland, Nassau the Home, and Hesse the Western. He decided not to interfere with the townships along the St. Lawrence and Bay of Quinte that Dorchester had named after the numerous progeny of the King.

High on their agenda was the Falls of Niagara. They set out in calèches for their first view. They breakfasted at the fine stone home of Robert Hamilton, merchant and legislative councillor. Hamilton was a former partner of Richard Cartwright, who had remained in the Niagara area after the Revolution. The Hamilton house stood at what was called The Landing, or Queenston, below the Falls. There, goods had to be removed from boats and carried up the steep mountain, above the cascade to an upper landing for transport in other vessels along Lake Erie. A firm friendship began between Elizabeth and Mrs. Hamilton, the former Catharine Askin, a daughter of the Detroit fur trader, John Askin. After viewing the great work of nature, they continued on to Fort Chippawa, close to the upper landing above the Falls. They spent the night with the Hamiltons. When they reached Navy Hall the next day, a message awaited Simcoe. Prince Edward was about to set out to inspect the garrison and defences of Upper Canada, and he expected to be at Newark in three weeks' time.[10]

Normally the Simcoes dined under a tree, which was cooler than inside the tents. On the evening of 16 August, Elizabeth was out for a drive when a thunderstorm blew in suddenly. Most of her blue and white Nankin china was broken when an oak bow above their temporary kitchen caught fire and servants hurriedly tried to save the delicate pieces. Meanwhile, the Queen's Rangers had been endeavouring to finish the work on Navy Hall. Even with extra help, by 19 August the place was hardly habitable. It smelled atrociously of fresh paint and damp plaster. They had no choice but to surrender the tents to His Royal Highness and make do with Navy Hall for themselves. The Prince and his entourage arrived the next day. From Navy Hall, Elizabeth wrote:

> we came here on a cold and blowing night. I sat by myself in a miserable, unfinished, damp room, looking on the lake, where it blew a gale, the Bear, a gunboat tossing about terribly, and not a cheerful thought passing through my mind ...

Fortunately, a letter from home eased her depression.[11]

Despite having to entertain royalty, Simcoe wrote to his two eldest daughters so that the letters could be sent on the ship that would be carrying the Prince down the lake. He advised Eliza to stay outdoors as much as possible, and he stressed the importance of reading. He hoped she would pass on the benefit of her instruction to Francis. She should study the Good Book, especially Genesis and Exodus, and the classics. A particular hero was Alexander the Great, and he hoped Francis would follow a military career. He never saw an unusual flower without wishing he could show it to his girls.[12]

He wrote to Charlotte in a lighter vein, as though he thought her less serious-minded:

> here I am & Mamma sitting in a very large Bower, fronting upon a fine river, & as high above it, as the sand cliff above the Shrubbery, with Sophia sitting upon the Table, little Francis with his bald Pole [sic] laughing & eating Bilberries.

He told her he would be completely happy if only the four girls were with them. He was delighted that Charlotte loved to dance. Perhaps he should learn to play the fiddle in order to accompany her. He was pleased she was growing fond of reading, and hoped she would make Francis fond of it too, and would teach him not to destroy too many birds, sail his little boats and fire his cannon "as Boys are apt to do." He was looking ahead since Francis was only fourteen months old.[13] (The letters would reach Wolford Lodge in November 1792. Miss Burges reported on the 20th that Eliza and Charlotte were delighted with their letters, but Harriet was perturbed that there was none for her. Mary Anne explained to the now five-and-a-half-year-old Harriet that when Papa wrote his letters he was not aware that she could read.)[14]

On 25 August, when Simcoe accompanied the Prince to Fort Niagara to inspect the garrison, he stood close to one of the guns when a royal salute was fired. This deafened him temporarily and left him with a searing headache that sent him to his bed for the remainder of the royal visit. The commandant of the fort, Major John Smith, was the Prince's host until his departure, to Simcoe's everlasting chagrin. Describing the headache Elizabeth wrote:

> [He] kept to his room for a fortnight. He had a gouty pain in his hand before & it is supposed the Shock of the Cannon firing so immediately above him fixed the disorder in his head. He has now recovered & has a pain in his foot, which perhaps would more effectually relieve his head, if it was more violent.[15]

The report of the cannon was less likely to have caused Simcoe's prolonged illness than his sleeping in Navy Hall. Paint at the time was very toxic, and the innate dampness of the building meant serious accumulations of mould. Breathing the mould each night would be sufficient to cause severe sinus pain, difficult to relieve until he was able to return to the airiness of their tents. To Elizabeth's regret, the visit of Prince Edward meant postponing their journey to Detroit until after the legislature could meet.

FOURTEEN
SIMCOE THE ADMINISTRATOR

During the summer of 1792, the residents of Upper Canada were voting in an election to send members to the first meeting of the provincial legislature. By proclamation before he left Kingston, Simcoe had divided the southern fringe of Upper Canada, where the settlements were developing, into nineteen counties. He had named some after his friends, Northumberland, Dundas or Addington, for example. Gathering votes in such an under- populated wilderness took time, but by September sixteen members had been selected. Counties with few voters shared representatives with others, while Glengarry on the St. Lawrence had two ridings, and Lincoln, on the Niagara Peninsula, had three. Leeds and Frontenac shared John White, the attorney general. Elected for Prince Edward County and Adolphustown Township was Philip Dorland, who refused, as a Quaker, to take the oath of office. (He was replaced by Peter van Alstine in June 1793.)[1] The counties were for electoral purpose; the unit of local government remained the district. Following the English pattern, Simcoe intended raising the militia as county units, and appointing a County Lieutenant in each:

In order to promote an Aristocracy, most necessary in
this country, which I mean to extend from time to time;
and have given them the recommendatory Power for the
Militia and Magistracy as is usual in England … [2]

On 16 September, the first Parliament of Upper Canada opened,
with all the pomp and ceremony Simcoe could arrange. He rode forth in
his full scarlet regimentals, escorted by Major Littlehales and Lieutenants
Talbot and Grey. A guard of honour of the Queen's Rangers, and some of
Colonel John Butler's disbanded Rangers who also wore green coats, lined
the route from Navy Hall to the Masonic Lodge building, where the
legislature would meet. The governor's party was followed by some
Iroquois men and women of the Six Nations, and others of the
Mississauga and Chippawa bands — local names for the Algonkian-
speaking natives of the Eastern Woodlands.

Elizabeth was arrayed in a gown made for the purpose in London.
She watched proudly, the band of the gown cutting into her swelling
waist; the Simcoe's seventh child was due in January. She was fatigued by
the evening, but she gamely attended a grand ball, and she was
meticulous in seeing that she spoke to every guest — members of
councils or legislature and their wives, and Simcoe's staff of civil servants.
She promised the governor to be quiet for the next few days, proud that
she had been such a good hostess to so many strangers.[3]

In his speech from the throne, Simcoe emphasised that Upper
Canada's was a British constitution. This implied a pyramid, with
monarchy at the pinnacle, an aristocracy in support of the sovereign,
and as limited a form of democracy as possible — truly high Tory
principles.

Two matters of extreme importance, the first to Simcoe, the second
to his subjects, were reserved lots and legal marriages. Under the
constitution, one seventh of the land in each township was to be
reserved for the support of the Crown, and another seventh to provide
funds for the clergy — Anglican, as far as the governor was concerned.
The reserved lots were not to be allotted in blocks, but in a
checkerboard pattern, so that they would be scattered throughout each
township. The man who worked out the pattern was Lieutenant David
William Smith, 5th Regiment, and the only son of Major John Smith.
Before the 5th was rotated to Niagara from Detroit, David had been
the chairman of the Western (Hesse) District Land Board. He had been
elected the member of the legislative assembly for Essex and Suffolk,
the most westerly counties.[4] (This system was to cause aggravation, as

the lots which remained unsold were a hindrance to contiguous development and a burden to roadbuilders who had to remove trees past unoccupied lands.)

During the years of war and displacement, many Loyalists had contracted marriages of doubtful legality. Loyalists held many certificates from magistrates, and Simcoe directed Chief Justice Osgoode to draw up a bill regarding these and future marriages, to be sent to England for approval. Because getting a reply would take time, Simcoe agreed to another bill that made provision for future marriages. Only Church of England clergymen could perform marriages. Only three reverend gentlemen qualified — John Stuart at Kingston, Robert Addison, now missionary at Newark, and John Langhorn, on the Bay of Quinte since 1787. Where no clergyman resided within eighteen miles, a magistrate could continue to perform the sacrament.

Another matter of particular concern to Simcoe was land granting. Lord Dorchester had set up a land board in each of the four districts, with a half-pay officer as chairman, to allot grants of land to Loyalists, who received their grants free of all charges, and to other settlers, who could receive permission to settle if they were thought to be of good character, and for payment of a patent fee. (At that time Captain Justus Sherwood, magistrate, was the chairman of the land board for Luneburg, now the Eastern District. Simcoe may have thought him too liberal with those whose claims as Loyalists were suspect.)

Simcoe disliked the land boards, but for the time being he tolerated them. He was more worried about interference in Upper Canada over which he had no control. The Indian Department headquarters were in Lower Canada; a separate department he requested was overruled. The same applied to land surveying. In charge of all surveying, was the elderly surveyor general Samuel Holland, in Quebec City. Deputy surveyors working in Upper Canada were subject to Holland's commands, not Simcoe's. Regular troops in both provinces came under the command of Major General Clarke. Meanwhile, Lord Dorchester remained in England, which left Simcoe free to communicate directly with Henry Dundas, secretary of state for the home department (and after 1794 the secretary of state for war and the colonies).

The autumn was unusually mild. By November the Simcoes were still not heating the canvas house, although Elizabeth did not specify whether one or two houses had been erected. She described the one she occupied as thirty feet long and twelve wide, divided by a partition to make a sitting room and a bedroom, and wall papered[5] She did not say where the others slept, whether the governor shared the canvas house, or used the second one, nor how Navy Hall was being used. It probably accommodated servants, aides and at times guests. Reverend Addison conducted services there on Sundays. Simcoe had a hut built for himself, above the Niagara River at Queenston. Inside he hung the tapestry, the gift from the Marquis of Buckingham. They had acquired pets, a grey and white cat that had adopted them in Kingston, and a dog named Jack Sharp. Elizabeth described him as a Newfoundland dog that had belonged to a Mr. Shane at Niagara. A hound they named Trojan joined the family circle and selected her as his special mistress, sleeping in her bedroom.[6]

On 3 December she visited Captain Henry Darling at Fort Niagara, to inspect his collection of stuffed birds and animals, which were of particular interest as they were local. Then on the 9th, Captain Joseph Brant arrived to pay his respects and dine with the governor. Elizabeth thought he might be cunning:

> He wore an English Coat with a handsome Crimson Silk blanket lined with black and trimmed with gold fringe & wore a Fur Cap, round his neck he had a string of plaited sweet hay, It is a kind of grass that never loses its pleasant scent.[7]

Brant, the wartime leader of the Iroquois warriors, held his captaincy in the Indian Department. He had been sent, financed by Sir William Johnson, to Rev. Eleazor Wheelock, then the headmaster of Moor's Charity School in Lebanon, Connecticut, where the pupils were promising Indian boys. There he improved his command of English. Soon after he returned to his own people he became an Anglican.[8] In 1775 Brant had made a journey to England, to seek help for the Six Nations in their struggle against the Americans. Little came of the journey; perhaps the most concrete result was his portrait that was painted by George Romney. Brant also made a striking impression on, among others, Hugh Percy, the 2nd Duke of Northumberland. His Grace was also the honorary colonel of the 5th Regiment and a general in the British Army who had served in North America during the Revolution. At that time, or when Brant came to England, Northumberland had been made an honorary Mohawk.[9]

The day after Brant came to dine, at Navy Hall, Simcoe set out to walk to Burlington Bay at the head of Lake Ontario, some fifty miles. He returned a week later having been "delighted with the beauty of the Country & Industry of the Inhabitants."[10]

Meanwhile Elizabeth had drawn a map of Canada and the United States. The dog Trojan, left in her bedroom while she went to have dinner, chewed the map to pieces, and she was obliged to paste it together. "The Gov. made some very pretty verses on the occasion":

> Awful Omen, prodigy unknown,
> In mystic manner Provinces devours,
> Shakes to the center Pondiaus throne,
> Scatters the Mississippi in its course,
> An o'r Alleganny plays with unresisted force.[11]

Having dealt with Trojan, Simcoe returned to one of his favourite themes, the superiority of all things British. His sense of the patriotic is typical of his other poems, and sadly, they are not memorable. Writing verses was an even more useful pastime as winter shut down navigation, and the only news from outside arrived carried by runners on snowshoes. Another pastime was endless games of whist. At first, Chief Justice Osgoode lived at Navy Hall, but by 31 December he had a house of his own. The Simcoes' seventh child was born at Newark on 16 January, 1791. Elizabeth did not mention the event in her diary but she did in her letters to Mrs. Hunt and Miss Burges. The baby was another girl, named Katherine, after Simcoe's mother, Katherine Stamford.[12] Elizabeth wrote to Mrs. Hunt asking her to register the birth at Dunkeswell. She decried the want of a wet nurse; feeding baby Katherine herself never occurred to her. The canvas house had proved quite comfortable during the birth. It had been boarded over to keep the snow from lying on it, and was quieter than the rest of their home;

> Pray give my love to Miss Hunt; tell her there are as many feathers, flowers and gauze dresses at our balls (which are every fortnight) as at Honiton Assembly & seldom less than eighteen couples. I have not attended them because I was, the greatest part of the winter in expectation of being confined.[13]

On 4 February, Simcoe set off on a much longer journey than the mere stroll to Burlington Bay. His objective was Detroit, travelling by way of the La Tranche River, "no European having gone that track & the Indians are to carry Provisions." Elizabeth was disappointed not to be with him, but she had not recovered her strength after the birth of Katherine. Simcoe's first stop was the Mohawk village on the Grand

River, where Captain Joseph Brant and a party of braves joined him to serve as helpers and guides. The "Gov. wore a fur Cap tippet & Gloves & Maucassins [sic] but no Great Coat. His servant carried two Blankets & Linen. The other Gentlemen carried their Blankets in a pack on their Back." The other gentlemen were Major Littlehales, Lieutenant Talbot, and Lieutenant David William Smith. Escorting them came a dozen Queen's Rangers. When the Mohawk warriors caught sight of the governor's party, they fired a feu de joie in welcoming "His Excellency, the Representative of the King, Their Father." The governor took with him a brace of pistols, a gift for Brant from the Duke of Northumberland.

Enclosed with the pistols was a letter from His Grace:

> My dear Joseph
> Colonel Simcoe, who is going out [as] Governor of Upper Canada, is kind enough to promise to deliver this to you, with a brace of pistols which I desire you will keep for my sake. I must particularly recommend the Colonel to you and the nation. He is a most intimate friend of mine and is possessed of every good quality which can recommend him to your friendship. He is brave, humane, sensible and honest. You may rely upon whatever he says for he will not deceive you. He loves and honours the Indians, whose noble sentiments so perfectly correspond with his own. He wishes to live upon the best terms with them. In short he is worthy to be a Mohawk. Love him as your own …
> Your affectionate friend and Brother,
> Northumberland,
> "Thorighwegri"[14]

During the governor's absence, Elizabeth found plenty to do. She was entertained on Sunday 17 February by some ladies of the Queen's Rangers at Queenston, now the headquarters of the regiment. The Rangers had built many huts as their new barracks. Elizabeth slept in Simcoe's hut, which held the tapestry from the Marquis of Buckingham. On 21 February a letter arrived from the governor. The La Tranche River, 150 miles from its mouth, was as wide as the Thames at Reading. He had re-named the river the Thames in honour of its English counterpart. Snow still fell as March arrived, and ice in the Niagara River, pushed by the strong current from the Falls, was piling into a great jam. Early spring was again a time of boredom. Getting about when the snow was melting was as difficult as they had found it in Quebec City.

Simcoe arrived at Newark on 10 March looking remarkably fit. His party had travelled 500 miles, part of the way by sleigh, but more often on foot or snowshoes. Life in the woods truly agreed with him. His only regret was lacking Elizabeth's company. He had sketched many maps which she was eager to redraw for him. He had agreed to send tools and seeds to the Moravian village in time for planting. After meeting the missionaries, he thought them fine men, doing good work among the Delaware people. The inhabitants had fed Simcoe's party and let them sleep in their houses. They were squatters, but they merited a grant of 5,000 acres. He had spent only four days at Detroit, and when he was leaving, the government ships in the harbour fired a salute. Simcoe had ordered prayers to be read in the woods on the Sunday of his visit. Forty attended, a small number, but the regular troops had their own chaplain. The 24th Regiment under Lieutenant Colonel Richard England, had replaced the 5th Regiment when it moved to Fort Niagara. The civilians at Detroit were mainly French speaking and Roman Catholic, residents whose forebears had settled along the Detroit River before the fall of New France.

Simcoe had eaten raccoons, which he found rather like pork and quite tasty. Jack Sharp, their Newfoundland dog, had a nasty brush with a porcupine. The long barbed quills, which adhered to his neck when he attacked the slow-moving creature, proved difficult to remove, and the dog was ill for some days afterwards. A party of natives who preceded Simcoe and his officers had built shelters of bark and boughs each day. When the governor's party stopped at five o'clock each evening, a meal was cooked and ready. After supping the officers sang "God Save the King" before settling down to sleep, feet close to a roaring fire. Best of all, Simcoe's expectations for the site of his capital were confirmed. The forks would make the perfect spot. The land along the Thames was excellent — a fine plain at the forks, dry and, characteristic of virgin forest, lacking in underbrush. Nearby was a spring of petroleum which they found by its strong odour. Three days after his return, the pressures were again affecting Simcoe's health. Though suffering from gout in one of his hands, he was anxious to begin work on the new capital, which he had decided to call New London. Rumours spread that Fort Niagara would soon be handed over to the Americans. In that event, Newark would be a tempting target. Britain and France were again on the verge of war. If the Americans renewed their former alliance with the French, they could destroy Newark in hours.

He sent John Scadding and one of his deputy surveyors, Augustus Jones, to the forks of the Thames to explore the site more thoroughly. He trusted Scadding's judgement in evaluating the land for agriculture. Jones had orders to lay out a line from the forks to Burlington Bay. Simcoe wanted his Rangers to build a road so that troops could reach Detroit by land. An enemy could easily cut off the Western District at Niagara. Of even greater importance than the capital was a safe naval base on Lake Ontario. He planned to take a party to explore the Toronto Carrying Place, so named because it was a portage route. He had heard that it had a fine harbour.

A matter that required legislation at the next meeting of the legislature was slavery. On 21 March he called an executive council meeting over an outrage committed against a black woman. Appearing before the council, Peter Martin a free black soldier of Butler's Rangers, testified to:

> ... a violent outrage committed by one Fromond, an inhabitant of this Province, residing near Queenston (or the west landing) on the person of Chloe Cooley, a negro girl in his service by binding her and violently and forcibly transporting her across the river, and delivering her against her will to certain persons unknown ... [15]

Martin's testimony was supported by William Gresley, who stated that Fromond had told him of his intention to sell "his negro wench" to some persons in the States. Gresley had seen the young woman, bound and screaming, conveyed across the river. He also said that he had seen a similarly bound black man, and had heard that many other people intended to "do the same by their negros." The council resolved to stop such "violent breaches of the peace" and a misuse of Canadian territory. They instructed John White, the attorney general, to draft a bill respecting slavery to present to the legislature when it convened in May.

When the weather turned hot in April, Elizabeth moved with the nurses and children to the hut above Queenston. The Queen's Rangers' mess supplied the meals. After dinner an officer escorted everyone back to the hut, and the band played until six o'clock. "Music adds chearfulness to this retired spot & we feel much indebted to the Marquis of Buckingham," she wrote on 3 April.[16] On the 5th she recorded the demise of Trojan, the map chewer. With the thermometer registering 78 degrees in the shade, 112 in the sun, the dog became ill. One of the soldiers mistook his condition for rabies and shot him. Elizabeth was angry. Shortly before he died, Trojan had showed that he was sane by running into the water to cool himself off.

On 10 April it snowed and they returned to Navy Hall. On the 18th Captain Lieutenant Aeneas Shaw arrived at Newark with his wife and seven children. The family had travelled through the United States by boat to the British fort at Oswego, where Shaw passed the winter with them. A native had helped them build huts and shoot partridges and ducks. On 2 May, Simcoe left in a bateau with seven officers to make a preliminary study of the site of Toronto, and was absent until the 13th. Elizabeth received letters from Mary Anne Burges, telling her how excited the four girls had been over the birth of their baby sister Katherine, for whom they were choosing presents. Aunt Margaret Graves was planning to move out of Wolford Lodge and was having a house built for herself on Lansdown Crescent in Bath. If the Simcoe's wanted to economise by putting a tenant in Wolford Lodge, the girls and the Hunts were welcome to stay at Tracey until the family returned from Canada.[17] When she received Mary Anne's letter, Elizabeth replied that Colonel Simcoe and she wanted the girls to remain in their own home. As for Mrs. Graves's move, she had half expected that the old lady would tire of the quietness of Wolford Lodge and crave a more interesting social life.[18]

On 13 May 1793, Elizabeth wrote to Mary Anne Burges:

> Coll. Simcoe returned from Toronto & speaks in praise of the harbour & a fine spot near it covered with a large Oak which he intends to fix upon as a site for a Town. I am going to send you some beautiful butterflies.

The situation at Newark was tense over the prospect of war with the United States. Although that country had proclaimed neutrality on 22 April, many Americans believed that a quick conquest of Canada would bring native resistance in the north-west to a halt. Simcoe felt helpless because of his lack of weapons and troops. He was eager to start work on a fortified naval dockyard at Toronto, but had to wait until the next session of the legislature was over. On the 14th, three Americans arrived at Newark, commissioners to negotiate with the tribal leaders of the interior. Disliking these men, and feeling ill, ELizabeth accepted an offer from Anne, wife of Lieutenant David William Smith, to recuperate at Fort Niagara. The children and their nurses went with her. Thus Simcoe's family was absent when the members assembled in late May for the 1793 session. Again Simcoe arranged due pomp and prayers.

On 4 June, the King's birthday, the governor held a levée at eleven o'clock in the morning. General Benjamin Lincoln, one of the American commissioners and a senior rebel officer during the Revolution, left an account of the ceremony. Lincoln noted the presence of several daughters of Sir William Johnson and Molly, Joseph Brant's sister. While "from the aborigines of the country [they] appeared as well dressed as the company in general." Their dignity impressed him.[19]

To Elizabeth's annoyance, the American commissioners were still at Newark, waiting for instructions from President Washington in Philadelphia, then the capital of the United States. The governor also resented having to accommodate the Americans, who could not leave until the various tribes had assembled at Sandusky, in the Ohio country. Meanwhile they held talks with Joseph Brant at Newark. They did not leave until 26 June. Seven of the native nations of Canada set out from Newark to the conference to show solidarity with their brethren in the United States. Lieutenant Talbot went ahead of them to carry papers to Colonel Alexander McKee at Detroit.

Even while the commissioners waited, Simcoe and the members of his legislature were hard at work. Two important matters concerned them. Simcoe wanted to abolish slavery. The members wanted local government by New England style town meetings. Since they belonged to the principal slave-owning class, they were horrified at the thought of losing their most reliable source of labour. With almost every man eligible for a grant of land, hiring workers was almost impossible. Simcoe was equally appalled at the idea of town meetings that meant sharing some control with ordinary folk. What followed was horse-trading by governor and legislators. Simcoe agreed to a limited form of town meeting, but one that would not meet regularly. The magistrates were empowered to call the meetings, and to issue warrants for the election of township officers, such as clerks, supervisors of highways, pathmasters and fence viewers.[20]

The members in turn agreed to a bill that would phase out slavery. No more slaves could be brought into the province. Adult slaves in Upper Canada must remain in servitude, but children born to slaves would be free at age twenty-five, and their children would be free from birth.[21] The slavery bill worked on by Attorney General White was modified accordingly. The session ended on 26 June. Simcoe was now free to move his family to Toronto, which would also serve as a temporary capital if American hostilities compelled him to move the government there.

On 20 July, 100 Queen's Rangers commanded by Captain Lieutenant Shaw, set out to begin work at Toronto. On the 28th, Captain Joseph Bouchette, of the *Mississauga*, reached Newark to take the Simcoes across the lake. (Bouchette had been a captain in the Provincial Marine during the Revolution.) They sailed on the 29th. The following morning Jean Baptiste Rousseau, a fur trader, came aboard to pilot the ship into harbour, which was formed by a long, curving sandpit, open at only the west end. Shifting sand made the entrance tricky, requiring a person with local knowledge to negotiate it safely. As the ship moved into the bay they could see the tents of the Queen's Rangers in a small clearing. (The sandpit is now Toronto Islands. A severe storm in 1858 broke through the eastern end, creating a gap and turning the spit and its lagoons into a little archipelago.)

The site for a naval base was the dry bed of a post-glacial lake, flat and somewhat swampy, punctuated by low knolls. It was bounded by two substantial streams. Simcoe named the easterly one the Don River, and the westerly one the Humber. Both flowed through steep-sided, flat-floored ravines between the lake bed and the upper surface of the shoreline. To the east of the Queen's Rangers' encampment, Garrison Creek emptied into the harbour. Beyond lay rising ground where the Simcoes decided to place the canvas houses, where they could catch the breezes. While the Rangers were clearing the site and erecting the houses, the Simcoes slept aboard ship.

By 4 August, the *Onondaga* had brought their horses from Newark, and Simcoe had dispatched it to fetch some guns from the fort on Carleton Island. The governor and Mrs. Simcoe rode on the peninsula, and to local landmarks. One was the ruins of Fort Rouillé, built by the French as a trading post, and evacuated in1760. They spent the night in the canvas house, and next day they brought the children ashore. On horseback the Simcoes discovered the cliffs east of the Don River, which they named Scarborough Bluffs, in honour of the long-popular Yorkshire spa. In the meantime, Alexander Aitken, a deputy surveyor, was laying out a townsite to the east of the garrison, ten blocks on a grid plan.

On 24 August, Simcoe received an official report that the Duke of York had distinguished himself at Famars, where his army had driven the French out of Holland. Simcoe ordered a Royal salute, and named "this station" York. The salute was fired by his few 12- and 18-pounder guns, joined by the guns of the *Onondaga* and the *Mississauga* and the Queen's Rangers' muskets. Among the natives was an Ojibway named Canise who picked up Francis, thinking he would be frightened by the noise. Francis seemed "delighted" by the sound.[22] The two-year-old, whose father had intended him for a military career, had made a promising start.

The naming of York was perhaps a trifle premature. In a counter attack some weeks later the, French repaired the damage by throwing back the Duke's forces.

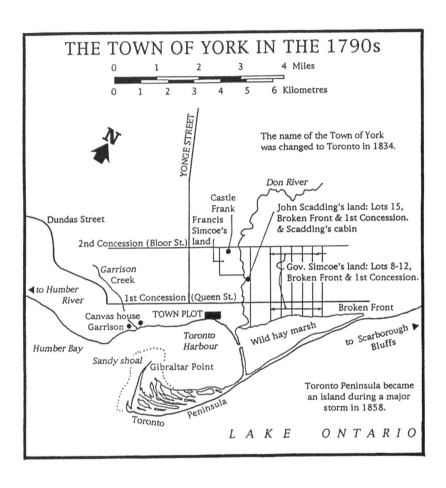

THE TOWN OF YORK IN THE 1790s

0   1   2   3   4 Miles

0 1 2 3 4 5 6 Kilometres

N

YONGE STREET

The name of the Town of York
was changed to Toronto in 1834.

Don River

Castle
Frank

Dundas Street

Francis
Simcoe's
land

John Scadding's land: Lots 15,
Broken Front & 1st Concession.
& Scadding's cabin

2nd Concession (Bloor St.)

Garrison
Creek

Gov. Simcoe's land: Lots 8-12,
Broken Front & 1st Concession.

to Humber
River

1st Concession (Queen St.)

Broken Front

Canvas house
Garrison

TOWN PLOT

Toronto
Harbour

Wild hay marsh

to Scarborough
Bluffs

Humber Bay

Sandy shoal

Gibraltar Point

Toronto Peninsula became
an island during a major
storm in 1858.

Peninsula

Toronto

L A K E   O N T A R I O

FIFTEEN
SIMCOE VERSUS DORCHESTER

Once the Ojibway people from the north and the shore of Lake Huron heard that the governor was residing at York, they began coming to satisfy their curiosity. Elizabeth thought them "extremely handsome & have a superior air to any I have seen, they have been little among Europeans therefore less accustomed to drink Rum."[1] She was right; transactions with the natives, conducted by John Butler, and earlier Sir John Johnson. They followed the long-established Indian Department practice of the liberal distribution of rum. Those from the north had not yet been wheedled into giving up tribal lands while inebriated.

On 28 August, four days after the naming of York, a gunboat arrived from Newark with a report from Detroit. The American commissioners had returned to the United States from Sandusky without making peace with the tribal leaders. The natives wanted the Ohio River as the boundary, and all white settlements beyond it removed. The Americans refused. Simcoe was bitterly disappointed. He had been hoping for a neutral aboriginal nation south of Lake Erie, as a buffer zone between Upper Canada and the Americans. He was more worried than ever that the war with France might spill over into North America. President Washington had declared the United States neutral, but he was allowing French privateers into American ports. The new French ambassador, Citizen Edmond Charles Genet, had sent agents into Lower Canada to stir up the French Canadians. Such activities alarmed Washington, who did not want war with Britain while his army was heavily committed against the tribes.

Early in September a letter arrived from James Bland Burges, warning Simcoe that a far greater threat than France was Catherine of Russia, who had territorial ambitions. Simcoe replied, "I ... from my Cradle have looked with dread on the aspiring Politicks of Russia; France may threaten the invasion but Russia can perform it." He referred to the 1793 partition of Poland by Prussia and Russia, adding, "I equally deprecate the darkness of Despotism, as the Lunacy of Liberty."[2]

By that time Simcoe knew that Lord Dorchester had returned to Quebec after his leave of absence. Simcoe was no longer his own man. Soon after the governor in chief's return, Bishop Jacob Mountain reached Quebec as the first prelate of the Canadas; earlier, the provinces had been a dependency of the see of Nova Scotia. Both Simcoes were pleased; the appointment should strengthen the Church of England in Upper Canada.

Captain Samuel Smith had left York with 100 Rangers, to open the road from the head of Lake Ontario to the Thames. "I hear they kill Rattlesnakes every day yet not a man has been bit tho they have been among them for 6 weeks," Elizabeth wrote. Smith sent two snakes in a barrel for her to examine. She found them "dark & ugly & made a whirring sound in shaking their Rattles when I touched them with a stick." The road would be called Dundas Street, in honour of Home Secretary Henry Dundas.[3]

On 25 September, Simcoe left for Lac aux Claies with a party of Rangers, Deputy Surveyor Alexander Aitken, Captain Henry Darling of the 5th Regiment, Alexander Macdonnell, Sheriff of the Home District, Lieutenant James Givins of the Queen's Rangers, and Jack Sharp, the Newfoundland dog. They reached the lake on the 29th, and renamed it Lake Simcoe — after the governor's late father. On the same date, Francis Simcoe's name was written on a grant of 200 acres on the Don River, where his parents would build Castle Frank as a summer home. Young Francis' was one of many grants the governor was awarding in the neighbourhood, and accepting grants commensurate with his rank. John Scadding received 253 acres on the east side of the Don River, and had begun building a cabin for himself.[4] Other officers of the Queen's Rangers had received grants (the list reads like a "Who's Who" of pioneer

Toronto.) Some civil servants and representatives were reluctant to move from Newark where they had suffered enough before procuring decent housing. Hannah Jarvis, wife of the provincial secretary, who had an acid tongue, commented, with the governor at York, the chief justice, attorney general, receiver general and secretary at Newark, and "acting surveyor general" at Fort Niagara, that "thus our government is to spend the Winter at respectable distances."[5] The acting surveyor general was Lieutenant David William Smith. Simcoe made the appointment and hoped it would be approved.

On 25 October the governor and party had returned from Lake Simcoe, after dividing into groups and becoming lost. They visited the village of the Ojibway Canise, but learned that he and his eldest son had died. Young Canise, their heir, gave the governor a blanket of beaver pelts. Simcoe enjoyed meeting another Ojibway named Great Sail. Because of losing their way, Simcoe's men had run short of provisions. They had decided to eat Jack Sharp, but his life was spared when they sighted Lake Ontario and knew they were nearly home. The dog, Simcoe admitted, was ungainly in a tippy canoe.[6]

A freight canoe arrived at York, the gift of the North West (fur trading) Company of Montreal. "It required 12 men to paddle, " Elizabeth noted. She had her first ride on 9 November:

> A Beaver Blanket & a carpet were put in to sit upon. We carried a small table to be used in embarking & disembarking for the Canoe cannot be brought very near the Shore lest the gravel or pebbles injure her, so the table was set in the water & a long Plank laid from it to the Shore to enable me to get in or out the Men carrying the Canoe empty into water & out of it upon their shoulders.

They had less than a "board between us & eternity" for the birch bark punctured easily. The natives always carried "Gum or pitch" to mend breaks in the bark.[7]

They made several trips to admire the land Simcoe had chosen for Francis. The boundary began at the top edge of the ravine through which the Don River flowed. From this bluff they had a fine view of the harbour, and the lake beyond the peninsula. Work began before the end of November on Castle Frank, a grand name for what would be a rustic log structure. The Grecian columns Elizabeth mentioned were trunks of white pine trees.

In November, Simcoe received a discouraging letter from Lord Dorchester. In response to Simcoe's report on plans to build defences at York, the governor in chief curtly told him that no new fortifications were to be erected at York, nor any other post. Simcoe did not have enough troops to staff any new posts, and none was available from Lower Canada. In fact, in the event of war, many of the soldiers on garrison duty would be withdrawn from Upper Canada to defend the more vital fortress of Quebec, the key to holding the country. Simcoe should strengthen his militia to defend Upper Canada. He countered, on 2 December, that Detroit and Niagara were indefensible, and he should choose safer locations — the Thames valley, Long Point on Lake Erie and York. If His Lordship would only to come to York, he could see the situation for himself. The Rangers were in comfortable log huts, and he had plans for a storehouse on Gibraltar Point, on the peninsula at the entrance to the harbour. He had paid close attention to his militia, but without weapons they were of no use:

> In the case of the King's troops being totally withdrawn and hostilities commencing by the Indians or the United States against this province, it does not appear to me possible that it can exist as a member of the British Empire.[8]

Simcoe relayed the content of Dorchester's letter to Henry Dundas. Loyalists and others had come to Upper Canada with the promise of land and a safe haven. Withdrawing troops would be morally wrong, leaving Loyalists, especially, vulnerable. Also, if the Queen's Rangers were ordered out of the country, Simcoe would have no authority left. Going over Dorchester's head turned out to be an error. Now that he was back in Quebec, all correspondence must pass through his hands.

While Simcoe was drafting his letter, Great Sail arrived with his wife and ten children. Francis handed around apples. "He shakes hands with the Indians in a very friendly manner, tho he is very shy & ungracious to all his own Countrymen." Elizabeth made a sketch of Great Sail, resolving to improve it later. She was impressed at the way their guests spoke, which to her resembled the great orators of Greece and Rome.[9]

On the 12th, Lieutenant Grey left York. He was going to join his father, 1st Lord Grey, in the West Indies. Simcoe and Talbot accompanied him as far as Niagara. They were back on the 22nd and Talbot was skating on the bay. Elizabeth wrote nothing about Christmas celebrations, but 27 December was so cold that water in the pail next to the stove froze. On 11 January 1794, the Queen's birthday, Simcoe ordered a twenty-one gun salute fired.

The cannon was loaded with pebbles, probably to conserve ammunition. At a dance held in the evening the ladies were "much dressed." On the 19th, they rode seven miles north to the log houses of some German settlers. On the 26th Captain Shaw's children set fire to some grass of a marsh close to the bay, which Elizabeth found picturesque. The next night she set her own fire to amuse herself. The last day of the month was mildly disastrous. A horse drawing hay across the bay fell through the ice and drowned, and John Scadding's cabin burned down. Nevertheless she was in high spirits. In March she would be going with the governor to Detroit, taking the children with them. The governor wanted to stay awhile and become acquainted with the French-speaking residents, to ascertain whether they were loyal or a possible source of help to the Americans.

March brought news of the execution of Queen Marie Antoinette of France, and Simcoe ordered a dance postponed. The weather was so bitterly cold that Elizabeth could hardly hold her cards though she wore three fur tippets. They divided the canvas house they used as a dining room by hanging a carpet, which helped somewhat, but the canvas ceiling had not been boarded over and most of the cold air came through it. Deer were scarce that winter, and when starving natives came often to York the Simcoes spared what they could, "inconvenient" when they were cut off from supplies until spring breakup. On the 14th, riding across the bay, Elizabeth felt her horse sink and threw herself off. The horse apparently wanted to roll in the snow, and she thought she prevented it crushing her because she struck it with her whip.

The next day Simcoe received an order from Lord Dorchester to proceed to the Maumee River as soon as navigation opened, to rebuild derelict Fort Miamis, sixty miles below Detroit and undeniably in United States territory. Dorchester had made a provocative speech, widely reported in the American press, that had inflamed the Congress. John Jay, the chief justice, was sent to England to open negotiations about the future of the British-held posts that were on American soil. Simcoe disapproved strongly of Dorchester's statement, and of this order. General Anthony Wayne, an old adversary, was leading an army reported to be 2,000 strong towards Detroit. Building a new fort across his path, Simcoe realised, was a hostile act, and unwise considering the weakness of his province. He had no choice but to obey.[10]

He proposed leading a small force, the 60th Regiment, then the Kingston garrison, the 5th Regiment from Niagara, and the Queen's

Rangers and marching towards Pittsburgh and Fort Washington (Cincinnati) to cut off Wayne's army from its source of supply, and either attack or starve it into surrender — a bold plan worthy of Simcoe's earlier campaigns.[11]

He resolved on a quick reconnaissance of the site of Fort Miamis (which British troops had evacuated after the Revolution). Again Elizabeth was disappointed. Taking his family into a potential combat zone would be foolhardy; if he should be killed Elizabeth must survive for the sake of the children. After Simcoe inspected the site, he returned by way of Lake Erie to Newark. He ordered Lieutenant Robert Pilkington of the Royal Engineers to take artificers, civilian or military, whatever he needed, and with a detachment of Queen's Rangers proceed to the Maumee River to begin construction. Pilkington shared with Elizabeth a talent and love of sketching.

In all this activity, Simcoe was still organising road building. By February 1794, the Queen's Rangers under Captain Shank had reached the halfway point along Dundas Street. Deputy Surveyor Augustus Jones assisted by four Rangers had been laying a line for a road to link York to Lake Simcoe, to be called Yonge Street, in honour of his Devon political friend, Sir George Yonge. They had begun the survey at the north end, Holland Landing (named for the surveyor general), and by 19 March they were back in York.[12] By then, Simcoe had left Newark with Pilkington and his work party again was bound for the Maumee River.

In her entry for 18 April, Elizabeth recorded that the sloop *Caldwell* had brought a cargo of pork from the Bay of Quinte. Her next entry was dated 2 May, when Simcoe had returned. On 19 April, Elizabeth had suffered a grievous blow. She wrote to Mrs. Hunt in May:

> It is with pain I take up my pen to inform you of the loss we have sustained & the melancholy event of our losing poor little Katherine, one of the strongest healthiest children you ever saw ... She had been feverish one or two days cutting teeth, which not being an unusual case with children I was not much alarmed. On good Friday she was playing in my room in the morning, in the afternoon was seized with fits. I sat up the whole night the greatest part of which she continued to have spasms & before seven in the morning she was no more ... She was the sweetest tempered pretty child imaginable, just beginning to talk & walk & the suddenness of the event you may be sure shocked me inexpressibly.[13]

Katherine was buried in the military cemetery near the huts of the Queen's Rangers, which Simcoe had named Fort York, on Easter Monday, 21 April 1794. A few days later Francis seemed unwell, and Elizabeth was panic-stricken. When Katherine died, Surgeon Macaulay was at Newark. Appalled that she might lose Francis, too, she sent for him. By the time Macaulay arrived in York, Francis was better. Of Katherine, Elizabeth wrote, "The loss of so promising a Child must long be a painful thing."

The governor learned of his daughter's passing when the ship bringing him from Detroit reached Fort Erie, at the eastern end of Lake Erie. The report claimed that Elizabeth was very ill, and he galloped the eighteen miles to Newark in scarcely two hours, over a road that was a quagmire from spring rains. He learned that Elizabeth was well, but "from the melancholy event in the family, which affected him in a less degree than it would otherwise have done if he had not been so frightened on my account."

When Elizabeth's letter reached Wolford Lodge, Mrs. Hunt had the unwelcome task of informing the four children, who had so long looked forward to becoming acquainted with Katherine. The following year a grave marker arrived from England, ordered by Mrs. Hunt, and inscribed "Katherine Simcoe, January 16, 1793 — April 19, 1794. Happy in the Lord." Preserved are two letters that illuminate the sorrow felt by family and friends. On 12 August, Mary Anne Burges wrote to her brother of her "great concern" at the sudden death of Katherine. Eliza received a letter from her great aunt, Elizabeth Gwillim, undated and written from Whitchurch. She reminded her great niece that all who die in infancy go to heaven. After this she continued, "Your brother wears Indian dress that is more becoming than English on the young."[14]

Still sorrowing from the loss of Katherine, Elizabeth was not happy about moving to Newark for the third session of the legislature. Francis had been healthier at York and she longed to remain in the wilderness community which, Lord Dorchester had decided was the capital. The expense of moving to York was justified, but a second move was out of the question. Neither the home secretary, Henry Dundas, nor his successor in 1794, William Bentinck 3rd Duke of Portland, was enthusiastic about the site on the Thames. Simcoe's frustrations, with Dorchester and the home government, were not helping his wife recover her equilibrium. To relieve her depression he suggested returning to Niagara along the shoreline in open boats. The thought of travelling helped more than anything else to restore Mrs. Simcoe's spirits.

They set out on 9 May, with the children and their nurses and other servants. The trip proved a disappointment because the weather was poor. Picnics under umbrellas were uncomfortable. They had brought a tent for the children and nurses, but the governor and Elizabeth slept in a boat. Near Forty Mile Creek (Grimsby) they bought good bread, milk and butter from a family from Pennsylvania for whom the governor had helped select land the summer before. Elizabeth described the shoreline accurately. The valleys of the streams that descend the face of the Niagara Escarpment were steep sided, and they often had ponds in them on the flat surface of the former lake bed. They reached Newark at noon on the 11th; the heat was oppressive.[15]

Lieutenant Pilkington, then supervising the work at Fort Miamis, sent Elizabeth sketches of Lake Erie, which she copied. The people at Newark were in a near-panic over war scares. If Newark were menaced, she wrote Mary Anne Burges, she would take the children to Quebec. Hostage-taking was a popular technique of frontier warfare. On 29 May, the *Mississauga, Caldwell* and two gunboats brought the members of the legislature to Newark. The speaker, John Macdonnell, member for the second Glengarry riding and the owner of Glengarry House, dined with the Simcoes. When Simcoe told him of their plan to send Elizabeth and the children to Quebec, Macdonnell thought that Quebec was more likely to be besieged than Niagara because of its importance. Simcoe disagreed. The Americans would try to seize Upper Canada, rather than attack such a well-fortified stronghold as Quebec.

On 4 June, the King's birthday, a ball was held in the council chamber. Thomas Talbot made the arrangements. Talbot, now a captain, would soon be returning to Britain, his tour of duty at an end. Francis' third birthday was on the 6th, but they delayed the party a day because Simcoe had to go to Chippawa. Mr. Speaker Macdonnell gave Francis a tiny cannon. The shots were barely two inches long, but they "made a good Report & pleased him much." The boy wore a rifle shirt and a sash which, with his dark hair and skin browned by the sun "gave him somewhat the air of an Indian." Some friend had relayed this part of the diary to Aunt Elizabeth Gwillim. A party of Senecas who came to Newark danced and sang. After they departed, Francis imitated them very well.[16]

At the session of the legislature, the members passed a bill to license retailers of wine and spirits, unpopular with most of the populace, but Simcoe was looking for sources of revenue. They also passed a new Militia Bill. Dorchester had had one passed in 1788, which appointed the first officers and made service compulsory for all men between the ages of sixteen and fifty. Simcoe's new bill extended the service to able-bodied men up to sixty, and permitted the militia to be used outside Upper Canada. He continued appointing county lieutenants, for as yet Dorchester had not forbidden them. The problem of arms for the citizen soldiers remained unsolved.

On 22 June they bid farewell to Captain Talbot, who sailed for Kingston on a merchant vessel, the *Gov. Simcoe*. (Talbot would resign from the army in 1800 and return in 1801 to promote land settlement.) The legislature sat until 7 July. Everyone worried about reports of General Wayne's progress. On the 13th another dear friend would depart. Chief Justice Sir William Smith died, and William Osgoode was ordered to Quebec City to replace him. To Simcoe's dismay, no new chief justice had been appointed for Upper Canada.[17] On the 17th, Simcoe returned to Navy Hall with a wounded finger. After sending for Surgeon Macaulay, Elizabeth asked how it happened.

"I was walking near the guard's tent at Queenston with a gentleman," he explained, "when a soldier aimed at an Indian's dog that had stolen some pork. The musket was loaded with pellets, and the gentleman, the dog, another Indian, and myself were all wounded. I gave the gun to the wounded Indian to appease him and I reprimanded the soldier." Dr. Macaulay probed the wound and wanted to remove the pellet but Simcoe, who had suffered enough, decided to let nature take its course.[18]

Meanwhile, the Queen's Rangers employed on Yonge Street were needed for military duty. Simcoe made an arrangement for the work to continue. A gentleman named William Berczy, a native of Wallerstein, Germany, arrived at Newark. He had brought a group of German-speaking people to New York State in search of land, but had had trouble over the high price demanded by "land jobbers" (speculators). He introduced himself to Simcoe and asked for land to the west of the Iroquois tract along the Grand River, admitting that the group he represented had already purchased some land there.

Simcoe persuaded him instead to accept a tract north of York in the newly opening Township of Markham.[19] The condition that Berczy accepted was that within a year from 15 September 1794, his settlers would complete Yonge Street, and open it from Lot 29, the point reached by the Queen's Rangers, to "the pine fort at Holland River." Having no authority to offer the workers wages, Simcoe allowed them more generous grants of land.[20]

On 8 August, Bishop Jacob Mountain and his brother, Jehosophat, a clergyman at Trois Rivières, arrived for a visit. On the 11th the Simcoes decided that Elizabeth should soon take the children to Quebec. She wrote to Ann Caldwell at St. Foy asking her to find a house for her to rent. On the 19th, Simcoe agreed to let Dr. Macaulay operate on his wounded finger. The surgeon found the shot after some agonising probing. On 25 August, by order of Dorchester, Captain Shank arrived from York with a detachment of Queen's Ranger, bound for the Maumee as reinforcements. On the 29th they received word of the battle at Fallen Timbers, where Mad Anthony Wayne defeated the native warriors. Wayne ordered the British garrison at Fort Miamis to surrender, but the commander, Major William Campbell of the 24th Regiment, refused.[21] Wayne withdrew when he found the fort stronger than he expected.

Simcoe was furious that so many Queen's Rangers had been ordered about by Dorchester. He had intended from the outset to use the regiment mainly to develop the country. Nevertheless, he was also in favour of fortifying Turtle Island, at the entrance to the Maumee, to block intruders from Lake Erie.[22]

He resolved to go to Detroit and stay awhile. In September he left with a party, and Elizabeth was ready to set out for Quebec. On the night of the 12th she boarded the *Mississauga*, escorted by John McGill, now with the local rank of captain, for Kingston. With them went Molly, sister of Joseph Brant, who lived at Kingston. She had been visiting her daughters at Newark. "She speaks English well & is a civil & very sensible old woman," Elizabeth wrote, scarcely hinting that Molly was well educated. While Mrs. Simcoe admired the "noble savage" she was ill at ease with a brown-skinned woman who behaved like a well-bred white lady. A fatiguing journey by bateau and calèche brought them to the home of Colonel Henry and Ann Caldwell at St. Foy on 24 September.

After finding a house, Elizabeth embarked on a happy social life once more. She found Lord and Lady Dorchester most kind and helpful. Maria, Lady Dorchester, was the young, vivacious wife to the elderly soldier, and compatible. At a party the Caldwells gave on 12 October, Elizabeth met Colonel George Beckwith, Simcoe's colleague during the Revolution, who was now the adjutant of the British forces in North America. Casually he mentioned that Mrs. Simcoe's father was Colonel Thomas Gwillim. At that Colonel Caldwell remembered Colonel Gwillim well, While visiting England after General Wolfe's death, he had stayed with Gwillim at his London house.

On 11 January, Colonel Beckwith called and offered his congratulations on Governor Simcoe becoming a Major General in the Army. Beckwith also thought that an honour would soon be forthcoming. Elizabeth tried not to be too optimistic. Simcoe had deserved a title, but whether he received one depended on which way the political wind was blowing.[23]

The person who would order the general's regimentals from Simcoe's tailor was Mary Anne Burges. In a letter dated 20 April, she repeated some preposterous gossip relayed to her by the Hunts. In the presence of someone they knew, Mrs. Graves had claimed that Mary Anne was pretending friendship for Elizabeth because she coveted General Simcoe. She informed the Simcoes that Reverend Edward Drewe had suffered a paralytic stroke while preaching. He was recovering, but Simcoe felt reconciled to Drewe's remaining in England. A journey to Upper Canada was now out of the question. Mary Anne added more bad news. George Spencer, appointed captain lieutenant in 1791, was still very ill. He was going to Spain in the hope of a cure from the "native air."[24]

The Simcoes also learned that they had lost a good friend in Exeter. William Pitfield, the apothecary at the hospital, had died. The notice appeared in the Exeter *Flying Post* on 13 February 1794.

SIXTEEN
MAJOR GENERAL

S imcoe meanwhile reached Fort Erie on 23 September and was on Turtle Island two days later. He marched with an escort to Fort Miamis, which was still unfinished owing to sickness. Major Campbell was also ill, and Captain Bunbury was in command. The governor sent for reinforcements from Detroit, which consisted of fifty Rangers. Back at Detroit he held a council meeting. Joseph Brant, who was present, criticised the British for not supporting the tribes. All Simcoe could do was promise to send a message to Lord Dorchester. He left on a ship and was back at Navy Hall by 18 October.

He did not comment on his conclusions about the French residents. He probably discovered that they disliked the Americans more than the British. He would have met some rustic characters who worked for the Indian department. Matthew Elliott had a whipping post in front of his house for chastising his many slaves. Simon Girty, raised among the Seneca people, was more like them than his white ancestors. (Called "the white savage" by American frontiersmen, years later Kentuckians would come to the Canadian side of the Detroit River for the joy of spitting on his grave.) Alexander McKee's mother was "of the country" as native women who married whites were called.

On the 25th, Simcoe wrote to his "Dear Girls." Mama, Sophia and Francis were in Quebec, but he expected that peace would come soon. He closed with, "Fear God & honour Mrs. Hunt & all who care for you." To Charlotte on 8 November he asked her to have "Mr. Scadding" (Thomas) cut down trees "without mercy" to improve the view around Wolford Lodge. He would soon leave Newark for York, and round the lake to Kingston, to meet Mama, Sophia and "the little dog Francis ... he thought himself so fine in his red stockings or leggings & Indian cloak that he acts as if he was twenty years old" but he was good natured.[1]

By the time winter set in, concluding that General Wayne would not attack Detroit at the moment, Simcoe returned to York and ordered all Rangers to follow him.[2] He mustered 400 Rangers, but not all were fit for duty. He had requested fresh recruits from England, but he was waiting for a reply. He had also advertised in Upper Canada, but few men would work for army pay when wages were higher for civilians in the labour-starved province. Jay's Treaty, whereby the British-held posts would be evacuated, was agreed upon in November. Oswego, Niagara, Detroit and Michilimackinac were declared on American soil. Simcoe assumed that garrisons would be reduced when the treaty was ratified, and he could again use his Rangers for developing the country. The military crises had passed with the defeat of the tribes at Fallen Timbers. Commissioners were now negotiating the surrender of a vast territory to the United States. The result, on 3 August 1795, would be the Treaty of Fort Greenville, signed by the Miami leader, Little Turtle, on behalf of the leaders of the confederation. Once the two treaties were in effect, peace would descend over the northwest.

Meanwhile, in Devon, now that she was thirty and still single, Mary Anne had restyled herself Mrs. Burges. Like Elizabeth's Aunt Elizabeth Gwillim at Whitchurch, "Mrs." implied a women in charge of her own household. Simcoe had asked her to place an order for a major general's regimentals with Mr. Cannon, his tailor, and to purchase books for his girls. Mary Anne replied that if a Captain Lowe could take them to Canada, that autumn or in the early spring they need not be insured. She had ordered books from a bookseller in Exeter who would send them to Wolford Lodge. The regimentals would cost £91, or £88 with a discount for prompt payment.[3]

Mary Anne was then making arrangements to become the guardian of her three-year-old cousin, the Hon. Julia Valenza Somerville, youngest of nine children of Colonel Hugh Somerville. Both her parents had died in recent months, and Julia would go to Mary Anne. Her brothers and sisters were to live with other relatives.[4]

Mrs. Simcoe's return journey to Upper Canada was notable for the uncertainties of driving on frozen rivers. She had admired Lord Dorchester's sleigh or "Dormeuse," which featured a large windproof hood of leather that made it possible to keep warm inside. She ordered one for her own use. At Cap Madeleine they had to go two leagues above the usual crossing and "even then saw water on each side of the carriage."[5] On Lake St. Francis the driver drove very fast to get across unsafe ice before it could break apart. When they reached the home of Major James Gray, they found that the governor had been there the day before, but not finding them had returned to St. John's Hall, an inn at Johnstown, where he and Major Littlehales had been staying for the past fortnight. At Johnstown, the administrative seat of the Eastern District, Simcoe had been conferring with local half-pay officers and other public servants on the needs of the St. Lawrence settlements. They had two fine rooms with good stoves. Outside the cold was intense, but the sky was a brilliant blue. By 20 February the Simcoe party left in the dormeuse and other sleighs for Kingston.

On the 23rd, at Captain William Fraser's in Edwardsburgh Township, snow began to fall heavily. Local men advised against setting out until the storm abated, but another guest maintained that they would have little difficulty proceeding. Since that was what the governor wanted to hear, they set off in light sleighs, leaving the heavy dormeuse to be fetched later. To oblige the governor, two men went ahead to "beat the way & hasten our Journey." At Gananoque the ice was extremely bad "so we drove as fast as possible as that is thought the safest way on rotten Ice."[6]

They reached Kingston on 1 March 1795. Elizabeth, ill at Johnstown, had recovered and she enjoyed driving with the governor as he inspected the Bay of Quinte, until a sudden thaw made it necessary to return to Kingston before the ice broke up. By the 21st, Simcoe was ill with the same infection that had stricken Elizabeth. He had to sit up in order to breathe, and Elizabeth stayed with him endlessly. She could find only a horse doctor; apparently the garrison surgeon was not available. Molly Brant, hearing of Simcoe's distress, sent Elizabeth a root. She thought it was "calamus ... which really relieved his Cough in a very short time."[7]

John Graves Simcoe was prone to respiratory allergies that made him susceptible to bronchial infections. Elizabeth did not specify how Molly Brant's root was used. Grinding and boiling to provide scented steam is a possibility.

By 12 May, Simcoe's family was aboard the *Onondaga*, waiting for wind and watching the launching of the new government ship *Mohawk* which came down so fast that the passengers feared she would strike the *Onondaga*. They sailed on the 15th, rain pelting down. Their entry into the harbour at York was traumatic. The captain was not sober and Trader Rousseau was away. Impatient, Simcoe ordered a lieutenant of regulars who admitted he knew something about sailing to pilot the ship. He brought the *Onondaga* safely round the sandpit, a happy ending and reminder of the Simcoes riding into Exmoor without an experienced guide.

They would soon have to leave for Newark for the fourth session of the legislature. Elizabeth took advantage of the short stay at York to visit Castle Frank, under construction on "Francis's Estate." On 4 June they celebrated the King's birthday with a dance, and on the 6th, Francis's fourth birthday, he gave a dinner for the soldiers' children. On the 9th the nurses, children and servants left for Newark on the *Onondaga*. The governor and Mrs. Simcoe, with a small escort, would follow the shoreline in the North West Company canoe. They reached Newark early on 16 June, and before they had settled in they had to play host to some not overly welcome guests.

The Duc de Liancourt-Rochefoucault was a French emigrant who had been living in England and was on a visit to North America. He arrived at Fort Erie on 20 June, accompanied by an Englishman, a French naval officer and a French marquis. The Duc had letters of introduction from the colonial secretary, now the Duke of Portland, and from George Hammond, the British ambassador in Philadelphia. Simcoe received then politely and offered them accommodation in Navy Hall, while he found out whether Lord Dorchester would allow them to enter Lower Canada. Elizabeth commented on the 22nd, "Their appearance is perfectly democratic & dirty" and she disliked them all. She was happier to see Mrs. John McGill (Catherine Crookshank), now settled in York in preparation for moving the government from Newark. Jay's Treaty was ratified on 24 June 1795, but the evacuation of the forts would be delayed some months.

The unwelcome guests were still there. The Duc de Liancourt, when writing his eight-volume *Journal for philosophical and commercial observation*, commented of Simcoe:

> In private life, Governor Simcoe is simple and straightforward; he lives in a miserable little wooden house formerly occupied by the Commissioners for the navigation of the lake. He is guarded there by four

soldiers who come from the Fort in the morning and return in the evening. There he lives generously and hospitable without ostentation: his mind is facile and enlightened; he speaks well on all subjects, more willingly on his projects than on anything else.[8]

Writing on 6 July, Dorchester, who actually apologised for inconveniencing Simcoe, told him to refuse a pass for the Duc de Liancourt. He did not want French, royalist or republican, among the French-speaking Canadians. The Duc left Newark for New York State on the 22nd. The legislature met on 6 July and the session ended on 10 August. The next day they dined with Mrs. Christian Tice, widow of Gilbert Tice, an officer in the Indian department. Her house was large, with a gallery along the front and plenty of shade trees, and far cooler than even the tents they had used above the Niagara River. Elizabeth asked Mrs. Tice if she could rent two rooms for a fortnight; the servants could stay in a tent nearby. Mrs. Tice agreed, and the governor could join them when he had the time. The stay lengthened into 2 October and the onset of a cold spell. They had enjoyed visits to the whirlpool below the Falls, and to Fort Chippawa, and on to Fort Erie for a council meeting with the native leaders. On the way, Simcoe fell ill, but he carried on as best he could. He went to Long Point in September, where a settlement was forming which he named Charlotteville, after the Queen. (Charlotteville became a township, and is now part of the town of Simcoe, in the Regional Municipality of Haldimand-Norfolk.) On 13 October the Simcoes left to spend the winter at York, sailing aboard the *Governor Simcoe.*

Elizabeth settled happily into the canvas houses, her main worry Simcoe's continued ill health. From the start, the Duke of Portland vetoed many of his plans. Portland disapproved of county lieutenants, mayors and aldermen as decreasing the powers of the lieutenant governor. When Simcoe proposed incorporating Newark and Kingston, His Grace refused permission. Simcoe feared more danger of independence if he did not create an aristocracy to control the lower orders and set an example. Portland appeared to be preparing the province for eventual annexation to the United States, which may have been close to the truth. The new home secretary was not anxious to encourage the rise of a new British Empire where it could be so easily attacked.

By November, William Berczy and his settlers were running out of steam. They had reached Lot 35, but Berczy was building up debts. Road building was just too costly to continue. In December, Deputy Surveyor

Augustus Jones informed David William Smith, acting surveyor general, on 24 December 1795, "His Excellency was pleased to direct me to proceed on Yonge Street to survey and open a cart road from the harbour at York to Lake Simcoe." Jones reported to the governor on 20 February that "Yonge Street was open from York to the Pine Fort Landing, Lake Simcoe." The governor so informed the Duke of Portland on the 27th. The land was excellent and had been opened for settlers.[9]

Meanwhile, the Simcoes were reading and re-reading letters from a packet that had come by sleigh from Kingston. In the packet was a long-missing shirt Charlotte had made for her father. Eliza and Harriet had written, but to Simcoe's chagrin there was no letter from Charlotte for him, probably because he had never thanked her for the shirt. On 12 February he obliged. "Mama, a better judge, says it is well worked and shows industry." He added, "Francis will be a fine plaything for you all." He hoped Charlotte would make him fond of reading. Sophia did not "love her books" and he was looking for Charlotte "to mend her taste." He expected to teach Sophia himself when he had time during the winter.[10]

Dundas Street and Yonge Street might encourage settlement, but they were essentially strategic roads of military significance. Dundas Street was there to bypass Niagara. Yonge Street was to link York via Lake Simcoe and the Severn River to Georgian Bay. Simcoe had already seen Penetanguishene, a future naval base for the upper Great Lakes. Certain people, notably Richard Cartwright, complained that roads linking existing communities would have been of greater benefit, but he did not have the defense of the province in mind.[11] Simcoe was planning to extend Dundas Street to York, and ultimately Montreal and Burlington as soon as he could make the arrangements.

The governor was feeling daily more unwell, mainly because of frustrations, first with Dorchester, and then with both His Lordship and the Duke of Portland. He had not been allowed independent departments. Requests for more troops brought some twenty recruits from England for the Queen's Rangers, a mere token. He had made a plan to establish a Canadian Regiment, to be raised by his half-pay officers. On 30 June 1794 he had submitted a list of officers for the regiment, and suggested that Captain Justus Sherwood (Loyal Rangers) and Lieutenant Hazelton Spencer (King's Royal Regiment of New York) had the contacts to recruit companies in the United States! Not only was Simcoe depending on Americans as his main source of settlers; he hoped to entice some to come as soldiers.[12]

Dorchester was upset when Simcoe allowed Berczy's workers government rations. Provisions were only for troops. Government ships were there for the use of the army. His Lordship had relented and for three months he allowed the Queen's Rangers to work on civil projects, but then he changed his mind and forbad such work.[13]

With the withdrawal of the British regular regiments, Dorchester informed Simcoe that 100 Rangers were to be stationed in two blockhouses, on the Canadian side of the Detroit River, and 100 more were to be at Niagara.[14] A bitter Simcoe poured out his feelings in a letter of protest. He had never disobeyed an order, and had done his best to carry out all instructions he had received. He particularly resented Dorchester taking over his very own regiment, sent for a specific task that had the sanction of the British government.[15]

On 18 April the family moved to the yet unfinished Castle Frank. Francis was not well, and Elizabeth believed that "a change of air" would improve him. They divided the large room with sail cloth, and pitched a tent in the inner part where they slept on wooden beds. They returned to the garrison when the time drew near to move to Newark for the fifth and last session of the legislature that could be held there. Soon after they arrived, the tiny community was plunged into mourning by the death of John Butler, the founder of the Niagara settlement and colonel of his famous Rangers. He was buried with full military honours in the family plot on 15 May, Whitsunday.[16]

The legislature met from 16 May to 3 June. Afterwards all civil servants must move to York without further delay. The 5th Regiment would be leaving in the summer, replaced by a garrison of Americans. Francis celebrated his fifth birthday on 6 June, and Simcoe drove Elizabeth to bid farewell to Mrs. Robert Hamilton at Queenston and to see other friends briefly. They left Newark by canoe, a boat following, on the 7th — their final journey of exploration on the margins of Lake Ontario and the Niagara Escarpment. The children stayed in the boat, but their parents borrowed horses and rode part of the way to the head of the lake, where the King's Inn stood, built by the governor's order to convenience travellers. A group of natives, encamped a mile off, came and greeted them with a volley of muskets "in our Horses' faces their usual mark of respect which frightened me and my Horse very much, he started & I shrieked, but the sound was lost in the Whoops of the Indians. They gave us the largest land tortoise I ever saw."[17]

Elizabeth described the plunge pool at Stoney Creek, a basin-like hole carved out more than a million years ago by the waterfall of an ancient river. This river had been obliterated during the last ice age, when the glacier scooped out the Great Lakes. For a time, the Niagara River dropped over the escarpment into the basin, before it changed its course to the present one. On 15 June, Joseph Brant arrived, bringing two of his sons and an escort of Mohawks. The boys, aged about ten years, Elizabeth reckoned, were to be put in school at Niagara. They gave Francis a boat, and his parents had him give them a sheep, a gift for the Mohawks' dinner. Elizabeth made sketches as they went.

Leaving the area around the King's Head, they reached the mouth of the Credit River, and explored it for three miles until they encountered rapids and turned back. They reached York on the evening of the 16th. The children went to Castle Frank because Francis was again ill, where Elizabeth joined them after a large party at the garrison. Meanwhile, Simcoe had applied for a leave of absence, to restore his health. On 14 July they learned that the leave was granted. They would sail on the armed frigate *Pearl*, Captain Samuel Ballard in command.[18]

The ship was at Quebec and would sail on 4 August, which did not leave much time for farewells. During the governor's absence, Receiver General Peter Russell would be the administrator of the province. They learned that Lord Dorchester had resigned, and would be leaving Quebec probably before they arrived there. Dorchester's successor, General Robert Prescott, was already in Quebec. On 21 July they left on the *Onondaga* for Kingston, to the salutes of other vessels in the harbour. They carried mountains of baggage and furniture, and many souvenirs of their five years in the Canadas — a sleigh for those rare occasions when enough snow fell around Wolford Lodge, a stove to help heat their home, and the canoe given by the North West Company.

For the journey down the St. Lawrence they changed to bateaux, sleeping in houses where clean ones were to be found, in tents or in their boats. At each set of rapids, the governor insisted on remaining in the bateau while they shot them, which he found exhilarating, but Elizabeth did not:

> The great width of the River adds terror to the scene which presents miles of foaming waves. We stopped a little while that we might not overtake or run foul of an immense Cajuex or Raft that was going down, however she struck on a Rock & we passed her ... The Gov. wished me to sketch, I believe he wished to take my attention from the Rapids ... Canadians pass the Rapids safely so many times every year, but one has to resist all that can affright the senses ... The Pilot to make himself appear brave was perpetually reminding us of the great danger which only his knowledge could save us from ...

They stayed a few days in Montreal, where Lieutenant General Gabriel Christie, the commander of the garrison, loaned them his coach to ride to church. Francis, who could only remember open carriages, called it a room on wheels.

At Trois Rivières they stopped to see the Reverend Jehosophat Mountain, the bishop's brother, and reached Belmont, the home of the Caldwells, on 5 August. The *Pearl* was waiting for them though they were a day late. The next day General and Mrs. Prescott called at Belmont. Prescott was elderly, and Simcoe wondered whether he should sacrifice his leave and stay to help out. Elizabeth was appalled at the very idea. If he did not take his leave, the government would think he did not need it, which would call his integrity into dispute. Her husband was too patriotic for his own good.[19]

They received a message from Bishop Mountain, offering to loan the Simcoes his house and carriage, since accommodation was almost impossible to find in Quebec that season. The Mountains' youngest child had died the night before, and they were going to Trois Rivières to stay with his brother Jehosophat. Gratefully the Simcoes accepted the offer. Mrs. Prescott had described to Elizabeth the dismal lodgings she rented while waiting for the Dorchesters to vacate the Château St. Louis.

On 16 August, at the bishop's home, they learned that the *Active*, carrying the Dorchesters, had been wrecked off Anticosti, but without loss of lives. The Dorchesters had been taken by schooner to Gaspé Bay. The *Pearl* left to take them to Halifax, and the Simcoes would have to wait until the ship returned to Quebec. On the 18th Elizabeth wrote: "The ship Adriatic arrived from Halifax [sic]. Dined at the Chateau Ther[mometer] 88. We are under great anxiety least Lord Dorchester should take the Pearl to carry him to England from Halifax."[20]

The *Pearl* returned on 3 September. On the 6th, a few days before they were to sail, fire broke out not far from the Mountains' house, and spread rapidly from roof to roof because the shingles were of wood. By that time the Mountains had returned. Once Simcoe was aware of the danger, he sprang into action and took command of the defense of the houses. He organised the crew of the *Pearl* to carry water, and saved the Mountain house and others in the vicinity, although all caught fire several times. Elizabeth had their trunks sent to Chief Justice Osgoode's house for safety, where they would spend the night. First they attended a ball at the Château, which itself had been threatened by the fire and had hoses trained on it to keep it damp.

They boarded the *Pearl* on Saturday 10 September. Some of their fellow passengers were the officers from the lost *Active*. They sailed in a convoy of some 130 ships, the armed *Pearl* and other Royal Navy ships guarding the merchant vessels. John Scadding left Quebec about the same time, although he may not have been on the same ship. Colonel and Mrs. Richard England were aboard the *Progress*, rumoured to have been captured by the French. On 20 September:

> At 12 two French Frigates & a Brig were seen. They soon took 6 of our merchantmen who not having obeyed the Pearl's signals were a great way ahead of us. We cleared for action. Captain [Leveson] Gower conducted me down two flights of steps into the bread room which just held me, the Children & my servant, there I spent 6 hours in perfect misery every moment expecting to hear the Guns fire, as we lay to for the Enemy. Never having been in real danger before, I had no Idea what it was to be so frightened.

The *Pearl* encountered considerable rough weather. They had hoped to disembark at Tor Bay, Devon, but the breeze was too stiff. By 12 October they were off Dover, still unable to land until the following morning. With several officers they dined at an inn in Deal, very glad to be in a room that was not heaving up and down.[21] They did not set out for Wolford Lodge immediately. Simcoe wanted to stop a few days in London to confer with the Duke of Portland, in order to justify the things he had done without proper sanction and to plead for the implementation of more of his projects. The Simcoe carriage finally drew in at Wolford Lodge on 22 October. During the damp, unpleasant autumn days Elizabeth admitted that everything seemed "so cheerless for the want of our bright Canadian Sun that the effect was striking & the contrast very unfavourable to the English climate."[22]

Simcoe had left a formidable legacy. He had laid the foundations for the future. His weaknesses as governor were a lack of experience, and a misplaced trust, especially in the granting of land. Despite orderly surveys, shifts in land policy caused confusion. Before his departure Simcoe tried to remedy the situation by abolishing the land boards and having all land petitions submitted directly to the executive council. The measure came too late. David William Smith (confirmed as Surveyor General of Upper Canada in 1798) investigated grants of whole townships, which Simcoe assumed would be filled with settlers. Of thirty-two such grants Smith found only six with many settlers, and "they were often simply moved from other locations in the province."[23] With all its faults, Simcoe's open-door policy had resulted in a population almost double that of 1791. His "late Loyalists" from the United States were almost the only source of new people. War with France precluded mass immigration from the British Isles which he would have preferred.

Undoubtedly Simcoe had too many bright ideas. His lengthy correspondence reveals a bombardment of his superiors, whether as soldier or administrator. His relationship with Guy Carleton/Lord Dorchester, whom he never met, casts the governor in chief in an unflattering light. Dorchester's biographer, A. G. Bradley, whose work was first published in 1907, is sympathetic to his subject. A 1955 pamphlet by A.L. Burt paints a less rosy portrait. Dorchester was also a man who covered up his mistakes and could show lack of judgement, as when he ordered Simcoe to rebuild Fort Miamis.[24]

Writing a summation of John Graves Simcoe in the *Dictionary of Canadian Biography*, S. R. Mealing concluded:

> The most persistently energetic governor sent to British North America after the American Revolution, he had not only the most articulate faith in its imperial destiny but also the most sympathetic appreciation of the interests and aspirations of its inhabitants.[25]

Ontarians will always remember Simcoe for the many places — urban and rural — which he named after people he wished to impress, or just for his friends. An exception is Saltfleet Township, now part of the City of Stoney Creek, named for a salt spring. Simcoe had sought a source of salt for food preservation and was delighted when his settlers found one. James Bland Burges, commenting that Simcoe "talks with his usual enthusiasm about the great work in which he is engaged," wrote his sister Mary Anne, that he would "do my best not to disgrace my new namesake." He referred to the Township of Burges (Burgess) in Leeds County, and he enquired about a land grant there. He might need a place of sanctuary should the Empress of Russia and the King of Prussia invade England.[26] Next door to Burgess is Bastard Township, named in honour of John Pollexfen Bastard, its true origin sometimes clouded by the passage of time.

SEVENTEEN
SAN DOMINGO

While the Simcoes were still in Upper Canada, a noteworthy gentleman paid a call at Wolford Lodge. The Reverend John Swete was touring Devon, visiting places of historic interest and houses of prominent people. In December 1794, he painted a word picture of the Simcoe house: "two stories and was coloured with stucco of yellowish tone." Swete knew the Simcoes were away, but he called to pay his respects to Miss Hunt:

> I could not help lamenting as I surveyed the wild and cultured beauties of the spot, that its worthy owner was absent from it in a less hospitable clime — but to the generous mind how weak is the voice in glorious ease when Honor calls. Was this that persuaded Col. Simcoe to quit his beloved rural shades — for the bleak region of Canada. Where as Governor of the back settlements is rendering service to his country by conciliating the Indian Tribes. He might well attach

189

Fame and Honor to himself when those happy ends
are effected.[1]

From the sacrifice, as Swete saw the then Colonel's time in the
Canadas. Simcoe had come home to recuperate. His convalescence was of
short duration. By the time the travellers reached Wolford Lodge on 22
October 1796, the government had selected a new assignment for Major
General Simcoe. He was to be sent to the French colony of San
Domingo, the portion of the Island of Hispanola now called Haiti. On
10 November, John P. Bastard wrote from Kitley, his seat in Devon,
advising Simcoe to take a "medical man" with him to San Domingo.[2]
Bastard would help look after Simcoe's family and be in touch with
lawyer Christopher Flood. Elizabeth was horrified at the very idea of her
General, now forty-four years old, going out to a fever island, the
graveyard of so many Britons. Simcoe, the patriot, was willing to accept
the commission, but he sought guarantees for the good of his family. On
10 December he wrote to the home secretary, the Duke of Portland:

> Having obtained His Majesty's gracious Permission to
> return to Europe, expressly on the advice of my
> Physician that it was necessary for the preservation of
> my life I should the Autumnal heats of Upper Canada
> during the present year, I need not state to your Grace
> the apparent impossibility of my remaining in the island
> of St. Domingo during the unhealthy season. I am
> therefore to request that your Grace will have the
> goodness to take the formal measures that the
> Commander in Chief of His Majesty's Fleet in that
> Station be especially directed to allot me a Frigate for the
> purpose of my return to Europe whensoever I shall think
> it necessary.
>   I have the honor & ... "[3]

Permission, a little grudgingly, was forthcoming. The Speaker of the
House of Commons was Henry Addington, who wrote hinting that on
Simcoe's return from Canada he would like to see his friend "employed in
forming and arranging the Yeomanry cavalry and Troops intended for our
defense" — a far cry from San Domingo.[4] Simcoe, meanwhile, had
rented a London town house at 53 Welbeck Street.

On 19 December he wrote to Prime Minister Pitt thanking him for
the provisions to be made for his son and family, and reminding him of

the unhealthy climate of San Domingo: "I have twice already been obliged to quit a Southern Clime to preserve my life."[5]

San Domingo had been a French royalist colony, one of France's richest; this was wealth built upon the backs of slave labourers. In 1789, 500,000 black slaves were working in the colony. Half of them were African-born, as distinct from those born into slavery in the colony, which implied a high rate of attrition and required the regular importation of fresh labour. When the slaves learned of the French Revolution, they seized the opportunity to be freed of their masters by rising in rebellion. The French in the colony, like those in France, were divided between royalist and revolutionary. By 1791 the slaves were well organised, and had found in their ranks an inspiring leader, the slave François Dominique Toussant L'Ouverture.

With the coming of the French Revolution, Simcoe was on the same side as an old adversary over the matter of slavery and the slave trade. In Parliament the leader of the anti-slave trade faction was William Wilberforce, but the man who had enlisted his help was Thomas Clarkson, a schoolmaster's son from Cambridgeshire. A member of the French *Societé des Amis des Noirs* was the Marquis de Lafayette. Visiting France, Clarkson met with Lafayette, and present were six "Deputies of Colour" including one Vincent Oge. They were bitter that white colonists of San Domingo were represented in the National Assembly, but the coloureds, or mulattoes, were not. Oge warned the members that if equal representation was not forthcoming, "a fire would be lighted up in San Domingo, which would not easily be extinguished." Back home, Oge led an unsuccessful uprising that was the precursor to years of war on the island. Oge himself was guillotined, but his demise did not affect the slave movement. Toussaint L'Ouverture and his followers were further encouraged in 1794 when the French National Convention abolished slavery. The slaves in San Domingo naturally sided with the republican faction, who were anti-slavery.[6]

The royalist French, fighting a losing battle, approached Adam Williamson, the British governor of Jamaica, their Caribbean neighbour. They asked Williamson to join in the war against the rebellious slaves and the French republicans in San Domingo. After some consultation with the home government, a British force of some 1,000 men landed in San Domingo in 1793. So began a venture which was doomed to failure. In August 1795, Williamson, now commander in chief of British possessions in the West Indies, came to the island. Of 982 troops landed, 630 were dead within six weeks. Between 1793 and the close of 1796, the British lost 7,500 men, mainly to yellow fever and malaria. They even recruited slaves to fight under French commanders. In May 1796, a further 7,000 British troops landed in San Domingo but the situation did not improve, rather it worsened. Prime Minister Pitt's solution was to send Simcoe to the West Indies as commandant and civil governor of San Domingo.[7]

Still the patriot, Simcoe felt he could not refuse the appointment. Before his departure he had considerable correspondence with Adam Williamson, then living in Avebury, Wiltshire. Because of Williamson's longtime service, he provided Simcoe with useful intelligence about the situation and background so that his colleague had an up-to-date briefing before he left England.[8]

In January 1797, Simcoe set sail for San Domingo, accompanied by a military staff. On the 20th, he wrote to Elizabeth from the vessel, "3 leagues off [the island of] Porto Santo" (thirty miles from Madeira). He mentioned that among the officers accompanying him were Major Edward Littlehales and Henry Darling, now a captain in the 5th Regiment, withdrawn from Fort Niagara the previous summer. They boarded another ship at Madeira and met an American officer who knew the Simcoes.[9] A month later they arrived at Port au Prince, the principal town of San Domingo.

Ironically, Simcoe, so strongly opposed to slavery, found himself leading a campaign that, if successful, would ensure the continuation of slavery in the French colony — three years after it had been officially abolished. His heart could hardly have been in his task, but he also believed in the maintenance of law and order regardless of personal sentiments. His stay on the island was brief. His health again suffered in the hot, humid climate. Worse, this was an ugly war. Neither side gave quarter. The hatred of the slaves for their masters, and fear of them by the white residents, meant brutal, excessive conduct by both contenders. Simcoe's order that "cruelties and outrages" must cease had no effect. Otherwise his campaign was partly successful. His forces took the basin of Mirebalais, north of Port au Prince, and they successfully defended the seaport of Saint Marc from an attack by Toussaint L'Ouverture and his followers. He informed London in mid-June that with 6,000 troops he could take the whole colony, but the government would no sooner send such a force now than when it had responded to similar entreaties from Upper Canada.

By August, an angry Simcoe had arrived back in England. He could not carry on without adequate troops and supplies from home, and he was ill from the few months in that disease-ridden climate. His superiors were not pleased by his premature departure. Henry Dundas, secretary at war, whom he regarded as a friend, did not bother to see him. The Duke of York, as commander in chief, even contemplated charging Simcoe with deserting his post. He still had a friend in the Duke of Northumberland. Writing from Syon House, his home at Isleworth, Middlesex, on 18 August, the Duke welcomed him home, and invited him to call upon him before returning to Devon.[10] Joseph Brant, to whom Simcoe had carried the Duke's letter and brace of pistols, had visited Syon House in 1775–76.

After a short stay in London, Simcoe returned to Wolford Lodge, greeted by an ecstatic Elizabeth and his daughters. Francis, by this time was boarding in Honiton in the home of the Reverend John Copplestone, who kept a small school in his rectory.[11]

Simcoe resigned both his San Domingo commission and his lieutenant governorship of Upper Canada. He was no longer willing to serve in Canada as anyone's subordinate. The Duke of Portland did tell him he could expect to become governor in chief of the Canadas when General Prescott finished his tour of duty in 1799. This appointment never materialised, perhaps because Simcoe made a peerage a condition of acceptance.[12]

Months later, when she found that her General had not received the appointment, Elizabeth was disappointed. She would not be able to renew acquaintance with all the good friends she had made in Quebec. Besides, if Simcoe was stationed there, with the Château St. Louis as their residence, they could take all their daughters. Francis could not accompany them because he must remain in England for schooling. The spring of 1799 would have suited her nicely because they were expecting their eighth child in July 1798.

The San Domingo excursion had cost the British dearly in lives and money. In 1798 they made peace with Toussaint L'Ouverture and thankfully withdrew from any interest in the place. The slave army turned back the French in 1802 when they tried to retake their colony. Having triumphed over two major European powers, the blacks established their state, the first in the modern world. (That state has never been free of problems since.) Later, when Simcoe asked the King for "two Brass Spanish guns" from San Domingo, a memorial to the island's last British governor, His Majesty assented and in due course the two cannon graced the hallway at Wolford Lodge.[13]

Due course implied lengthy negotiations, not the only example of Simcoe's persistence. He wrote to the Duke of York, requesting him to ask His Majesty to confer on him "the token of Approbation which I most earnestly entreat your Royal Highness" to help him obtain "two or three small brass field pieces [that] were brought away from the Spanish Ports to Port au Prince":

> [they] were too difficult in their management & too curious in their construction to be of much military service; & were not used as being in no respect equal to the British Guns of nearly the same Calibre.... My humble request therefore is, that His Majesty will be pleased to give permission that I should obtain two of those Cannon, & that your Royal Highness would graciously condescend to order such permission into Effect.[14]

The Duke informed Simcoe that he had the King's consent. He had notified the Master General of Ordnance. When the cannons did not arrive, Simcoe wrote to the ordnance people, who replied that no one seemed to know which cannons he wanted, and where they lay. Simcoe tried again, because he had heard that all ordnance stores removed from San Domingo were to be sold to the United States of America:

> I shall not fail to desire that these two guns may be excepted from it; but the Directions ... may be rendered more effectual if you can describe the Guns in so distinct a manner as to prevent the Ordnance Officer at Jamaica from mistaking them ...

He then enlisted the aid of a former colleague at San Domingo, one William Spicer, who contacted the Commissary at Port Royal, Jamaica, where the San Domingo ordnance was housed. Eventually Spicer informed Simcoe that the guns were en route to England. They were next lodged in the Tower of London, without carriages. Simcoe ordered some built, to his specifications. (The guns — two 4-pounders — arrived at Plymouth on an ordnance sloop on 24 August 1800, two years after Simcoe had requested them.) [15]

When he first returned from San Domingo, Simcoe was without an active role to play. He had had promises, but little else. He had antagonised some of the establishment, but he still retained some powerful and influential friends.

PART V
GUARDIAN OF THE WESTERN DISTRICT

Throughout 1797, Napoleon Bonaparte was annexing territories to France. In Ireland, growing unrest led to open rebellion in 1798. In June, the rebels were defeated near Wexford. Napoleon took Egypt, but in August, Admiral Nelson won the Battle of the Nile, which cut off the French there from Europe. Meanwhile, a French force landed in Ireland, which surrendered in October. By December 1798, Britain had agreed to an alliance with Russia. In 1799, Britain and Hyderabad divided Mysore between them. A coalition against France was signed by Britain, Russia, Austria, Turkey, Portugal and Naples. By September 1799, the Duke of York was commanding an army in Holland.

Britain captured Malta in 1800. By December, an Armed Neutrality Act of the North had been signed by Russia, Sweden, Denmark and Prussia, to counter Britain's right to search ships of all countries. In 1801, the United Kingdom of Great Britain and Ireland was proclaimed. In March, Czar Paul I (son of Catherine II) was assassinated. Britain seized Danish and Swedish islands in the West Indies, and the Treaty of St. Petersburg acknowledged Britain's right of search.

With the Peace of Amiens, 1802, Britain and France ceased hostilities temporarily. Napoleon proclaimed himself the First Consul of France for life. In December, Peshaw of Poona surrendered his independence to the East India Company. The United States purchased the vast territory of Louisiana from France in April 1803. Hostilities between Britain and France resumed in May.

By 1804, war had broken out between the victorious East India Company and Holkar of Indore. Hobart, Tasmania, was founded in October, and Bonaparte was crowned Napoleon I in December. The highlight of 1805, on 21 October, was the Battle of Trafalgar. Nelson, the victor, was mortally wounded. Britain upset the United States by closing her West Indian possessions to American trade. That December, Napoleon defeated the Russians and Austrians at the Battle of Austerlitz.

In 1806, Britain occupied the Cape of Good Hope. With the death of Pitt, the Ministry of All the Talents succeeded him, and passed the act abolishing the slave trade. France and Prussia were now allied against Britain. In April, Britain declared war on Prussia after that country seized Hanover. By October, Napoleon had occupied Berlin, and he took Warsaw that December. In the meantime, Simcoe had died in Exeter on 26 October.

EIGHTEEN
THREATS FROM FRANCE

Early in January 1798, Simcoe received a letter from William Windham, an under secretary to the Secretary at War Henry Dundas:

> Sir,
> His Majesty having been pleased to appoint you to serve as a Major-General on the staff of Great Britain with one Aide de Camp I am commanded to signify to you the King's Pleasure that you do obey such orders as you shall receive from His Majesty; the Commander in Chief [the Duke of York] or any other your Superior Officer,
>
> > I have the honour to be,
> > Sir,
> > Your most obedient humble Servant,
> > W. Windham.[1]

Simcoe was to command the forces of the West of England with particular responsibility for "Most of Devonshire and Part of Somerset." His military superiors were Lord George Lennox, the military governor of Plymouth and a full general in the army, and Lieutenant General Richard Grenville, who held an overall command for the western counties of Cornwall, Devon and parts of Somerset.

The threat of invasion by Napoleon and his armies was now very real. On 22 February 1797, three French frigates had shelled Barnstaple, in North Devon.[2] The long coastline of south-west England was doubly vulnerable, first from the Continent, and second from Ireland. In December 1797, a French invasion fleet had sailed for Ireland without being discovered. Only a combination of bad weather and bad seamanship had prevented a French landing.[3] The fleet had returned to France, but her troops might try to threaten England from across the Irish Sea. Simcoe and his military and civil colleagues had orders to make every preparation to repel the French, should they land, and to ensure that the invaders could not live off the country. He set about his new role with characteristic vigour and all the energy and enthusiasm he had thrown into the American War and Upper Canada. Again his fertile brain formulated ideas for the defense of his command, and he bombarded his superiors with them.

He could call upon civil colleagues of the Lieutenancy and the Magistracy, and he had at his disposal a mixed crop of fighting men — regular army, Militia and units of Volunteer Infantry and Yeomanry. The Militia was raised by a ballot system operated by the lord lieutenants of each county. (In Upper Canada he was astute enough not to refer to them as "Lord.") Under the Militia Acts of 1758, each parish constable was required to submit a list of all men aged eighteen to forty-five. From these lists, men would be selected by ballot. Men not wishing to serve could persuade someone to act as a substitute, usually by offering an agreed sum of money. Where numbers of enrolled Militia were inadequate, a Supplementary Militia Ballot could be implemented. This form of 18th century conscription was not well received, but conscription rarely is.

The lord lieutenant of Devonshire was Hugh Lord Fortescue. Members of the Militia were subject to military discipline and law and were paid. The Volunteers were an adjunct of the Militia, and were under the same command structure. Parishes within the county raised their own Corps, usually organised by the local gentry and clergy or by committees. The government supplied the Volunteers with arms and some clothing, but most expenses were met by the men themselves. The Corps that were of cavalry, whether gentlemen, yeomen or tenant farmers, had to supply their own horses.

Plans for the evacuation of livestock, wagons and foodstuffs involved the civilians of the farms and villages. Most important, the Militia and Volunteers had to be trained into an efficient fighting force. Preparations involved all the western counties, though Simcoe's responsibilities were Devon and the small section of Somerset.

The Devon and Exeter General Open Standing Committee began to function in April. Normally, meetings were held in Exeter Castle, with Lord Fortescue, or Lord Clifford of Ugbrooke House, Chudleigh, as chairmen. The committee coordinated the preparations and implemented legislation enacted for the defense of the Realm, together with instructions from the Secretary at War. As a member of this committee, Simcoe advised the members on all military matters. Preparations did not wait for the formation of this committee. On 30 January, the first constructive steps were taken, the establishment of the Posse Comitatus or Defense Lists (which were separate from the Militia Ballot Lists).[4]

Lord Fortescue ordered a return submitted listing all males resident within each parish, specifying who could be recommended as "Chief and Petty Commanders." Orders went out to the petty constables of the parishes within their constablewicks to comply with the decisions of the committee. They were for raising and establishing a "Civil Power" for general defense, and to suppress any riot or insurrection or rebel invaders, and to recommend, if the number to be levied on any parish exceeded 100 men, two or more "proper and fit persons from which may be chosen a Chief Commander" and also proper persons to be petty commanders over every twenty men. Others were to be chosen as directors of stock and drivers. A return was to be prepared of the numbers of "waggons," carts and cart horses in each parish that could be "used for the removal of Dead Stock or conveying Soldiers or Baggage etc." All returns were to be submitted by 19 February.

The High Constable for Hemyock, where Simcoe owned the castle and other property, did not issue the order until 7 February. This left little time to complete the considerable task. The parish's return listed 240 men and recommended as chief commander the local parson, a common practice and in this instance the Reverend John Land. Many of the surnames on the return are to be found in the village to this day — Clist, Farrant, Moon, Pring, Hart, Salter, Wide and Lowman. Families throughout Devon tended to stay firmly rooted in their rural communities for many generations.

The first part of Hemyock's return, "A," named three other chief commanders, Robert Farrant, yeoman, Edward Lutley, and Robert Fry, sergemaker (who was also the high constable). Ten petty commanders were listed. Occupations of the men included husbandmen, labourers, weavers, thatchers, a butcher and a baker. Thirteen were wool combers; the woollen industry was important in the village. Transport numbered six wagons, twenty carts and sixty-four horses.

The second part, "B Live and Dead Stock" showed 470 oxen, 237 cows, 270 young stock, 1,296 sheep and 202 pigs. Dead stock (harvested crops in store) comprised 144 quarters of wheat, 60 of oats, 35 of barley, 73 loads of hay, 15 of straw, and 201 sacks of potatoes. The information was vital to the lord lieutenant (and later to the social historians of the county).[5]

On Friday 13 April, the committee met again. Simcoe was listed only as "Esquire." Plans included the removal of "the aged and the women and children from the path of the invader." A printed notice set forth the general principles for executing an "Act of Parliament made and passed in the 38th year of the reign of his present Majesty King George the Third intitled:

> An Act to enable His Majesty more effectively to provide for the Defense and Security of the Realm during the present war and for indemnifying persons who may suffer in their property of such measures as may be necessary for that purpose.

The order asked for more returns — names of all men dwelling within the parish between ages fifteen and sixty, showing those incapable of active service owing to infirmity, and accounts of males under fifteen and over sixty, and of females "within such Parishes Tythings and Places by age, infirmity or other cause incapable of removing themselves from danger." This and other returns were really a census. Emergency planning was comprehensive (and useful to later historians and genealogists).

Simcoe set out to meet all the newly appointed civilian commanders as well as his military subordinates. He undertook tours throughout Devon and his part of Somerset, and Elizabeth often accompanied him. Bubbling up was the Irish question. Aunt Elizabeth Gwillim, writing from Whitchurch on 28 March, thought the Irish situation looked ominous. Many people disapproved of Mr. Pitt's solution, union with Great Britain and Catholic emancipation. The Catholic Duke of Norfolk, she maintained, was already making the country disloyal. She hoped the next baby would be a boy.[6]

On 13 May, Elizabeth described some of the Simcoe wanderings in a letter to her friend, Miss Elliott. They had been to the South Hams area:

and I have lately been a fortnight from home, which affords me an opportunity of telling you how much I wish you had seen the pretty scenery I had lately viewed — you would scarcely tho believe yourself in Devonshire were you to travel in that part of it called South Hams near the sea coast — the vallies [sic] are extremely rich, but the villages in Gloucestershire being so different from the dispersed cottages and little churches in the East of Devon ... but neither the Dart nor the river at Ivybridge at all enchant me as they used to before I'd seen the rivers of Canada.

Sharpham, near the River Dart, was the home of John Pollexfen Bastard's younger brother, Edmund. John P. was the colonel of the 1st Devon Militia, and Edmund was the lieutenant colonel. Apparently in the Militia, the colonel was the commandant; in regular regiments the lieutenant colonel was usually the commandant, and the colonel was an honorary rank. Pollexfen was a family name. In the 17th century, their ancestor, William Bastard, had married a Pollexfen heiress whose home was Kitley. It became the family seat, passing to John P.

The "Genl" often rode nine hours a day on horseback without suffering ill effects. However, about three weeks before, he was seriously ill with "gout in his stomach":

> ... because Ld. Somerville would have his Yeomanry received in the worst weather possible, in order that he might be no longer detained from the Agricultural Society; at the same time making his farmers lose a day during the sowing time — and obliged the General to pay a Physician a fee, the worst mode of spending money; but I hope it will be a warning to him in future not to omit changing wet clothes.[7]

Lord Somerville was Mary Anne Burges's cousin, the eldest brother of her ward. The Hon. Julia Valenza Somerville was growing up at Tracey, and at Wolford Lodge she was like another sister to the Simcoe children.

Simcoe's relations with the aristocracy and gentry were reasonably good, but occasionally problems would arise, such as the harvest taking precedence over the timing of troop reviews. The Simcoes did establish strong friendships with a number of distinguished West Country families, the Coleridges of Ottery, for example, and in particular the Cliffords of Ugbrooke, the wealthiest Roman Catholic dynasty in Devonshire.

The name Coleridge is well-known. Samuel Taylor Coleridge was the poet. His brother, the Reverend George Coleridge, was the headmaster of The King's School, at Ottery St. Mary. That year, Francis Simcoe, now nearly eight, had become a pupil at King's (a school that still exists). Another brother, James, was a lieutenant colonel, and an aide de camp to General Simcoe. When fear of French invasion was at its height, Colonel Coleridge would climb, each morning, to the top of the Hilly Field at his home, Chanter's House. From there he could see Wolford Lodge. He would focus his telescope on a certain window and if a towel was hung from it he was to hurry to the Simcoe house immediately.[8]

During their tour in May, the General and Mrs. Simcoe had visited Ugbrooke, the Clifford family seat. This was the first time the families had met. Elizabeth, usually suspicious of Catholics, was favourably impressed. "Ld. and Lady Clifford are very worthy pleasant people; he has a great taste in drawing and she is one of the most amiable women that can be and nothing of a modern fine lady."[9]

Charles, 6th Baron Clifford of Chudleigh was a deputy lieutenant of the county, assistant to Lord Fortescue, and on the Devon defense committee. He also commanded the Volunteer Companies at Chudleigh and Teignbridge. He had a remarkable younger brother, the Hon. Robert Edward — soldier, military analyst, translator of learned works, topographer and cartographer, collector of maps and books, Fellow of the Royal Society, Fellow of the Society of Antiquaries, suspected spy and much more. He met and corresponded with John Graves Simcoe for many years, often supplying him with books he sought, particularly military ones. Robert Clifford was educated in France. In 1758, King Louis XVI gave him a commission in Dillon's, a regiment of Irish Jacobites, in the French service. The colonel proprietor was Lieutenant General Count Arthur Dillon, a cousin of Robert's by marriage. Robert had tried to enter the army in England, but he was barred by a law prohibiting Catholics holding the King's commission.

Robert left the regiment in 1791 and divided his time between England and France. He studied the development of military thinking and training, which had reached a high level of efficiency in France. He knew how the French operated, and his knowledge of the material, maps and plans made him useful. He shared confidential information with Simcoe, whom he looked upon as one of the more forward thinking senior officers in England.[10]

Simcoe was full of more ideas as a result of the tour of inspection, and he submitted many reports to Lord George Lennox. (He was a younger son of the 2nd Duke of Richmond. His son Charles became the 4th Duke, who in 1819 died of rabies soon after being sent to the Canadas as governor in chief.) General Lennox gave Simcoe his wholehearted support, and ordered him to place his ideas before a special Devon Standing Committee at a meeting on 15 May.[11]

Offers of aid poured in to the committee from all over the county. Morale was high, patriotism strong. More companies were added to the Honiton Volunteers. From the village of Starcross, on the River Exe, came an offer of service and boats from the local bargemen. A letter from Secretary at War Henry Dundas was read at the meeting, suggesting that gamekeepers might be formed into a corps of sharpshooters. Simcoe, familiar with German Jaegers during the American Revolution, probably agreed.

At the meeting of the committee on 15 May, Lord Clifford was in the chair. They discussed a plan for driving livestock away from areas most exposed to invaders and for "proper places of assembly" from which to travel to places of "General Rendezvous." Each parish was to choose an assembly place for livestock, dead stock, wagons and supplies, and a route from there to two selected rendezvous, Dartmoor for Devon, and Somerton for Somerset. The final choice would depend on where the French landed. Simcoe produced a list of county bridges to be reserved for use of the troops or "to be crossed only by cattle."

Superintendents of parishes were ordered to prohibit civilians from using the turnpike roads, which must be left open for the King's use. Conductors and overseers responsible for livestock should carry provisions for a few days, a blanket and tools for breaking down hedges. Those in charge of dead stock must destroy hay, corn and cattle, horses not for public service, carts and wagons before seeking a place of safety, in other words, scorched earth. Only those who followed instructions would receive compensation for losses. Returns from all over Devon poured in to Exeter Castle. For Simcoe, this was the beginning.

The matter of his pay as a major general was cleared up in a letter from Under Secretary Windham on 26 June. He would receive the pay from the date of his commission, 3 October 1794, to 29 November 1796 inclusive, and for the time he spent in San Domingo.[12]

June brought the insurrection in Ireland that ended with the defeat of the rebels at Vinegar Hill on the 21st and the entry of British troops, led by General Gerard Lake, into Wexford. By that time Elizabeth was awaiting confinement. A second son, John Cornwall Simcoe, was born at Wolford Lodge on 7 July and baptized on 2 August. His sisters rejoiced for, as Eliza had written her great aunt Margaret Graves, they had "girls enow."[13]

August saw French help to Ireland, too little and much too late. Some 900 troops landed, after the insurrection had been quelled, and all of them surrendered. French prisoners of war were a dilemma for Simcoe. Many were being brought to Plymouth, to be housed somehow. (Not until 1806 when Dartmoor Prison was being erected was the problem of the incarceration of French prisoners solved.)

Lord Clifford, active and valuable to Simcoe, wrote wondering whether the General might bypass the rules and obtain a King's commission for him despite his religion. Simcoe replied, with regret, "His Majesty is unwilling to sign any commission for Noblemen or Gentry of the Roman Catholic persuasion." However:

> In this predicament I beg to concur in the opinion of Sir [Francis] Justice Buller, and to advise your Lordship to act as if you had received your Commission ... till the Enemy land no overt act is called for, it being solely between you and your Company whether they choose to obey your orders, the Volunteers not being under military law ... and when that shall be the case, your Lordship's commission as Deputy Lieutenant most certainly will be superior to that as a Captain of a Troop, at least within the Hundred or County ...[14]

Lord Lennox authorised exercises for troops encamped at Stanborough Heights, Milbourne Down, Berry Head and a few other places. Simcoe chose Saturday and Monday the 22nd and 24th of September, weather permitting. On the 22nd, troops at Milbourne would attack and capture outposts of the camp at Stanborough, then retire, "firing a salute in honour of the day." On the 24th, troops from Stanborough would attack the camp at Dartington, but would be checked at the River Dart, to "exemplify the total impracticability of a foreign Invador passing our Rivers and fastness when the County shall rise as one Man & be properly arranged to oppose them." He wanted all the Volunteer Yeomanry Corps to participate. He claimed he was preparing the troops for "Invasion or Insurrection"; this last seems odd in view of the enthusiasm the Devonians were showing for the cause.

Berry Head was particularly important as a defensive site, a headland outside the fishing town of Brixham, capped by an Iron Age fort. Stanborough Heights also had an ancient hill fort. Simcoe had sketch plans drawn, showing field patterns and parkland. Much of the exercise took place on high ground southeast of Dartington Hall. He referred to an "old Roman redoubt" in Dartington Park, a scene of some of the action. He was pleased with the exercise, which concluded with the "Combatants" gathered in the park to sing God Save the King which ."..had a fine effect amidst the picturesque scenery of the Dart."[15]

In October, four-month-old John Cornwall Simcoe was inoculated and developed smallpox. On the 13th Mrs. Gwillim wrote from Whitchurch that she hoped "our little Man" was safe from all danger of the smallpox for his life:

> ... but as Chicken Pox is about who ever inoculated him ought to be particularly careful of mistakes ... but by your mentioning the ninth day it looks as to be the right sort the other drys [sic] away sooner.[16]

She was wrong. Little John developed a severe case from which he would never make a complete recovery.

The burden of defense, Simcoe was convinced, must fall upon the cavalry. In that event, he wrote Lord Fortescue, he would need more, preferably two regiments of regular cavalry. The Somerset regular cavalry was at Taunton, the Militia Devons at Exeter, and provisional regiments (incorporated militia) of the Devons were in South Hams and North Devon. A return towards the end of the year shows where Simcoe's troops were located — "Return of the Distribution of Troops Under the Command of Major-General Simcoe ... 7th November 1798. In Barracks & Cantonment":

1st Somerset	Militia 10 Companies Exeter
North Devon Militia	4 Companies Biddiford
	2 Companies Barnstable
	2 Companies Torrington
Col. Warneford's Infantry	4 Companies Ashburton & Buckfastleigh
	2 Companies Chudleigh Bovey & Adjacents 1st Devon
Militia	2 Companies Totness
	3 Companies Berryhead
	1 Company Kingsbridge
	1 Company Dartmouth

	1 Company Modbury
	Detachments Staddon Heights
62nd Regiment of Foot [regulars]	9 Companies South Molton
4th Devon Militia	2 Companies Newton Bushell Abbot
	2 Companies Shaldon Teignmouth
	Dawlish Starcross
	2 Companies Sidmouth Sidford
	Ottery Otterton
	1 Company Topsham
	1 Company Exmouth
East Somersets	2 Companies Columpton
	2 Companies Tiverton
	2 Companies Crediton
	2 Companies Honiton
1st Royal Dragoons [regulars]	3 Troops Exeter
	1 Troop Taunton
	3 Troops Taunton
Surrey Line Cavalry	1 Troop Barnstable
	1 Troop Tavistock
	1 Troop Totness
	1 Troop Modbury
Royal Artillery	Detachments Staddon Heights,
	Barnstable (with North Devons)
	Exeter (with 1st Somersets)
	Berry Head (with East Devons)
	Exeter Torbay[17]

The return did not encompass the Volunteer Corps, one of which may have been of very youthful members — the older boys at The King's School who wrote to General Simcoe:

> ... We trust, Sir, that the small spark of the PATRUS AMOR which now warms our young hearts will, by this instance of your favour be breathed into a flame to animate us like our brave Ancestors in the defense of our Country And suffer us to assure you that the present occasion may be considered the happiest moment of our lives ... Wherever we shall think on you, Sir, the character of the second Scipio will recur to our minds, who is reported, when retired from the din of war and the fatigue of State Affairs to have spent his time in innocent amusements with Children. His ungrateful country alas; hastened the death of a man whose family had been the cause of preserving its liberty ... God save the King.[18]

It was signed "Captain Beague, Ensign Bacon, Sgt. Bastard" and twenty other young warriors, including two Coleridges. Publius Cornelius Scipio was the conqueror of Carthage, of whom Simcoe would approve.

A system of rapid communication was vital. Riders rode express, which implied non-stop, changing horses. Some riders were at key points, ready to carry dispatches and were efficient for the time. Simcoe had difficulty over toll roads, where keepers were uncertain who should pass without payment, until an order was relayed from Exeter:

> Government allows the Major general of every District a carriage and ten horses for his Majesty's Service and also 3 horses for his Brigadier Major ... to pass Toll free and directed the Gate Keepers not to demand any.[19]

The County Committee for Internal Defense received applications for commissions in the Volunteer Corps that required the approval of Lord Lieutenant Fortescue. Only "gentlemen" were supposed to be eligible. When an application arrived for a Brixham innkeeper named John Underhay, Simcoe was appalled. He wrote Fortescue on 16 December 1798:

> I am confident there is no one person of the Magistracy or Lieutenancy of the County would have recommended

a Tavern Keeper to obtain a King's Commission … and I should as I conceive, betray my professional, and not only that, but my political duty, did I not do my utmost to have the King's Commission rescued from so vile a prostitution.[20]

Underhay, however, had considerable support in Brixham. Sir Francis Buller, a Justice of the Court of King's Bench, informed Fortescue that Underhay was "the most considerable man at Brixham Quay." The applicant was a land owner who had great influence over the local people Fortescue accepted Buller's opinion and granted the commission as commander of the Brixham Volunteers.

Each commander was issued with a booklet entitled:

THE SOLDIER'S COMPANION; CONTAINING INSTRUCTIONS FOR THE DRILL, MANUAL, AND PLATOON EXERCISE, AS COMMANDED BY HIS MAJESTY. INTENDED FOR THE USE OF THE VOLUNTEERS OF THIS COUNTRY. TO WHICH IS PREFIXED A FEW OBSERVATIONS ON FIRST FORMING A MILITARY CORPS.

Meetings were to be at the most convenient times and situations not to interfere with other engagements, such as harvesting. Nothing in the book suggested that tavern keepers were excluded. Simcoe's intolerance could have been because of an "Indisposition." To Lord Clifford he wrote that favourable weather might help. Between visits to troops he did not have time to recover.[21]

Wolford Lodge was his headquarters, and scarcely a relaxing place for man or woman. His agents began looking for a suitable property somewhere in the Budleigh area. Elizabeth and the children, and where possible Simcoe himself, needed to be able to get away from the hubbub.

Simcoe's pay was substantial, but not for one of his commitments. In addition to pay as a major general on the staff, he now was the honorary Colonel of the 22nd Foot, the Cheshire Regiment. His annual income as major general was £655, plus £114 "forage allowances on taking the field." As colonel in a Regiment of Foot his pay was £410.12.6d. and £91.5.0d. forage while in the field[22] He undoubtedly dipped into part of the income from his estates to cover some expenses.

NINETEEN
TROUBLED TIMES

The pace of life at "Brigade Headquarters" — Wolford Lodge — was frantic as 1799 dawned. A steady stream of people came and went; an equally steady stream of correspondence flowed from Lord George Lennox at Plymouth, Lieutenant General Richard Grenville in Somerset, and Lord Fortescue, not to mention Simcoe's replies. On 10 January Mrs. Gwillim wrote her niece, sympathising over General Simcoe's attacks of gout. In March, Simcoe admitted to one of his commanders, Lord Rolle, whose seat was at Bicton, that he was using an amanuensis to write his letters because of the pain in his right hand. On other occasions Elizabeth had helped him, but just now she was too worried about her children to spare the time. Francis and Caroline were down with whooping cough, a deadly killer of children. They recovered, but little John Cornwall Simcoe, still struggling to survive, died on 20 March, at age nine months. His was the first burial, on the 23rd, in the plot the family had chosen, at some Cistercian ruins near Wolford Lodge.[1]

The Simcoes found the retreat they had sought, at the small town of Budleigh Salterton, about four miles east of Exmouth at the mouth of the

River Otter. At the time Budleigh was attracting sightseers, a prelude to its life as a popular holiday spot. The "Salterton" part was derived from salt pans nearby. Artist Sir John Millais made the town famous by his painting depicting Sir Walter Raleigh as a boy, on the beach. Raleigh had been born at Hayes Barton, a farmhouse at East Budleigh. One visitor to Budleigh whom Simcoe probably knew was James Lackington, a wealthy London bookseller who had been born in Wellington, Somerset, only ten miles from Wolford Lodge. Simcoe, the avid collector, may have done business with Lackington.

The new house was situated on high ground with a commanding view along the coast in both directions. The dwelling may have begun as a fisherman's cottage. It was enlarged over the years, and was eventually known as Simcoe House, then Little Hill, and again Simcoe House. Judging by the amount of his correspondence that was dated Budleigh, Simcoe spent considerable time there from 1799 onwards.

He was too pressed to attend a meeting at the Guildhall, Taunton, on 9 May, where John, Earl Poulett, was in the chair. The meeting passed a resolution:

> That General Simcoe is entitled to the Thanks of this Meeting for the comprehensive view he had taken of the Subject of the defense of the countryside and the means which he has suggested for that Object: and that this Meeting will by every means in their Power endeavour to carry those Means into execution.[2]

Deputy lieutenants and esquires attending learned of French plans that had been sent to the Committee of Secrecy, House of Commons, entitled in French "Instructions for the March and Operations of General Humbert" (incidentally the same man who had led the French troops to Ireland in August 1798). The document proposed a landing on the western peninsula of England, and to establish the French in Devonshire. Humbert was to cut off communication between Plymouth, Dartmouth and Portsmouth (in Hampshire). He was to avoid the stations of the many garrisons unless he saw an opportunity to promote a "Commotion." In fact, social unrest had begun to spread and there had been riots in the West Country. The French assumed that their invading army would live off the country, the very thing Simcoe had sought to render impossible. The landing never materialised.

On 20 May, John P. Bastard wrote to discuss the Duke of Kent's appointment as Commander in Chief of the British Army in Canada, a position Bastard had hoped would go to his friend.[3] A few days later Lord Clifford was writing about a forthcoming muster of the Kingsteighton and Chudleigh cavalry:

> I mean to give a little Fete to the Troop in the Old Camp on the King's Birthday. Col. Slade lets me have his band. The Park will appear to great advantage but I fear you & Mrs. Simcoe will be too much occupied to honor us with your presence on the occasion.[4]

He was correct, for the General was planning two reviews, one at Woodbury Common for the Devon troops, the other at Curry Moor for those of Somerset. Woodbury Common is a large area of beautiful high heath between Exmouth and Ottery St. Mary, commanding superb views of the Exe Estuary and the Sidmouth gap. At a high point is an Iron Age hill fort, a site used for military training before and since. The review, before Lord George Lennox, was spectacular — 139 artillery with horses, 734 cavalry and 2,748 infantry, including the Honiton Volunteers, who were special to Simcoe. The some 900 horses represented a lot of dung. A dispute arose between Lord Rolle, Simcoe and others over who was entitled to take the dung away — one of many disputes between Rolle and Simcoe that would in time lead the former to challenge the latter to a duel. Simcoe declined; common sense prevailed.[5]

Curry Moor is situated on the Somerset Levels, an area of low-lying land long ago reclaimed from the sea — a very distinct and fascinating landscape. The review, before the commander of the "Western District" Lieutenant General Richard Grenville, was successful. Grenville wrote a letter of appreciation on 26 June:

> I am anxious to take the first opportunity of impressing to the Commissioned and NonCommissioned Officers and Privates of the different Volunteer Corps of cavalry and Infantry belonging to the County of Somerset, who passed before me in Review on Curry Moor this morning, the great satisfaction I derived from every part of their conduct.[6]

Simcoe duly passed on Grenville's praise to the troops and received similar comments from Lennox. The good impression was the result of Simcoe's enthusiasm and professionalism. One of his right hand men at this time was Henry Darling, whom he had known at Fort Niagara, now serving as his brigade major. Simcoe next moved his headquarters to Plymouth. Both Lennox and Grenville were taking leaves of absence. On 28 November 1799, the Exeter *Flying Post* reported: "Major-General John Graves Simcoe, to be Commandant of the Garrison at Plymouth, in the absence of the Governor and of Lieutenant-General Grenville."

Despite the worry over a French invasion, Simcoe had petty matters to distract him. Lord Rolle, as Colonel of the South Devon Militia, was acting illegally in staying at his home in Bicton, rather than at headquarters in Exeter. Rolle's Lieutenant Colonel Elford brought this to Simcoe's attention. Rolle incidentally had rubbed many people the wrong way. When he raised the matter with Rolle, the colonel suggested buying a house in Exeter. The dispute dragged on until Simcoe decided that Rolle could sleep at Bicton. Lord Fortescue, who slept at his home, Castle Hill, north Devon, and John Bastard, who often slept at Kitley, had established a precedent.[7]

At Plymouth, Simcoe's time was heavily committed to paper work — inspection returns from the region, requisitions, troop movements and myriad others. He must have kept a diary during the American Revolution, on which his *Journal* was based, but scraps of paper in his handwriting deal with day-to-day military matters. Elizabeth was with him in Plymouth following the death of baby John, and she was expecting their ninth child. The new arrival was a boy, born at Plymouth on 28 February 1800.[8] They named him after Henry Addington, the then Speaker of the House of Commons and a childhood friend of Prime Minister Pitt. Owing to pressure of work in Plymouth, Henry Addington Simcoe was not baptized at Dunkeswell until 2 June 1801.

Before the birth of Henry, General Simcoe had been approached by Sir Charles Stuart to join him on a military expedition to the Mediterranean, as second in command of a force of 15,000 men. Simcoe declined because he did not want to leave Elizabeth until after her confinement. When Lord Grenville (William Wyndham Grenville) of Pitt's inner circle renewed the offer, Simcoe consented, but by then the Duke of York had appointed Sir Henry Paget as Stuart's second in command. Stuart persuaded the Duke to appoint Simcoe to be Paget's superior. An enthusiastic Simcoe went to London to prepare, but at the last minute the expedition was called off. On 30 April, Simcoe wrote to Francis, now nearly nine years old:

> My dear Son,
> The expedition on which I was going has been laid
> aside, to my great Mortification as an English gentleman

& an English statesman, but to my great satisfaction as the Father of Francis Simcoe, whom I shall hope to find a very good boy on my return to my command in Devonshire, which will be shortly.[9]

He now had enough free time to increase his holdings. He acquired Pitpark at Budleigh Salterton, other small parcels nearby, and Windsor Farm in the parish of Luppitt, close to Wolford Lodge. John Scadding was the tenant of the farm.[10] Defense preparations, however, continued, especially a buildup of Volunteer troops. The lord lieutenant accepted a new corps of Infantry for the Hundred of Hemyock, which included Dunkeswell.

By August, Elizabeth and their older daughters were at Whitchurch, called there because of the final illness of Mrs. Elizabeth Gwillim. Elizabeth's aunt breathed her last on the 6th, and was laid to rest in the family plot in St. Dubricius churchyard. Elizabeth would miss the knowing letters from this aunt, as sensible as Aunt Margaret Graves was sometimes silly.

In September, authorities were worried about signs of civil unrest in the West of England, even more than the threat from across the English Channel. Unrest resulted from poor harvests in many parts of the country. Not large producers of grains, Devonians imported them from other counties whose farmers now had no surplus to sell. Prices were high and demands large in the greater Plymouth area, where the military, civilians, and the off-shore fleets all required provisioning. Prices of food rose causing hardship. A handbill displayed in the Shambles, Cullompton, threatened bloodshed similar to that in France:

> Now see the youke is taken of[f] from them now they have provision at so reasonable a price as any person could wish ... their [sic] is nothing wanting in this Country only Courage & then we should be released of our burden.[11]

Disturbances known as Bread Riots occurred at many centres, including Honiton. Grenville ordered Simcoe to send the 2nd Somersets to Bristol to help quell the disorders. On 1 January 1801, union with Ireland (without Catholic emancipation) came into effect, which added the Cross of St. Patrick to the flag. The same day, Under Secretary at War William Windham wrote to Simcoe:

Sir,

The King having been pleased to appoint you to serve on the Staff in Great Britain as a Lieutenant-General, with Aides de Camp, I am commanded to acquaint you, It is His Majesty's Pleasure that you do obey such Orders as you shall receive from His Majesty, the Commander in Chief, or any other your Superior Officer,

I have the honor to be ...[12]

The Simcoes were then celebrating the festive season with a grand house party. Under the General's direction, family and guests staged a masquerade, which Caroline described in a letter to Mrs. Hunt who was then living in Exeter.[13] Guests appeared as characters from Shakespeare. General Simcoe as Prospero introduced everyone. "Mrs." Burges was "the drollest figure in the room" as a witch from Macbeth. Julia Somerville was Moth with enormous wings; Eliza, Thisbe, Charlotte, Pyramus; Harriet, Wall; Sophia, Moonshine; Francis, Lion. A band from Honiton played for dancing, and a "pedlar" distributed presents. In attendance were the children of James Coleridge, whom Caroline called "Captain" although he was a Militia Colonel. Elizabeth was a spectator; her tenth child was expected in the spring. House parties, with a pageant or masquerade, became a tradition as the children grew old enough to enjoy the play-acting. Simcoe wrote the scripts, usually in rhyme, on patriotic themes.

In March 1801, Simcoe's military career seemed about to take a turn for the better. Pitt resigned on the 14th over the rejection of Catholic emancipation, and Henry Addington became prime minister. On the 23rd, at Wolford Lodge, Elizabeth gave birth to her seventh daughter. They named her Katherine, after the sixth daughter who had been buried at York, Upper Canada.[14]

On 10 January, Simcoe had replied to a letter from Henry Addington respecting Vice Admiral Horatio Lord Nelson:

I rejoice that Lord Nelson is to be employed & am much indebted to you for any conversation with him in which my name was mentioned for I believe him (whatever may be his foibles) to be governed by a true heroic and English Spirit ...[15]

Perhaps Simcoe counted Lady Hamilton as one of Nelson's foibles. He was now second in command of the Channel fleet; his superior was

Earl St. Vincent Admiral Sir John Jervis. Nelson had joined his flagship, *San Joseph,* at Plymouth. There he discussed the Baltic problem with Simcoe. Nelson later wrote Henry Addington that he was very much impressed by the General.[16]

Lieutenant General Grenville wrote on the 18th, that he had heard from the Duke of Kent that Simcoe would continue on the staff of the Western District. The command would pass to Simcoe "as the eldest [i.e. most senior] General on the Staff."[17]

Lord Clifford, writing on the 27th, congratulated Simcoe on being given the western command, and relayed a conversation he had had with Earl St. Vincent at Tor Abbey, one that he was not expected to pass on. St. Vincent raised the possibility of Simcoe taking a command in the Baltic. Clifford warned St. Vincent that Simcoe would decline it.[18]

The situation in the Baltic was serious. Denmark, Sweden and Russia had placed an embargo on British ships. The Danes had occupied Hamburg to prevent Britain trading with north Germany. Operations would be necessary to prevent an alliance being formed between the league of northern nations and the French. Simcoe, Clifford, St. Vincent (about to become First Lord of the Admiralty) and Prime Minister Addington, had discussed the situation at length. A fleet should be sent. Simcoe, as usual, recommended an operation far more massive than even Addington, his friend, could contemplate. He wanted 25,000 infantry, 10,000 cavalry and 5,000 volunteer engineers.

He recommended, as the first priority, "take absolute possession of Copenhagen ... Cronenburg and the Island of Zealand" and the destruction of the arsenal at Copenhagen. The Danes should be persuaded that a British force was an army of deliverance, because they had been forced into the alliance with Sweden and Russia for fear of being overrun by those countries. The British must be "Strong as the times" and if the islanders of Zealand were not convinced by "persuasive tactics" Britain should annex the island and deport the inhabitants. Strong stuff indeed.[19]

On 1 February Admiral Lord Nelson arrived in Tor Bay, on the *San Joseph* (he later transferred his flag to the *St. George*). He went ashore to meet with St. Vincent concerning the Baltic campaign. Nelson would be second in command of the fleet under Admiral Sir Hyde Parker, and His Lordship recommended embarking 10,000 troops. He thought Simcoe was the only general capable of leading such a venture.[20]

As Lord Clifford had predicted, Simcoe was reluctant. To Addington on 1 February he wrote that while His Lordship wanted him to command the troops for the Danish-Swedish-Russian expedition, especially as "Sir C. Grey" had declined:

I mentioned Stuart or Lord Moira, under whom I had rather Serve than Command, because in case of Command, really and truly, I should be at a loss for a second, should Government leave such a nomination to me, & therefore I should prefer the serving with either or both of those excellent Officers, who perfectly know that I would neither betray them, nor the Service of my King and Country.

He concluded his letter with: "It was with Sir Hyde Parker as Admiral, that I recently formed my best hopes of the Conquest of San Domingo..."[21] Simcoe had informed Pitt and others that he wanted foreign service, yet he backed away from this opportunity. On 12 March, Parker and Nelson sailed with fifteen ships of the line, two fifty-gun ships, frigates, brigs and 1,000 troops. A month later the Danes agreed to an armistice, thus avoiding a confrontation with the Russians in the Baltic.

Simcoe turned his attention to the home scene. Lord Rolle had "a rage for popularity" for he ordered his tenants to bring their grain to market at reduced prices, or risk non-renewal of their leases.[22] Law and order was vital, especially in a time of riots that came to a head in March and April. The main authority was Lord Lieutenant Fortescue, assisted by a number of deputies, law officers, magistrates and the military, and to a lesser extent by high constables and parish constables.

Simcoe inspected a large part of his command. On 10 March he sent a report to the adjutant general. Meanwhile, he wanted good maps for his officers to use. He had frequently produced his own operational and campaign maps. He had turned to Robert Clifford for assistance when he was expecting a French invasion. On a national scale, the Board of Ordnance was undertaking a trigonometrical survey of England. In 1791, a Royal Artillery officer, William Mudge, was appointed to the survey, and he became its director in 1798. Plymouth-born Mudge had begun working in Devon in 1795. On 28 August 1800, he advertised in the Exeter *Flying Post*:

... in order to execute the commands of the Master General of His Majesty's Ordnance for the Survey of Devon and Parts of their adjoining Counties, Somerset and Cornwall, to erect Staffs and Staffs with Flags attached to them ... is it [sic] therefore earnestly requested that no Person will molest or throw them down, as such Proceedings will unavoidably be productive of much inconvenience.

It was signed "Wm. Mudge, Captain of the Royal Artillery, Director of the Trigonometrical Survey, Dunkery Beacon, Aug. 22, 1800."[23]

The French were far ahead of England at scientific map making; their army had a corps of surveyors who added topographical detail that might be of military significance. In England, maps were produced by a publisher named John Cary. His maps were on a scale of five miles to the inch — and Napoleon had acquired a set of Cary maps of southern England.[24] Robert Clifford made Simcoe a set of base maps on which he could place relevant detail, rather than have his officers accept details on comprehensive maps that might not be accurate, and in any case were too busy to be read quickly. (As yet the Board of Ordnance maps were not available.) Clifford made him "Skeleton" maps using Cary's large ones as a base on which he retained all towns in capital letters on oil paper. These he engraved on large copper plates from which he could make any number of copies, and add such information as was required on each: "This could be of great use for officers going to outposts as in 5 minutes they may take their post from the general map & keep it in their orderly book." They were what Simcoe required — a general view at a glance.[25]

Simcoe sent his detailed plan, "The Defense of Devon" to Robert Clifford, who replied:

> You have noted the assailable parts, at least with respect of the south of Devon; am sorry the North of Devon has not been considered with equal accuracy, for though the Enemy may not invade by that part ... (particularly as Bristol was one of their grand objects Last War) it may be found necessary to bring convoys to the North by sea for the Defense of the County.

The Exe, the Teign, the Dart and the Yealm would afford landing places — "the Enemy having landed must send out foraging parties" for food and detachments to wage the war. Simcoe also sent to Clifford drawings of "entrenched camps" at Roborough Down and Buckland Down, which Clifford thought "mostly beautiful."[26]

Later, Clifford sent Simcoe the map, on two sheets,

> but the division is natural. I coloured the roads in the little one to show how much clearer it would look, and the roads you may wish to make military roads need only to be washed over with pale red which would make

them appear a sand colour over the yellow ... The rivers
are done with a pen rather soft.[27]

Simcoe received reports on more riots, and an eye-witness account
from a Mr. Fanshawe at Newton Ferrers — forwarded by Lord Clifford.
A feature of these uprisings was the lack of real violence, only plenty of
intimidation. One form was to force farmers to sign agreements to sell at
affordable prices. Many rioters belonged to the Volunteer Corps, and
even some of their officers, the very people expected to help calm the
situation. The Reverend Pratt, parish priest at Luppitt, characteristic of
most of the clergy, offered assistance for the restoration of tranquility. In
March, when serious riots broke out in Somerset and Devon, Simcoe
ordered troops to Cullompton, Honiton, Tiverton and Oakhampton,
and moved a squadron of cavalry from Dorchester, in Dorset, to Chard
and Ilminster, Somerset. Exeter mobs were descending on neighbouring
villages such as Exminster, Kenn and Broadclyst.

James Coleridge, writing on the 28th from his home at Ottery,
described how he dealt with a mob at Exmouth. He gave all who had
taken an oath, to exonerate themselves by bringing Coleridge their arms.
A Major Hull later sent Coleridge a letter warning him of a farmers'
meeting, to make decisions that would be disagreeable to the people,
resulting in more disturbances. His letter was carried by an "orderly," a
man whose job it was to deliver messages and await replies so that the
exchange might take only hours. Simcoe replied:

> It is not proper to trust people with arms from the Duke
> of York to the Drummer, who will not support the petty
> Constable in aid of the laws of the land — however I
> regret the measure they must in that case be disarmed.

Coleridge reported on other threats, and advised testing the
Volunteers, and if they refused to assist the civil power they should be
disarmed immediately. At a meeting in Ottery St. Mary, "The Gentlemen
and the farmers ... had agreed on an acceptable price of twelve shillings a
bushel for wheat, and "every inhabitant have it in proportion to their
families." Good sense was beginning to prevail. The people at Exmouth
told Coleridge:

> Give us whatever quantity the stocks in hand will afford
> and at a price by which we can obtain it, and we shall be
> satisfied. We will not accept any Subscription from the

gentry, because it enhances the price and is a hardship on them.

He blamed the trouble at Exmouth on "Hucksters" from Honiton, who had bought at a low price on the market, owing to threats from the mob, and would sell at a higher price in Exmouth. Many of the Volunteers agreed to support civil power. He wanted to believe them.[28]

To curb the unrest in Honiton, the local magistrates issued a declaration because they had heard of the "riotous Proceedings of the People tending to awe the Farmers, and by those Means to prevent them from bringing their provisions to market in the usual Manner":

> We are determined to the utmost of our Power, according to Law, to prevent any Force or Compulsion from being used to induce them to sell their Grain but at their own Choice; and that we will attend to give them the Protection which the Law affords.

However, they recommended to those who had been prevailed upon to join "any Riotous Proceeding of the Nature above stated" to cease such conduct, thus avoiding the consequences of such actions. The signatures of the magistrates read like a list of Simcoe friends: John B. Cholwich, Francis Rose Drewe, William Tucker, Reymundo Putt, Richard Graves, J. [John] Kennaway, J.G. Simcoe, Edward Honywood, and H. [Herman] Drewe.[29]

A troop of dragoons en route to Somerset would halt in Honiton on market day. Simcoe informed Cholwich: "Gentlemen were also going to be in attendance." They did not succeed; "with all our endeavours butter was sold to the mob for 8d" a pound, a result of intimidation. He wrote Fortescue that Devon and Somerset were in a state of anarchy. Yet hardly anybody seems to have been seriously hurt in all the disorderly behaviour. The lord lieutenant, and Simcoe, had their informers who reported that in Plymouth, dock workers were demanding higher wages and collective action over food prices. In Totnes the mobs turned on the corn merchants, one of whom, Giles Welsford, demanded prosecution of the alleged ringleaders. The riots began to subside in April. When Lord Fortescue sent a county justice, the Reverend Thomas Kitson, to investigate allegations in Totnes, he found that witnesses no longer wished to testify. Some felt intimidated, but others thought their grievances were being rectified.

In coastal Brixham, where John Underhay commanded, certain fishermen and townsmen, with some Volunteers, planned to pressure farmers to lower their prices. Underhay called a meeting where Volunteer officer Lieutenant Pridham produced an agreed price list for goods that he claimed had come from Dartmouth. The majority decided to put these prices to local farmers, traders and merchants as though they had been recommended. Three Volunteer officers, Pridham, Captain Sanders (Underhay's deputy) and William Collier, accompanied deputations to the farmers, traders and merchants, claiming they went to prevent violence. Simcoe then learned of a plot for the Brixham men to join forces with sailors of the fleet when it anchored in Tor Bay. The action was supposedly foiled by a change in the wind that sent the fleet down the channel.

Lord Fortescue ordered the Volunteer officers prosecuted for rioting. Sanders, Pridham and Collier were tried and acquitted. The Brixham Volunteers were disbanded. Underhay, who had played no part in the riots, lost the command Simcoe had never wished him to have in the first place.[30]

TWENTY
A BRIEF PEACE

As the spring of 1801 progressed, Simcoe was groping for ways of curbing the unrest. He wrote to Lord Forestcue:

> I trust under Your Lordship's recommendation Gentlemen of spirit and distinction will readily and universally stand forth on especial occasions and execute and enoble the Constitutional office of Constable.

Such men should unite with the military to bring about good order. Yet he sympathised with the plight of the common people. Their grievances were not against the Crown and State. They were not planning a French-style revolution, but they were vulnerable to professional agitators. He relayed to the Duke of Portland, the home secretary, an opinion Lord Somerville had sent him:

> The loyalty of our common people is meritorious. I can trace nothing like subversion in their riots. Their

221

condition is truly pitiable. Not a loaf of bread at any bakers, not a loaf of bread to be seen in the markets ...[2]

There had been trouble at Plymouth docks, but the men had admitted "improper conduct" to the local commander, Richard England, a major general and another colleague from Simcoe's Upper Canada days. Simcoe had been less understanding of the dockyard workers, who, he thought should be crushed because their work was essential. Cornwall was now quieter and the problems were subsiding in Devon and Somerset. He admitted that people were "driven by want." Honiton Magistrate Honeywood wrote that the better off inhabitants had subscribed for the relief of "the lower orders" and the community "without the least interference with the farmers at our markets." Simcoe approved and made a "handsome donation."[3]

Colonel James Coleridge acknowledged that professional agitators had been at work in Ottery St. Mary:

> ... the Ottery mob was visited by delegates from Exeter who had come there for the *express purpose* of fixing the prices the name of one is Baker, he is a joiner & lives in Exe Lane, Exeter ... Another person came from Chard or Ilminster by the name of Ewings. They neither of them *acted openly* & were disappointed in their intentions as the plan was resisted and compleatly [sic] defeated.

People realised there was a scarcity, and rioting did no good, which would lead to the restoration of order. Coleridge also told Simcoe that young Francis, at The King's School, had had "two more of his teeth removed by Mr. Hodge." Reverend George Coleridge, Francis's headmaster, wrote on 30 April, "It must give you, Sir and all Xtrian Parents great, satisfaction to find the subject of religious education in the public schools started."[4]

While Ottery and vicinity was quieter, in Plymouth strong measures were indicated. John Bastard informed Simcoe that the Volunteers had marched against the dockyard men. In ale houses the toast was "Damnation to all who will or have taken the oath of allegiance." Simcoe asked Lord Fortescue for a list of magistrates and "Gentry" willing to act as Peace Officers, complaining of the "listlessness and want of energy in the higher classes of people."[5]

Simcoe wrote to several men of influence asking what was

happening in their neighbourhoods. The Reverend T.E. Clark, of Clayhidon, in the Blackdown Hills, wrote that his parishioners had behaved well. The Reverend John Land of Hemyock found the poor suffering but they had refused to take part in "the tumultuous & disgraceful Proceedings of that Town." Robert Russell, an Exeter carrier, offered the use of his horses and wagons.[6]

Parliament had passed an act "Making better provision for the Maintenance of the poor and for diminishing the Consumption of Bread and Corn" in January, but moving through the system took time. People were to be encouraged to use cheaper substitutes for wheat, oats and barley. The Gentlemen of Exeter raised a total of £3,000 to import corn and flour from outside Devonshire, one of many schemes to alleviate the plight. Poverty now was not confined to parish poor, but embraced a wider group normally self-reliant. By 9 May the efforts of leaders of society had been effective. Simcoe's role had been as coordinator and adviser. The overall responsibility lay with Lord Fortescue whose work Simcoe praised as a "Herculean task." Fortescue was to visit Wolford Lodge the following day, and Simcoe was sending "a man to meet you at the Half Way House. He will guide you the Simcoe's new way" — a route bypassing Honiton. At this time, politicians were mooting another appointment for Simcoe. He heard that he might be placed in command of Ireland. Nothing came of it, and he wrote to Lord Fortescue, "I presume I am too young.".[7] He was forty-nine years old.

The Duke of York had lauded Simcoe's appointment to the West Country, and he appeared quite content to leave him there. Overall command carried prestige but day-to-day chores did not. Mr. W. James of the Wellington Volunteers in Somerset complained that his corps had been issued with Prussian muskets that were too heavy when bayonets were attached. Where to house French prisoners was still plaguing him:

> The removing of so large a number of prisoners as are now at Plymouth would always be difficult if not impossible but the intersection of the County by the Mountains of Dartmoor will probably be the means of preventing them falling into the hands of the enemy. [8]

He had made a point of becoming familiar with many leaders of the clergy. Now he stressed the important role they must play in the event of invasion. On 30 July 1801, he wrote to the Bishop of Bath and Wells that the clergymen should stay in their parishes for as long as possible, and seeking his opinion, to relay it to the members of the Somerset Defense

Committee, that would meet at Taunton Castle. In August he sent instructions for the county deputy lieutenants to follow if the French landed. Alarm posts should be set up within the Hundreds, parties of Volunteers would support local magistrates, crossroads were to be destroyed in Devon, Somerset and Cornwall, the three counties now under Simcoe's command.

He had heard from Robert Clifford in June, who thanked him for sketches of Alexandria. On 4 August, Clifford wrote again, from London, to discourse on continental troop movements. He had acquired books for Simcoe, gratifying for a man who loved enlarging his library. Another correspondent was William Osgoode, who had retired as Chief Justice of Lower Canada and was living at 16 Mitre Court, Paper Buildings, in London's Temple.[9]

Bishop Fisher, of Exeter, remained in regular contact with Simcoe. He was dismayed that the churches of the city were too small to accommodate the "lower orders." Soldiers garrisoned in Exeter should be able to attend divine service, or he might provide them with a chapel. An unused church near the Fore Street might suffice. Several clergymen would, for the pay the government allowed, gladly officiate.

Among Simcoe's close friends was Archdeacon George Moore, whose home was in Cathedral Close, near where the General had grown up. On 26 September, Moore had written him, recalling seeing Captain John Simcoe's death notice in the *Gentlman's Magazine* : "I see by the paper that Lord Fortescue intends to honour the General Court at the hospital on Tuesday with his presence in order to dispose of Mr. [William] Pitfield's Legacy." Pitfield, the apothecary, would have been gratified, "had he lived to see the day."[10]

On 1 October, Britain and France signed preliminary peace terms. Now Simcoe was able to turn his mind to acquiring more land. When he had enquired about purchasing common, or waste, lands before he left for Canada, the time was not right. Now, the government had passed the Enclosure Act of 1801. Large areas of the Parish of Dunkeswell could be purchased and fenced. Commissioners had been appointed to process claims. General Simcoe's name was on a list of applicants as "The Lord of the Manor of Dunkeswell otherwise Bowerhayes." Of his properties, the list specified "occupiers or tenants of each."

These included Wolford Lodge, Little Wolford, Shaptons and Marleshayne occupied by Simcoe himself and Thomas Scadding; Bywood occupied by Henry Farant; Manleys by Richard Webber; Dunkeswell Grange by William Marks; Horwoods by William Burrough, and other smaller properties. On the list were the commissioners' observations on timber and other trees on the waste lands. Simcoe's claim was "Allowed, except as to the proportional Parts of the Soil claimed by several Proprietors of Lands in Right of their Lands, & allowed them by us; & except the proportional Value of the Trees on the Waste, to which such Proprietors of Lands (being allowed their claims to the Soil) will be entitled under such claims." Simcoe was able to enlarge his already considerable estates. In addition to gains in Dunkeswell, he acquired Cleave and Moors (occupier Thomas Scadding) in Awliscombe, to the south, and in Hemyock village, where he already owned the Castle. On the 1802 Land Tax Return of Hemyock, Simcoe is shown as the occupier, although he did not reside in the Castle. In 1803 the occupier was Brian Mordan.[11]

In his work *General Views of Agriculture of Devon*, C. Vancouver wrote that Simcoe had enclosed 1,200 acres of the Blackdown Hills, and planned to build two or three farmhouses, and annex 300 acres as holdings for each. The commissioners valued the waste at six shillings per acre. Under proper management the value would treble in a few years. The author admired the General's "culture of exotic as well as native trees in the country."[12]

Early in 1802, Elizabeth took her daughters and little Henry to Budleigh Salterton. She was unwell and hoping that the bracing air of the coast would improve her. She was back at Wolford Lodge in time for Simcoe's fiftieth birthday, on 25 February 1802. Simcoe had asked the Reverend John Pratt, vicar of Dunkeswell, to conduct a service suitable for a Christian educated by a "most pious and excellent mother":

> There is a text in Leviticus I believe that particularly enforces purity of heart in those who inspire to military commands, as mine in all views is a military family it may not be amiss in a more especial manner to inculcate the 'Remembrance of a Creator' to those who shall engage in the solemn duties of protecting their Country, at the times from enemy insurpation.

The service was held in the drawing room. Simcoe had decided on a family chapel made from the Cistercian ruins. The burial plot, where John Cornwall Simcoe lay, would be adjacent to the chapel. Work was well under way, and he planned to have a service of dedication when it was finished.

The threat of invasion was receding. On 27 March 1802, Britain and France signed the Treaty of Amiens, which bought a temporary peace.

About the same time a twelve-year-old boy named John Bailey became a member of the domestic staff at Wolford Lodge, rising from cleaner of cutlery to coachman. Literate, although his spelling reflects the broad Devonshire he spoke, he left a memoir invaluable in telling the Simcoe family story from 1802 to 1850.[13] The original Bailey manuscript is the property of Margaret Partridge, a descendant of John Graves Simcoe:

> ... now genral Simcoe when living foloed the same plan by early rising he formly very ofton would be ether out riding or walking at 5 or 6 o clock in the morning with mr. scading planing about the planting of the plantacions and ofton genral and mrs. simcoe would be out taking a ride in the canadia snow slides when the snow wase deep thoos canadia sno slides as aney one may supoze do not go on hevey and dead byt slip on the snow that a poney fold very well draw it ...

Bailey recalled that when Simcoe stopped to speak to a labourer, the man, as was expected, removed his hat. Simcoe asked him to put his hat back on but the labourer felt he could not wear it while talking with the General, whereupon Simcoe took off his own hat while he and the worker had their chat. Bailey thought Simcoe "a very liberal gentleman." However, when trades people called at Wolford Lodge, Simcoe, fond of military precision, had them march to the house two by two, with fife and drum. They received their orders and marched off in the same fashion.

The day the Treaty of Amiens was signed, a gentleman, John Voss, wrote enquiring about the history of Hemyock Castle. Simcoe was convinced, no surprise, that it was of Roman origin. It resembled a drawing he had seen of a Roman fortification near Cairo. Voss, who had been certain the castle was of 11th-or-12th century origin, diplomatically agreed with Simcoe. (In fact, the castle was a manor house of Norman origin. A licence to "crenellate" (fortify) was granted by King Richard II at the close of the 14th century.)

On 3 April, from 5 Edwards Street, Portman Square, London, Robert Clifford wrote that he had obtained books his friend wanted. He could not find Kirwam's two works on manure (part of the Agricultural Revolution had been applying this fertiliser, rather than depending on fallow of fields). Robert was sending Barnel in four volumes "to complete your set on Forsyth's War (unbound)." He had found *Claireux on Geometry* for Miss [Eliza] Simcoe, and two copies of *The Battle of*

Culloden. The books had cost two pounds, which he asked Simcoe to send to his sister, Laura, at Ugbrooke House.[14]

Command of the Western District ceased on 24 May. Simcoe's letter of gratitude appeared in the Exeter *Flying Post* on the 20th. He thanked Major General Richard England, at Plymouth, for the "support and assistance he has uniformly received from him during its continuance ..." and he extended his appreciation to the staff officers, the Royal Artillery, the Cavalry and Infantry for their "spirit and discipline ... seconded by the Militia, yeomanry and Volunteers ... any army of France ... would speedily have been destroyed, and all apprehension of invasion would for ever have been at rest."[15]

His success in Devon in May was undermined by word that his beloved Queen's Rangers were to be disbanded, to take effect by 25 October. The lieutenant colonel commandant was now David Shank, while Samuel Smith was the major. Shank would return to Britain, but Smith and most of the other officers would remain in Upper Canada, with substantial land grants to give them a stake in the province's future. John McGill, on the Legislative Council, was particularly effective in handling accounts and as an administrator.[16]

Now that England was at peace, Simcoe was able to look to his estates, and take a holiday. In July at the invitation of the Royal family, he went with Elizabeth to Weymouth for a regatta. He went riding with the King and the Duke of Gloucester, while Elizabeth visited Maiden Castle, an Iron Age fort and the largest prehistoric monument in England. Miss Mary Hunt joined them for dinner. She was now a tutor in the household of Princess Charlotte, the only child of the Prince of Wales and his hoyden wife, Caroline of Brunswick The Prince and his daughter were also at Weymouth, the reason Miss Hunt was there.[17]

Simcoe had a talk with the King about being appointed Commander in Chief in Ireland, where, he informed Elizabeth's cousin William Walcot, Henry Addington had told him he would only be sent if Ireland was in danger:

> ... be it so, no man has more prosperously attained the object of his public life than myself, and I thank God, without bestowing a thought on the unworthy treatment I have met with from Ministers.[18]

After they returned home, Simcoe was on edge. He wondered whether he should run for parliament again. He was negotiating through William Walcot to sell Elizabeth's properties in Northamptonshire, so that he could consolidate his holdings in Devon. He had found the enclosures a great advantage:

> The Commissioners who reduce all its parts to money, for the purpose of division, have estimated my allotments in their present state, at upwards of Five Thousand Pounds per annum; and I have purchased all that has been sold, and mean to bid for the remainder that is to be sold to pay the expence; the amount will be less than Five Thousand Pounds.

He would thus unite Wolford, Bywood and Windsor, nearly 10,000 acres "in a ring fence ... I wish you could come and see us and suggest agricultural improvements.":

> I have no estate that does not pay me nearer five than four per cent; and had I no family to provide for, for which purpose it is right to accumulate from income, I could extend my purchases to an immediate four percent, to any amount.

He was succeeding as Lord of the Manor, yet so many promises had gone unfulfilled, even though his close friend was the Prime Minister. At Weymouth, he told Walcot, he had paid his duty:

> ... and met as usual, with the most kind treatment, from the best friend I have ever known: His Majesty advised me not to hurry in selling, as many persons must soon want to purchase Estates on their return from foreign stations, and told me to have my Estate valued, above all things.[19]

Wolford Chapel was now complete and the time had come for its dedication. Aunt Margaret Graves arrived from Bath, her first visit to Wolford Lodge since she had moved out while the Simcoes were in Upper Canada. Simcoe wrote to the Reverend John Pratt requesting him to conduct the ceremony "before our most valued Relation Mrs. Graves" wished to return to Bath:

> The chapel stands on the ancient precincts of a former church and over the bones of those who have departed

centuries ago; circumstances that led me to prefer this
site to the convenience of placing it adjoining the house.

The family motto inscribed in the chapel was "as for me and my
house, we will serve the Lord" (Joshua 24:15). The ceremony took place
on 23 August 1802.[20]

After Mrs. Graves left Wolford Lodge, the General and Mrs. Simcoe
rode to Ugbrooke to visit the Cliffords. In the autumn they went
travelling accompanied by Eliza. When his gout flared up, Simcoe
returned home, while Elizabeth and Eliza went to London. On 11
November, Simcoe informed William Walcot that he would soon be
sending an abstract of the title deeds to Aldwinkle, Elizabeth's birth place.
He was writing in a comfortable chair, reading history and waiting for his
gout to subside.[21]

Robert Clifford wrote on 30 November from the Hotel d'Orléans.
He was taking advantage of the peace to visit his old haunts. Of the
general situation in France, he warned his friend that French policy was
the "Destruction of England."[22]

With the spring, Simcoe was spending considerable time in London.
Robert Clifford's prediction, unfortunately, turned out to be right. On 18
May 1803, Britain declared war on France. Britain refused to part with
Malta, and Napoleon was interfering in the affairs of Italy and
Switzerland. This news sent shivers up Simcoe's spine. Robert Clifford was
still in France. When he failed to arrive on the first mail packet after news
of the resumption of hostilities became public, garbled rumours spread.
Three English gentlemen had been hanged as spies, one of whom was
likely Robert. During an emergency debate in parliament, John Bastard
spoke on the fate of the English gentlemen. Simcoe drafted a letter to Lord
Clifford commiserating over the fate of his "unfortunate brother."[23]

Out of the blue, Robert arrived in London. He had been detained,
but a former officer of Dillon's (Irish Jacobite) Regiment recognised him.
He was temporarily released on Friday 20 May, on the understanding
that he would not try to leave France until the next mail packet sailed on
Monday. Robert boarded an English vessel that same Friday night, and
brought along:

> ... 200 weight of maps, plans and manuscripts of France
> and its environs which would in all probability have got me
> to the Temple [prison] ... and as I had an order to let them
> pass at Dover, from the Treasury, they are safe in England
> without them being opened since they left Paris ...

With the help of Lord St. Vincent, Robert gained free entrance to the Admiralty, which "saved me £20 tax for my maps etc ... I always fall on my legs, though sometimes gouty."[24]

Now that French threats had to be taken seriously again, Simcoe's mind turned to national defense. On 7 June he wrote to the Duke of York to suggest building a set of towers along the coast, like those the Romans had erected in the Mediterranean. In 1794, the British had had difficulty taking such a tower at Cape Mortella, Corsica. He recalled that a tower had once stood in Plymouth, and he was enclosing some plans.[25] (A series of Martello towers was built along the coast in 1804, and in the 1830s around Kingston, Upper Canada.)

The General and Mrs. Simcoe had visited London, where they leased a house in Somerset Street, off Portman Square. They saw his old friend Thomas Milles, before going to Stowe to see the Marquis and Marchioness of Buckingham, thence to Bath and Wolford. To William Walcot, Simcoe wrote that he was fully occupied with enclosures. He was acquiring another 800 acres, and planning roads and out-buildings for the various new farms. (Enclosures have a bad reputation for depriving the common folk of grazing land for their animals. The old system was inefficient and needed reform. Simcoe's reports on creating new farms added far more to the agricultural economy than what was lost through privatisation of the common lands.)

Simcoe told Walcot that he had received a gift from "our Justices" some old armour he would "place in Battle array in the passage which leads to my Library." He curtailed his book purchases when a farmhouse that burned down had to be replaced. He had bought Gorwell Farm in Hemyock, and some smaller properties, all with tenants. While in London, he trusted John Scadding implicitly, even to dealing with the enclosure commissioners, and with Lawyer Christopher Flood.

Simcoe was again a lieutenant general on the staff, by authority of the King. His subordinates were Major Generals Thomas Garth, cavalry, Richard England, infantry, and John Calcraft, assisted by Messrs Grosvenor and Cawell, militia. The lord lieutenant reactivated the Devon Standing Committee, usually chaired by Fortescue himself. Again returns were compiled. Simcoe's days were filled with inspections, surveys and field exercises. He had little time to spend with his family. Constant inspections proved the best method of keeping a good standard of efficiency. He travelled extensively, into Cornwall as well as Somerset and Devon — the inspecting officer for the entire Western District. Recruitment resumed for Volunteer Corps and individual companies, especially of light infantry. In the orders he issued, he stressed devotion to duty and discipline.

John Bailey described the 1st and 2nd companies of the Honiton Volunteers, who exercised at Wolford. After practising firing, the General would treat them to "a nice dinner have tables fixe throo the avennue for 2 hundred of them the band at the frunt of the house playing some livley tuns ..." the Luppitt Artillery under Captain Pearce would meet at the battery on St. Cyres Hill, to practise and to fire salutes on the King's birthday. Bailey described a mock battle between "French" and "British." The soldiers numbered 10,000, the spectators 20,000. The French retreated to Hembury Fort when the firing grew too hot. Just where Simcoe could have put 10,000 troops, let alone so many onlookers on a less -than-spacious site is a mystery.[26] The various local companies were part of the Devon Corps. The Volunteer Pay List and the Returns have been preserved in the Public Record Office.[27] A typical infantry company consisted of a captain, lieutenant, ensign, three sergeants, three corporals and sixty-three privates.

Simcoe was again in touch with William Mudge, now a major, who offered such "Topographical assistance as the material of my office are able to afford." Mudge would soon be based at Chudleigh, where he planned to consult Robert Clifford, who meanwhile, had been arrested as a spy. Lord St. Vincent had asked him to undertake "A Grand Military Expedition through Kent." Robert wrote to Simcoe on 13 August that he had been at Chatham, Rochester and Dover: "The day after my return I went to Sheerness, where I was taken up for a spy, but was soon liberated as I had a letter from Lord St. Vincent to the Commissioner." Sheerness, on the Island of Sheppey, in the Thames estuary, he thought indefensible, which implied that Chatham was insecure.[28]

Property owners were not always happy to find fortifications on their territory. John Perring, who owned land at the mouth of the River Yealm, was not pleased to find a battery under construction on his side of the river. Simcoe had intended placing it on the Plymouth side, and when he decided it should be across the water, Perring was livid at not being consulted. Major General Mercer, of the Royal Engineers, had been too zealous in carrying out his orders. Work began before Perring could be notified. John Bastard, a mutual friend, smoothed the situation, but only temporarily. Perring complained to Lord Hobart, now Secretary at War, thus involving the Army Legal Department. Simcoe wrote many letters; fewer would have sufficed had Perring not been wealthy and a former Lord Mayor of London.[29]

Throughout the summer, new companies were raised. Defense

returns arrived at Wolford Lodge, again the command post. One order required "the Name of any Foreigner resident within their respective parishes in which Description Americans are included."[30]

To the Devon Standing Committee, Simcoe recommended a chain of signals along the coast — a system of beacons that dated back many centuries and had been used when the Spanish Armada had threatened invasion. Devon beacons were at Culmstock and Dumpdon Hill, both near Wolford Lodge. In Somerset, beacons shone on high points at Castle Neroche (in the Blackdowns), Borough Chapel, Glastonbury Tor and Beacon Hill near Shepton Mallet.

By September, Whitehall sent permission to extend recruitment to 12,000 men. From St. Mary's Castle, near the Scilly Isles off the toe of Cornwall, Simcoe received entreaties from Daniel Lyman, the captain in command of the islands. The tone of his letter implied that he had served with Simcoe in North America. He wanted the resources to defend the Scillies. Simcoe was sympathetic but, shades of Upper Canada, defending the Scillies was not a priority, and he could do nothing for Lyman.[31] Meanwhile, on 3 October he called a meeting at Wolford Lodge of representatives from all the parishes in the Hundred.

The visitors felt reassured to have the commander in chief resident in their area, but people in certain parts of Devonshire felt very neglected. On 19 November, Lieutenant Colonel H.J. Downe, commanding the 1st North Devon Regiment of Volunteer Infantry, wrote from his headquarters at Bideford. He complained that he had not "a single regiment of the line or artillery of any kind on the north coast as far as Lands End." He had only Volunteers to depend on and no speedy means of communication should the enemy land. Downe, too, considered a system of coastal beacons. Simcoe again was sympathetic, but official thinking favoured a direct assault from the Continent, not a threat from the French using Ireland as a base.[32] The war with France dragged on, dominating a lifetime for the young as well as their elders.

TWENTY-ONE
UNIVERSALLY LAMENTED

If John Scadding was a right-hand man, Christopher Flood was another. To Henry Addington on 3 December 1803, Simcoe wrote:

> I can only repeat that I was much beholden to Mr. Flood for his attention to my children when for years I was absent from them in Public Service in Canada. This obligation is of the most permanent nature.

Flood had been a useful counselor during the food riots, and he continued giving Simcoe good professional service. Now he sent the General a copy of new legislation to assist him in calculating his income tax. It had first been levied in 1799, and abolished in 1802. Income tax was introduced again in 1803, and Simcoe had appealed to the lawyer. As the owner of so many pieces of property, and with his army commissions, Simcoe's finances were complex. [1]

He received a letter dated 5 December from Charles Yorke, member of Parliament and for a short time Prime Minister Addington's secretary at war. A firm opponent of Pitt, he was now acting home secretary. Yorke's letter concerned an offer from Robert Russell to form a "Corps of Waggoners." His Majesty approved, but the Corps would not need to be armed or exercised. Nevertheless the members would not be exempt from "Militia or Ballots." Officers could be commissioned by the lord lieutenant. Russell's patriotism was also business. Aiding the cause would lead to opportunities for gain later on. In time he was a successful banker in Exeter. [2]

Simcoe made his last will and testament in 1803. Elizabeth would be his sole executrix, and apart from legacies to his children, his principal beneficiary. William Walcot of Oundle, John Pollexfen Bastard of Kitley, and longtime friend Thomas Milles, were appointed trustees of Simcoe's properties in England and of lands granted to him in Upper Canada.

In February 1804, John Bastard, in his role as Colonel of the 1st Devon Militia, reminded him of the thorny matter of quartering troops at local inns. So many troops were squeezed into the district between the rivers Dart and Yealm that officers were allowing their men to find their own lodgings. As the district had but one "Pot House Ale House" he might have to move some troops inland. Inn keepers did not mind billeting soldiers who were stationed for a time, but they objected to provisioning troops that were just passing through. For the first they received allowances, but all too often they served the transients without remuneration. They complained to Simcoe that they could not afford the expense. The number of inns in Honiton "does not exceed 21 and 15 are very small pot houses." They asked to be relieved of the burden of the troops passing and re-passing daily. [3]

Following the renewal of the war, discipline had become a problem in some of the Volunteer Corps. Unlike the breaches of discipline during the food riots of 1801, those of 1804 were a more general form of rowdiness. Acting Secretary Yorke recommended that infractions be dealt with by regimental court martial. In March, a drunken volunteer had struck Sir John Kennaway, the high sheriff of the county and a neighbour of the Simcoes. A retired servant in the East India Company, Sir John had purchased Escot House from Sir George Yonge. While Kennaway's attacker was in jail awaiting a regimental court martial, another volunteer incited people to release him. Magistrate Lord Rolle dealt with the "inciter."

Colonel Tyrwhitt, of the Stannary Volunteers, finding two offenders guilty at their court martial, sentenced them to corporal punishment, and ordered them drummed out of the corps. Simcoe admitted that even the few lashes administered had caused grumbling in the ranks.[4] When Lord Clifford had asked his friend to help him get a King's commission, Simcoe had replied that he did not need one, as volunteers were not subject to military law. Yet military law governs sentencing at a court martial. Either the law had changed, or the court martial was less than legal.

Some of Simcoe's correspondence dealt with the health of the troops.

His Inspector of Hospitals, J. Borland, M.D., submitted a report on the condition of the barracks and hospitals. He had already visited Truro and Pendennis, in Cornwall, and he recommended enlarging the hospital at Berry Head. It could accommodate only nineteen men, but it should contain "5 sick men for every 100 men the barracks can accomodate." He wanted separate circular cooking houses, and ranges of "railways" erected along the length of the barracks "on which beds and bedding ought to be exposed to the air in fine weather; as there was no room for cleaning sheds, iron hooks could be placed alongside the railways for men to attach their belts when cleaning them."

Most of the rooms were at ground level, which meant that the floors became encrusted with dirt. Scrapers and dry brushes would serve "rather than constant washing which encouraged a damp atmosphere and consequently invites disease." [5]

On 31 July, Elizabeth gave birth to their eleventh and last child. Anne (sometimes spelt Ann) was "received into the church" on 30 July 1805.[6] Incidentally, after losing John Cornwall Simcoe, none of the family letters refer to inoculation for Henry, the second Katherine, or Anne. Their parents may have decided that they would risk catching smallpox in the course of events, rather than by what was known as elective infection.

By August 1804, Simcoe had learned that Lord George Lennox was dying. He wrote to ask the Duke of York that he be considered as Lennox's replacement. He was informed, rather tersely, that his application would be submitted to His Majesty with others from general officers. In time, an impersonal circular reached him, addressed merely to "Sir":

> I have received the Commander in Chief's direction to request that you will adopt such Precautions & give out such orders as you may judge necessary for the Preservation of the Game in the District under your Command and to prevent the interference of the Officers with Manorial Rights of the Gentlemen of the Country and above all to secure the Farmers from any

inconvenience and damage which might arise from Officers and Soldiers trespassing over their lands ... [7]

Fortunately, Simcoe had the comfort of good friends. Vicary Gibbs, then living at Bromley, Kent, wrote happily of his appointment as Chief Justice at Chester: " ... in the point of emolument I am a considerable loser" (but the job led eventually to his appointment as Attorney General).

The Bishop of Exeter sent the Simcoes an aqua tint of Niagara Falls, the work of his younger brother, Captain George Fisher, Royal Artillery. Elizabeth, in particular, admired his artistry. She remembered George making the sketch ten years before when he was stationed in Upper Canada. Mrs. Fisher, the Bishop added, sent her best regards to the General and Mrs. Simcoe, "and the young ladies, not forgetting the little Captain [Francis]." [8]

From London, Robert Clifford enquired of his brother: "You do not mention the General, what is become of him, I fear he will not be pleased at the change of Ministry." [9] Henry Addington, rigid and high Tory, was not the man to head an administration in wartime. With some encouragement he resigned, and accepted a peerage — pushed upstairs as Lord Sidmouth. Pitt was again the prime minister, which was bad news for Simcoe, who could not expect any advancement from him.

For Christmas 1804, the family took a holiday in Bath, a departure from their usual vast house parties where Simcoe staged masquerades on patriotic themes. Eliza, now twenty, was the recorder. (Her diary, with sketches, belongs to descendant Margaret Partridge.) "Papa," Eliza wrote on 29 November, was not well enough to go to the Pump [Room]." Instead he "sent for the waters," which were supposed to restore the imbiber to good health. On 11 December Major Henry Darling, the General's A.D.C., joined them, bringing dispatches. On 21 December, "Papa, Major Darling and Francis went to the top of Malvern where is the remains of an old camp..." [10] The view from the top of the Malvern Hills was very fine (thought to have been the inspiration for the work of Sir Edward Elgar, patriotic music Simcoe would have admired). Francis had just completed his first term at Eton. In contrast to his father's experience, under the popular headmaster, the Reverend Joseph Goodall, Francis passed some of the happiest days of his life. [11]

DUELLING OVER DUNG?

Returning to his work, Simcoe confronted a trivial problem, again the question over who should benefit from dung left where large numbers of horses congregated. The dung in question was on Woodbury Common, his adversary, no surprise, was Lord Rolle. As the principal landowner in the area, Rolle complained that Simcoe had authorised the removal of the dung but, as the lord of the manor, the dung was his, to sell or distribute to local people. Rolle wanted clarification on the question of "importance to every British Subject whether the orders of a General is to overturn the Lord of the Manor's established right etc."[12]

The tedious correspondence reinforces the picture of Simcoe as a man with a patient streak, as the letters over clarification piled up. Lord Rolle's staff had blocked some who attempted to remove more dung. Finally, the matter was referred to the Duke of York. The vague response from His Grace's Quartermaster General Brownrigg was: "conceiving it was the custom to dispose of it for the advantage of the public." No one had the right to dispose of the dung without the authority of the commander in chief, but, general practice was that dung usually formed part of the remuneration given to the proprietors or occupiers of land under culture and the lord of the manor where it was common land. The purchase price should be reclaimed and placed at Lord Rolle's disposal.

Simcoe probably expected this verdict — after the defense of property rights from the circular on the subject that he had received. Records showed that, elsewhere in the country, dung had been sold and the proceeds passed to the quartermaster general's office. Finally, from Whitehall, Simcoe received orders dated 4 July 1805:

> ...in making arrangements for ground on Woodbury Common ... the dung made at camps shall be at the disposal of the Proprietor care being taken that the sum of money to be paid by the public is decreased in Proportion to the calculated amount of this advantage. [13]

The relationship between Simcoe and Rolle grew so bad that John Bailey, in his idiosyncratic spelling, recalled Rolle's challenge: "... there was a duel chaling but Lord role offered to fight with his fiestes but that way general simcoe would not except..." He was quite right. Gentlemen used swords or pistols; fists were for ruffians. (At the coronation of Queen

Victoria, Lord Rolle, nearing age ninety, tripped on his robes while ascending the steps of the throne and rolled to the bottom. Thus fell the rolling Rolle, fair game for punsters.)

NEW HOPES

In March, 1805, the Earl of Moira informed Simcoe that the death of the member of Parliament for Honiton left an "open seat" and he offered him the chance to stand as candidate. Simcoe declined, as he had already told Mr. Flood to "exert himself in favour of [candidate] Mr. Bradshaw." He gave Moira to understand that had His Lordship been in Pitt's administration his response might have been different.[14]

Simcoe, meanwhile, dreamed of a magnificent library to house his growing collection of fine books. He had asked an Exeter man, John Kendall, to prepare plans. John was the son of Edward Kendall, who had been stonemason for the Dean and Chapter house of Exeter Cathedral. John Kendall, in his father's footsteps, had been Cathedral stonemason. He had also studied under James Paine of London, a designer of country houses. On 23 July 1805, Kendall submitted his plans, with the estimated cost £170.[15] The record does not show whether Simcoe accepted the offer, but John Bailey later wrote of a magnificent room at Wolford Lodge, created during renovations.

Robert Clifford, now at 10 Welbeck Street, London, had acquired two more "military works" for his friend. He had also approached a stonemason about a window Simcoe had designed for his library, which would cost £200.[16]

Life was now comparatively quiet at Wolford Lodge. Simcoe had given up hope of a more prestigious command, preferably active service overseas, but he continued doing his duty as commander of the West of England. Military exercises were still important in the training of his troops. He received Lord Fortescue's permission to use suitable areas at East Budleigh, Budleigh Salterton, Colaton Raleigh and Aylesbeare — all convenient to his coastal retreat.

A weak point in his defences was Berry Head. Despite failing health, Lord Lennox visited the site and reported to Simcoe that the steep ascent from the beach was "not so cut away as to prevent people ascending and descending" but it could be defended adequately with "hand-grenades and pikes"…[17] (Berry Head was not put to the test, except by large colonies of sea birds who assault the cliffs annually.)

Life in the West of England was reasonably calm, but news from overseas signalled great rejoicing. Lord Nelson had been victorious at the Battle of Trafalgar; euphoria dampened by Nelson's death. John Bailey recalled that people within earshot mistook Simcoe's exuberant celebrations for the arrival of the French:

> … genereal simcoe sent to captain pearce to send the Luppitt artulery with thare cannon at the end of St. sirues hill thare to fire a salute it wase then 8 o'clock at night the people of honiton was rather alarmed hearing the cannon so very near them the guns wase herd very plain at axminster and many parts of devonshire general simcoe hade a very grand dinner party all the head gentery of the neiburhood wase present the greet new room wase fitted up buetefule moor than five hundred lamps lighted up in the room.…

The lamps were set up to form a crown and G.R. (George Rex). Some fifty carriages brought guests to a grand ball. Outside Wolford Lodge, round a great bonfire, more cannons were fired, Bailey recorded, with "greet joy." The servants worked very had because the following morning they had to prepare for a "Young Ladys ball."

Wolford Lodge was then undergoing renovations. Lady Clifford enquired how the work was progressing. To help out, Lord Clifford was sending the General "Sir Joshua Reynolds account of Vanbrough buildings" for his perusal. "Pardon all faults, (Amase?) is strumming the harp and all the children dancing and making such a noise I can hardly write."[18]

William Mudge was still working on the survey of Devon. On 14 November 1805, Lawrence Palk of Haldon, south of Exeter, informed Simcoe that he had sent Major Mudge's plans to Major Darling's office at Exeter as "you will direct that Lord Clifford may convey them to Wolford Lodge." Palk had penciled in some alterations and added a new road that ran from Exminster over the Exminster Marsh to the River Exe where there was a regular ferry to Topsham. Robert Clifford may have studied the plans in his capacity of consultant to John Cary, the map publisher. Palk was enthusiastic over an idea Simcoe had for a triumphal arch, to be erected on the Plymouth Road in honour of the late Lord Nelson.[19]

Simcoe was on his way to London when Lord Nelson's body arrived, preserved, not in the good navy rum of legend, but in a cask of good French brandy. The funeral was set for 9 January 1806 at St. Paul's Cathedral. To his chagrin he was:

… ranked as a squire because I came too late to town to go with the Commander-in-Chief … [At St. Paul's] I deserted the low company I was in & got between two Highland Centinels.

He found the ceremony impressive but "too theatrical." He had seen Admiral Berkeley, the Duke of Kent, Lord Sidmouth and Colonel William Spencer, who had agreed to assist with the "determination of Francis." Spencer offered to help Francis, then fourteen, obtain a commission in the army. Simcoe had decided not to have his elder son enter the navy.[20]

Hopeless as his wish for an active command seemed, Simcoe persisted. He maintained that the Duke of York had promised him Plymouth and then broken his word. Addington, now Sidmouth, had also promised him Plymouth, but that went by the way with the return of Pitt. He had once been promised the governor generalship of Canada, but that, too, had come to nothing.

On 10 February, his luck began to change. Pitt had died on 23 January. The new ministry was a coalition led by William Wyndham Lord Grenville, brother of his dear friend, the Marquis of Buckingham. Lord Sidmouth was now Lord Privy Seal in what was known as the Ministry of All the Talents, whose motive was reform. Simcoe suggested a command in Italy, but on 10 May, Lord Moira, now master general of ordnance in the new government, wrote that he was being "saved for better things."[21]

Francis, meanwhile, had decided on his future. He wrote to his mother on 28 June 1806 from Eton that he would make the army his career, and Lord Moira was going to assist him. William Walcot had advised him to follow a legal career, but fifteen-year-old Francis was not interested. "Cholwich," whom he had told of his decision, had attended a cricket match. He had also met "Sir J. and Lady Poole, Mr. Osgood[e] and Mr. and Mrs. DeLuke."[22] He meant Jean André Deluc, the eminent Swiss geologist, author of a three-volume work, *Geological Travels*. His journeying that summer included visits to Mary Anne Burges, who introduced him to the General. Her friend Miss Elliott also offered him hospitality. A daughter of Admiral and Mrs. Elliott of Colchester, she was now living at Egland House, near Wolford Lodge.

Oddly, Francis did not mention his father in his letter, nor suggest that his mother pass a greeting to him. This was not the only instance where Francis appeared to distance himself from his father. Simcoe's daughters wrote "Father" but Francis put "My Father" when he mentioned him at all. The Lieutenant General's expectations may have been hard on the boy. They were alike in many ways, and Simcoe himself would have been amazed had he suspected his elder son was afraid of him. He loved all his children without reserve but, not unusual, tension existed between father and heir.

Jean Deluc visited the Simcoe house in Budleigh Salterton. The General took time off for an excursion and loaned him John Bailey as a guide. On a Simcoe horse, with Bailey and Miss Elliott's gardner, Henry Rowe, as his escort, Deluc set off for the home of Sir John Trevelyan at Nettlecombe, Somerset. They stopped at Simonsburrow, above Hemyock, to examine a "burrow believed to be the grave of a Saxon warrior Sigmund." He was particularly intrigued by the fossils he examined in the limestones and shales of the Blackdown Hills. Deluc found Simcoe impressive: "I shall never forget that excellent man, whose character endeared him more to me even than the services of which I was then indebted to him."[23]

At the time, for Simcoe, life was quickening. In November 1805, India and Great Britain signed a peace treaty. A Board of Control, usually called the India Board, was created to monitor British possessions in the East Indies and the affairs of the East India Company. On the board was Lord Sidmouth's brother, John Addington, which may account for Simcoe's name being suggested for the Indian command. Lord Moira, in a personal letter, enquired whether his friend wanted to be Commander in Chief in India. Moira had not spoken to anyone as yet, until he could know Simcoe's reaction. Then the Marquis of Buckingham wrote that his brother, Thomas Grenville, President of the India Board of Control and First Lord of the Admiralty, wanted him to take the position in India.[24]

On 27 July, Simcoe wrote Thomas Grenville:

> I cannot hesitate a moment in saying that the command
> therein pointed out is not suited to my inclination nor
> to that experience nor sort of ability that I believe myself
> to possess.

With surprising haste, his sense of duty and patriotism overwhelming him, Simcoe had a change of heart. On the 28th he informed Moira:

> My Lord,
> Mr. Grenville, through the marquis of Buckingham,
> sounded me in respect of India. This Command I
> declined by last night's post, thinking the

communication private and optional. Today I received a very flattering letter from Mr. Grenville stating that Lord Minto was as desirous as himself of the appointment, & that such were the sentiments of the *Duke of York* I cannot but consider the Commander-in-Chief's opinion as a command & therefore have consented.

He warned Moira that his letter was *confidential,* although if the Duke of York knew, it would not be a secret. "I wait with great composure to learn whether in the interim between my acceptance & prior refusal, any other person volunteers a banishment to India ... "[25]

Word of Simcoe's appointment soon spread. On 7 August, Robert Clifford wrote to his sister-in-law, Mary Lady Arundell of Wardour Castle near Salisbury, that Simcoe had been named C. in C. in India and would shortly be arriving in London. Robert Russell, the helpful Exeter carrier/banker, sent his congratulations.[26]

Simcoe would have preferred a command in Europe rather than "gain the treasures of the East" as he had told Thomas Grenville. King and Country came before his personal feelings, especially as the order came from the Duke of York. Gilbert Elliot-Murray Knynymound, 1st Earl of Minto, would be the new Governor General. Plans were interrupted when the administration learned that Napoleon was intending to invade Portugal to dethrone the Royal family and partition the country. A naval squadron must be sent immediately to Lisbon with Admiral Lord St. Vincent and Lieutenant General Sir James St. Clair Erskine, 2nd Earl of Rosslyn, to report on whether Britain should support Portugal by sending troops. Simcoe would be going. Moira told him he would have rank as a full General in Portugal.

Simcoe left for Plymouth to embark on H.M.S. *Illustrious.* He took Eliza with him as far as Ugbrooke, at the invitation of Lady Clifford. Eliza had been unwell, and Elizabeth trusted that the change of air would restore her. Writing from Ugbrooke to Miss Hunt, Eliza recalled her mother's distress over the Portugal venture: " ... to have a husband torn from her and sent on an expedition is hard." The family felt that he was fit to go to India, but not to undertake the mission to Portugal. Eliza was the first person her father had told when he thought he would be sent to India, and she had been flattered that he had confided in her.[27]

On 2 September, Simcoe wrote to Elizabeth from Lisbon. He was taken ashore and for a short while he convalesced at Coimbra. He wrote to Eliza from there that he was feeling somewhat better.[28] To Elizabeth he admitted that he had been ashore, and had gone to St. Vincent's ship *Britannia* to visit the naval surgeon:

> … & well I did so, for I was seized with the asthmatic paroxysm on my return, which lasted seven hours, during which period I exhausted the whole artillery of medicine for my recovery, but being skilfully attended by the faculty, & most affectionately nursed by my friends & servants, I thank God that I am perfectly convalescent.

He admitted the cause of his illness, which he blamed on the "Hurry of the voyage" crowded into one cabin with eight other men. While they were aboard, the *Illustrious* was being painted "white lead on the outside & verdigris [green oxidated copper] within." In fact, he was being slowly poisoned.[29]

St. Vincent could see that he was dying. On 25 September he ordered him home — on the very vessel that had been the cause of his suffering.[30] The *Illustrious* reached Tor Bay on 20 October, where Simcoe was carried to a sloop stationed there to protect the Brixham fishing fleet. From Topsham on the River Exe, he was taken to Archdeacon Moore's house in Cathedral Close. An express message reached Elizabeth, who was in London with Eliza and Charlotte, shopping in preparation for India. They hastened to Exeter, arriving in time to find him still alive. He died on 26 October 1806, about the time that Mary Anne Burges, her own health poor, arrived to comfort her friend.

Sir John Kennaway, aided by Colonel James Coleridge and Major Henry Darling, implemented funeral plans worthy of so high-ranking an officer, plans prepared by Simcoe himself. Kennaway arranged for the Sidbury and Sidmouth companies of artillery, with two guns, to fire one minute guns from twelve noon until one o'clock. There could be no military displays in Exeter itself because an election was in progress. Soldiers must not be permitted to intimidate voters. The Exeter *Flying Post* reported on 6 November, a Thursday, on the funeral two days before:

> On Tuesday the remains of the late much lamented General Simcoe, were removed from his apartments, at the rev. Archdeacon Moore's in this city, to his family seat at Wolford Lodge, for interment. The funeral was most respectably attended; three mourning coaches followed the hearse, in which were the chief mourners,

the confidential friends of the late general, and his servants. After them came the general's carriage attended by two servants in deep mourning on horseback. In succession we noticed the following gentlemen in carriages: Generals Thewlis and Thomas, with the staff, lords Clifford and Graves, sir Stafford Northcote, sir Wm. Pole, sir John Kennaway, the High-sheriff, admiral Richard Graves, Mr. Baring, Mr. Morshead, colonel Chester, colonel Coleridge, major Dickenson, Mr. Dalrymple &c. All the troops having quitted this city on account of the election, the Exeter regiment of volunteers assembled at the three mile stone on the Honiton road, to pay a compliment to the departed general. From thence his remains were escorted by a squadron of dragoons, the volunteers assembling at various passes to line the road, whilst the procession passed on. At Honiton the troops were all drawn out, and minute guns fired. In short, every respect which could be paid to an esteemed, and much lamented commander was shown on this occasion. The body was interred by torch light, about six in the evening.[31]

John Bailey mentioned military units dear to the General's heart — the East Devon Yeomanry Cavalry, which he had raised personally, and the Dunkeswell cavalry troop of his tenants. The Militia was preceded by the 3rd Dragoon Guards, one leading Simcoe's horse (not the loved Salem who must have been long dead), boots reversed in the stirrups, his arms on the saddle. When the procession reached Wolford Chapel, thousands were waiting:

> The Church field was crowded. The Luppitt Company of Artillery was there with the guns, which were fired when the body was put in the grave, which shook the very house of Wolford.[32]

Elderly Aunt Margaret Graves, who did not attempt to attend the funeral, wrote to Eliza, her favourite correspondent, that time was the best healer. She sent kindest wishes to "Mother and her dear children" especially six-year-old Henry, who was too young to understand what he had lost.[33]

TWENTY-TWO
LIFE AFTER THE GENERAL

Tributes to the late General were limitless. Admiral St. Vincent wrote Major Henry Darling on 27 October: "He was worthy of all our admiration & regret, for a more gallant Soldier or honourable Gentleman neer existed ...." Others who praised him were the Bishop of Exeter from Warwick House, London, to the Reverend Edward Drewe; Lord Sidmouth: "I cannot but look upon the death of this great & good Man as a national Calamity" and Jean Deluc wrote in the same tone from his home in Windsor.[1]

John Ross Robertson stated that Mrs. Simcoe went into seclusion after her husband's death. Nothing could be less accurate. She could not afford to mourn long, not as his sole executrix, not with three very young children to raise, not with her husband's other business to clear up. In the first place, Eliza had a relapse, and Elizabeth escorted her to Ugbrooke where Lady Clifford gave her tender care. Next, Simcoe's will had to go for probate. According to the will, among the properties Simcoe left her were Mansells, Tencery and Cropfields, Little Southey, Southey plot, part of Daws, and Great Southey, and part of Sheldon Grange in Dunkeswell.

She also owned a small plot in Awliscombe known as Cleaves and Moors. As she studied the volumes in the library, she realised that she would keep those that would interest Francis, but she would have to give some away. She immediately thought of Robert Clifford, and she invited him to come to Wolford Lodge and choose maps and books that he would like to have.[2]

In Upper Canada, Simcoe's land grants amounted to some 5,000 acres, in his name or Francis's, that required attention. She was in touch with Captain John McGill, still on the Legislative Council in York. McGill had to provide information on bills he had paid as provisioning agent for His Majesty's forces in Upper Canada while Simcoe was still in the province. After Simcoe left, McGill was promoted inspector general of public accounts, a new office established by Peter Hunter, Simcoe's successor in 1799. Elizabeth informed the Audit Office that she could not prove from vouchers she had that some £5,183 paid to Peter Russell, administrator after Simcoe left on leave, had been repaid. She assumed that Russell, as receiver general, kept things in good order.[3]

This was but one of many problems she had to sort out with the Audit Office or Whitehall, to satisfy everyone that Simcoe's various accounts had been settled — pertaining to Upper Canada, San Domingo, Portugal, the 22nd Regiment, or for his command in the West of England. This involved endless letter writing and hunting down proof that nothing had been overlooked. Strangely enough, Simcoe had not received his commission before he left for Portugal. Henry Darling arranged to have one drawn up. Through the long drawn out process, Elizabeth's trusted helper was Lawyer Christopher Flood.[4]

Her other tower of strength remained John Scadding. Now Elizabeth, not the General, rose early and rode about the estates with Scadding, newly married to Melicent Triggs and expecting the first of three sons. He still had his 253 acres on the Don River at York, where his neighbour, James Playter, was looking after his interests. (John returned to York in 1817 or 1818. He was in his sixties, but he believed his sons would have a brighter future. He was killed in 1824 while clearing land, struck by a tree that collapsed unexpectedly.[5]

At Christmas 1807, Francis Simcoe left Eton. Lord Moira, a full general in the army and honorary Colonel of the 27th (Inniskiling) Regiment, used his influence to secure an ensign's commission for Francis in his own regiment. The commission had been signed at Horse Guards on 30 October 1807. Two battalions of the 27th were fighting on the Continent, but a new 3rd Battalion was training at Enniskillen, Ireland. Francis would be joining it in the spring of 1808. Elizabeth had paid

£400 for the commission and arranged for her elder son to receive an annual allowance of £100. Before embarking for Dublin, Francis spent a month in London with Lord Moira, who became very fond of his young protégé. On 9 January1808, Elizabeth wrote to Moira, thanking him for introducing "Ensign Simcoe" to his commanding officer, Lieutenant Colonel Samuel Graham.[6]

Francis's battalion moved on to the campaigns of the Peninsular War, where he was soon promoted lieutenant, again by purchase. The commission was signed on 22 December 1808. Serving in Wellington's 4th Division, he was with the reserves at Bussaco, Portugal, and at the three sieges of Badajoz, Spain. In the last, on 6 April 1812, he was killed in action. Division Chaplain George Jenkins wrote to Elizabeth that he had found Francis's body in the breach, and had him as decently buried as circumstances would permit.[7]

Mrs. Simcoe's diary, published in two versions, created the impression that Francis was her favourite. She never mentioned Sophia, nor Katherine who died at York, except as "the children," yet she made many references to Francis. These were undoubtedly inserted from her letters to Mary Anne Burges, who often asked for news of Francis. Elizabeth herself avoided writing about what the children with her were doing because she was sensitive to how much the four girls in England were missing her. In some places in the published diary, Elizabeth answers Mary Anne's direct questions, which were added later to the version she sent to Wolford Lodge. The same applies to the many remarks about Francis, added to the main diary after his death two months short of his twenty-first birthday. (Mary Anne counselled Elizabeth on how to deal with Sophia's temper. Nothing is in the diary, but Sophia was on hand to see that none of her mother's complaints were inserted.)

Two other young men known to the Simcoes who died during the Peninsular War were sons of M. and Mme. Ignace de Salaberry, and of Sir John and Lady Johnson. Lieutenant de Salaberry fell at one of the early sieges; Captain James Johnson, 28th Regiment serving in the 2nd Division, died a few days before Francis. He was killed, not at the main siege, but while the 2nd Division was to the southeast, ready to check Marshal Soult, known to be approaching with French reinforcements.[8]

At the time the bad news about Francis reached Devon, Mary Anne Burges had not long to live. She had moved from Tracey, which she had leased, to Ashfield, a smaller house that she purchased. She died on 10 August 1813, in the arms of twenty-one-year-old Julia Somerville, the young woman Mrs. Burges and the Simcoes hoped might become Francis' sbride. Charlotte wrote to Miss Hunt that she had never seen her mother so depressed as she was over losing Mary Anne.[9] (Four years later, Julia married her first cousin once removed, Sir Francis Bond Head Baronet, the sixth lieutenant governor of Upper Canada, whose conduct helped foment a rebellion in 1837.)

Elizabeth Simcoe had suffered enough. Sorrowing that her dearest friend was gone, she took stock of her situation, a father who never saw her, a husband dead at fifty-four, and Francis. She had given enough to the military; Henry, intended for the Royal Navy by his father, would enter the church. He followed Francis to The King's School and Eton, and in 1818 he matriculated at Wadham College, Oxford, and received his Bachelor of Arts degree. He served as curate, and then vicar at the two-point charge of Egloskerry and Tremaine, in Cornwall.[10]

Henry's vocation was in keeping with his mother's greatest source of comfort as years passed. Her church became the centre of her world, involving her in the daily life of Dunkeswell. She expected her daughters to be equally dedicated, each carrying out specific tasks for the well being of the poor people of the parish. She embraced the evangelical movement within the Church of England. To combat worldliness — and the influence of the Methodists — clergymen should be better educated and keep the sabbath. There were not enough churches to hold everyone. A memorial to her zeal, and that of her daughters is Holy Trinity Church, built from the stones of Dunkeswell Abbey and Simcoe funds. The Simcoes also helped finance the restoration of the churches of St. Mary's Hemyock and St. Nicholas Dunkeswell. In St. George's Anglican Church at Sibbald Point on Lake Simcoe, Ontario, is the Simcoe window. It was made by Simcoe's daughters and shipped from their workshop at Wolford Lodge to Susan Sibbald, a friend of Eliza Simcoe who had emigrated to Upper Canada.[11]

Of the daughters, only Anne, the youngest, married, and not during her mother's lifetime.[12] John Ross Robertson assured his readers that Mrs. Simcoe forbad her daughters to marry. There may be a grain of truth, but other factors were even more influential. Great Aunt Margaret Graves helped to instill a prejudice against marriage, which deprived a women of her independence. Admiral Graves took over Margaret's fortune, and willed part of it to his nephew, Richard, which the lady never forgot. Simcoe, too, had taken control of Elizabeth's assets, although he used them wisely and left her much better off than when he married her. An unmarried woman with little money faced a hard life, but the Simcoe daughters had less need of husbands because they had independent means; not enough to make them victims of fortune hunters, but sufficient for them to take care of themselves. Mrs. Graves, who died in late 1808, left each of the five eldest £1,000. When William Walcot died, Henry Simcoe was his principal heir, but all the Simcoe daughters received legacies. They stood to inherit still further sums from their mother's estate, which might have influenced some of them not to cross Elizabeth. Two daughters, at least, Charlotte and Sophia, had their father's determination. Had they wished to marry, no one could have stopped them.

Henry Addington Simcoe did marry during his mother's lifetime, and like his parents he had eleven children. Nine were by his first wife, Anne Palmer — five sons and four daughters. With his second wife, Emily Mann, he had two more daughters.[13] All of his grandchildren were born to his daughters. John Graves and Elizabeth Posthuma have many descendants, among them John Vowler and Margaret Partridge, as well as Bill Vowler and his son Tim and daughter Laura, and Dr. Anne Cole (who added Simcoe as her middle name). None bear the surname Simcoe, although there might have been one exception.

John Kennaway Simcoe, Henry's second son (the first son, Henry, had died at age twenty-five) inherited Wolford Lodge. This John died childless in 1891, and the heir was now Arthur Linton, a grandson of Henry Addington Simcoe's eldest daughter, Anne Eliza. One of her daughters married a Linton. Their son, Arthur Linton, added Simcoe to his name in order to inherit the arms of John Graves Simcoe, but like so many other male descendants, he was childless.

The family fortune, once so substantial, had been dissipated. In 1923, Wolford Lodge was partly destroyed by fire, and Arthur Linton Simcoe sold it to a Brigadier Kemball. At the time, most of the contents still intact were also sold. Among the disposed-of effects were the two Spanish cannon that had been in San Domingo, which Simcoe had retrieved after considerable persistence. The guns, cast in Spain in 1747 by a famous gunfounder, Mathias Solano, went for £25 to a buyer from Surrey. In 1940 the purchaser presented them to the the Leatherhead Urban District Council. Still in perfect condition, they are on display in the Mariner's Suite at the Leatherhead Leisure Centre. What Simcoe would have thought of this fate defies description.

Wolford Lodge was sold again, to Alfred Le Marchant in 1926. This owner built a new Wolford Lodge on the site of the destroyed one. In one of the transactions, Wolford Chapel was sold separately. To preserve the chapel and its grounds the English publisher, Sir Leicester Harmsworth, bought them and he offered them to the people of Ontario. At the time of Harmsworth's death, the Ontario government was still debating whether to commit funds for the upkeep of the chapel and grounds.[14]

By 1966, the government had become conscious of the value of recognising Ontario's heritage. In a ceremony held at Wolford Chapel, Sir Geoffrey Harmsworth, Sir Leicester's son, presented the title deeds for the chapel and grounds to the premier of the day, John Robarts. Sir Geoffrey's gift included the easement for the right of way that guaranteed access over his property to visitors. In May 1989, the John Graves Simcoe Association (now part of the Ontario Historical Society) hosted a Simcoe Weekend. Guests received lunch at the present Wolford Lodge, owned by Mrs. Pamela Mitchell, the daughter of Mr. Alfred Le Marchant and his wife, Turdis. Her husband, the Very Reverend Patrick Mitchell, KCVO,then the Dean of Windsor, conducted a dedication ceremony. The chapel is still used regularly for worship such as on Good Friday.

Elizabeth Simcoe lived until 17 January 1850, her eighty-eighth year. By the time she was buried beside Wolford Chapel, only six of her children remained. Her daughters Charlotte and Harriet had died in 1842 and 1845. The five surviving daughters, Eliza, Caroline, Sophia, Katherine and Anne, bought 11 Lansdown Crescent in Bath, where they could have a livelier social life than at isolated Wolford Lodge. Just short of her fiftieth birthday, in 1854, Anne Simcoe married John Alford in Paddington, Middlesex, now part of Greater London. The marriage certificate showed that she was a daughter of a "General in the Army" and Alford a labourer and farmer's son. Anne had married below her station, and not with any of her sisters as witnesses.

The land grants in Upper Canada had been sold long since. Henry had inherited the 5,000 acres from his father. John McGill, who warned Henry that taxes would soon eat up such profits as he might make, helped in selling the lands. They did not bring high prices because so much cheap land was available. Very few of the reserves for clergy and crown had been sold. The vacant lots were interfering with the orderly development of the countryside and were one of the causes of the rebellion in 1837. Castle Frank burned down in 1829, the last Simcoe property remaining in Upper Canada.

A few years after his death, subscribers in Devonshire raised funds for a memorial to John Graves Simcoe. The famous sculptor, John Flaxman, carved the marble monument that now stands in the south choir wall of Exeter Cathedral. The inscription reads:

Sacred to the Memory of
JOHN GRAVES SIMCOE
Lieutenant-General in the army and
Colonel of the 22nd Regiment of Foot

Who died on the 26th day of October, 1806
Aged 54
In whose life and character the virtues of
the Hero, the Patriot and the Christian
were so eminently conspicuous that it may
justly be said he served his King and
his country with a zeal exceeded
only by his piety towards his God.

Across the bottom below the main inscription is a tribute to Francis Gwillim Simcoe:

During the erection of this Monument
His eldest son
FRANCIS GWILLIM SIMCOE
Lieutenant in the 27th Foot,
Born at Wolford Lodge, in this County,
June 6th 1791. Fell in the
Breach at the siege of Badajoz
April 6th 1812, in the 21st year
of his Age

Of the two, Francis died utterly unfulfilled. He had been desperate for a promotion to captain, and was denied it because of the hidebound army rule that all lieutenants who had served longer in the regiment had the right to purchase promotions ahead of him, a matter of seniority, not ability. Francis never attained that seniority. One way of jumping the queue was by leading a "forlorn hope," the party who went first into the breach during a siege. A lieutenant who survived the command of a forlorn hope automatically received his company. Francis may have thrown away his life at the bloodiest battle of the Peninsular War in an attempt to win his captaincy.

Opinions on the importance of John Graves Simcoe are as diverse as their authors. Some see him an an upper-class English snob, others as a man who never lived up to his early promise. He was an imperialist, but in the most positive sense of the term. John Gellnor, who edited the 1962 version of Simcoe's military journal, viewed Simcoe's four and a half years in Upper Canada/Ontario as "an incident in a life he wanted to devote to professional soldiering." Most would agree that he emerged from the American Revolution as the finest commander of light troops in the British Army. Certainly, what Simcoe sought was an important, active military command. Despite many opportunities while Britain was constantly at war, Simcoe "the strong-willed and self-confident military autocrat, is really a tragic figure."[15]

The tragedy lies less with the man than with his early, unexpected death when he was about to realise his dream of an important active command, and the peerage that would be his reward. With that honour this man, of relatively modest but most respectable origins, would have placed his wife and children where he wanted them, among the best people in the land. That he did not even achieve a knighthood may be blamed on the system of the time where the right friends outweighed ability. Of the seven men who were lieutenant governors of Upper Canada (before it was united with Lower Canada in 1841) only Simcoe and Peter Hunter never had titles other than their military ranks. (There once was a Lord Simcoe, a hotel in downtown Toronto; it has been demolished.)

Even Simcoe's sternest critics have to agree that he was a man of honour, who valued loyalty — to King, country, wife and family, friends and the men who served under his command. While he valued his contacts with the aristocracy, he retained the common touch. Many of his aspirations for Upper Canada failed, because he was a man of his own time, and place, whereas Upper Canadians were North Americans who believed in upward mobility. They did not accept that each person had a place in society, and should keep it. Despite certain attitudes, Simcoe treated individuals with decency and understanding whatever their station in life.

At the heart of Ontario's "Golden Horseshoe" which curves around the western end of Lake Ontario, lie the streets of Simcoe's original Town of York. Renamed Toronto in 1834 when it was incorporated, the city has grown to more than two million people. In the capital of the province, John Graves Simcoe has not been forgotten, and he is the acknowledged founder (despite Dorchester's hand in the selection, or Simcoe's fervent desire for the site of the present London, on the Thames). Ontarians have been slow about celebrating a rich heritage, but they are improving. The acceptance of Wolford Chapel was an important step. Another was the city fathers' proclamation that Civic Holiday (August Bank Holiday) would be known as Simcoe Day.

The Queen's Rangers live on in the modern Militia unit in Toronto, the Queen's York Rangers, an amalgamation of two earlier regiments. The members applied for, and received, the right to add "1st American Regiment" to their official name. The addition symbolises descent from the Provincial Corps of the American Establishment, Simcoe's original

Queen's Rangers, 1777–1783. The regimental colours, restored, have a place of honour in the mess of the Queen's York Rangers. Her Majesty the Queen appointed His Royal Highness The Prince Andrew, Duke of York, Colonel in Chief of the Queen's York Rangers (1st American Regiment). The appointment was gazetted on 20 September 1997.

Various actors, even descendants, and others, have portrayed John Graves Simcoe on the holiday, usually in his green Queen's Ranger coat. In 1995, Toronto celebrated "200 Years Yonge," the bicentenary of the opening of Yonge Street. The tall, imposing Lieutenant Governor, the Honourable H.N.R. Jackman, attended functions in the red coat faced dark blue of a major general in the army, Simcoe's rank in 1795. (Oddly enough, Sir George Yonge's name does not appear in Simcoe's correspondence after his return to England in 1796. The friendship apparently passed into history sooner than the roadway.)

Throughout his time in Upper Canada, notwithstanding having so much vetoed by Lord Dorchester (himself a pompous and less than heroic military commander), Simcoe left his mark, and he tried to protect the territory as well as he could. Attack, rather than defense, was his style when he suggested carrying the war into Pennsylvania, to avoid letting American troops get too close to his domain. He did much by his own presence, and that of his government. Under the Quebec Act of 1774, territory that was established as Upper Canada had been reserved for the native tribes. Governor Haldimand agreed to allow Loyalists to settle inland because the refugee Iroquois wanted them nearby for protection.

Had those Loyalists been accommodated somewhere in the east, Upper Canada might well have been overrun by land-hungry Americans — much as happened in Kentucky, Ohio and Texas. In each case, settlers flocked in and then demanded annexation by the United States. In the 1790s, American settlers did flock in, most with Simcoe's own blessing, at a time when Britain, at war with France, could not spare more troops to protect the settlements. Those Americans came, not to unorganised territory where they could make their own rules, but to a British province with an established government. Without the Loyalists, the need they created for a province, and Simcoe's work, the Dominion of Canada might well have ended at the Ottawa River.

While Simcoe's command in the West of England did not become active, it was the most important of his life. Attempting to fortify the long peninsula south of the Bristol Channel was even more difficult than trying to defend Upper Canada. Even on home ground Simcoe was worried that Volunteer citizen soldiers might not stand up to the French. In Upper Canada he begged for more regular regiments, and again in the

West Country. When he did not receive the backing he believed he needed in San Domingo, he withdrew from a situation that the government soon recognised as hopeless.

When Eliza Simcoe wrote that her mother and family were alarmed at the General's going to Portugal, but not to India, their premonition was correct. He might have flourished on the long sea voyage to India, but the hastily commissioned *Illustrious* killed him.

ABBREVIATIONS
PUBLIC ARCHIVES

AO — Archives of Ontario, Simcoe finding aid F47.
/WCSL Copies of materials in AO from the West Country Studies Library, Exeter

CWC — Colonial Williamsburg Collection
Sim/Corresp. Cruikshank, Ernest A. Corresp etc.
DCB — Dictionary of Canadian Biography
DNB —Dictionary of National Biography

DRO — Devon Record Office.
DRO/Sim — Simcoe Papers
DRO/PR/Dunk. etc. — Parish Registers
DRO/Land Tx — Land Tax Returns
DRO/Lieut. — Lieutenancy Papers
DRO/LTD — Dunkeswell Land Tax
DRO/LTL — Luppitt Land Tax
DRO/LTH — Hemyock Land Tax
DRO/LTA — Awliscombe Land Tax
DRO/LTEB — East Budleigh Land Tax
DRO/Dunk/encl — Dunkeswell Enclosure

EPS — Elizabeth Posthuma Simcoe
FRYER/HA — FRYER/Hilary Arnold Genealogy
JGS — John Graves Simcoe

NA — National Archives of Canada
NRO — Northants Record Office Parish Registers NRO/PR/Cott etc.
PRO — Public Record Office, London
SOM/RO — Somerset Record Office
Vowler — John Vowler Papers
WCSL — West Country Studies Library Exeter *Flying Post* WCSL/EFP

PRIVATE COLLECTIONS

Bailey — John Bailey Memoir, coll. of Margaret Partridge
Drewe — Drewe Family Papers: Francis Drewe Genealogy
Partridge — Other items, coll. of Margaret Partridge
Vowler — John Vowler Papers

PREFACE
1. Fryer, Mary Beacock. *Elizabeth Posthuma Simcoe.* (Toronto: Dundurn 1989); *Our Young Soldier.* (Toronto: Dundurn 1996).

CHAPTER 1: "Young Graves"
1. FRYER/HA p. 258. The date was probably New (Gregorian) Calendar, although this calendar commenced on 14 (formerly 2) September. The Act of Parliament was passed in 1750.
2. Wolford-Simcoe Papers, v. 1, p. 20. Metropolitan Toronto Library. Here is a rare instance when Simcoe was referred to by a given name, rather than his initials.
3. Copy of material in Avon Registry Office, Parish Register. Here the name is Catherine; in all other documents it is Katherine.
4. Robertson, John Ross. *Diary of Mrs. John Graves Simcoe.* (Toronto: Briggs, 1911, pp. 14-16; Riddell, William R. *The Life of John Graves Simcoe.* (Toronto: M and S., 1926, p. 18).
5. CWC JGS Papers, HS 30.6 Folder 2 item 14.
6. Riddell, JGS, p. 32
7 FRYER/HA p. 257.
8. Prob. 6/161. Prob. 11/1458, PRO, relates to JGS's own will.
9. WCSL/EFP [Editor] Trewman's Exeter *Flying Post.* 29/3/1787; 16/8/1787.10
10. Martin, Ged. "The Simcoes and their Friends." *Ontario History* vol. 69, no. 2, June 1977, p. 110. Sir Francis Head described Simcoe's daughter Katherine speaking broad Devonshire.
11. Austen-Leigh, Richard A., ed., The Eton College Register, 1753-1790.
12. Prob. 11/1458, PRO.
13. Lyte, C.M. *History of Eton College 1440-1875.* (London: 1875, pp. 332-36.
14. WCSL, AO coll., reel 9, item 36, Milles to JGS, 27 Nov. 1768.
15. Reel A605, F23, (William Bocawen [sic] to JGS, 1797), Simcoe Papers, NA.
16. Lincoln's Inn Admission Register.
17. The Army List 1771.
18. The Army List 1775.
19. Drewe, Genealogy by Francis Drewe of Ticehurst, Sussex, and Broadhembury, Devon.
20. AO Reel 9, item 52,WCSL.

CHAPTER 2: "The Field, Not The Forum"

1. Riddell, p. 459; Chudley, Ron, *A History of Craft: Master Masons in the Province of Devonshire.* 1980.
2. AO, Reel 9 item 43 (Milles to JGS, 18 Apr. 1774), WCSL.
3. The Army List 1774.
4. Strachan, Hew. *British Military Uniforms 1768-96.* (London: Arms and

Armour Press,1975), p. 180.

5. AO. Reel 9, item 47 (Jan. 1775); poems in reel A605, F23, NA.

6. Biography of Samuel Graves, DNB.

7. Ibid.

8. Riddell, p. 47.

9. Drewe, Edward, "Military Sketches by Edward Drewe." 1784; Richard Polwhele, *Poems by Gentlemen of Devon-Cornwall.* 1792, np.

10. Simcoe, John Graves. *A Journal of the Operations of the Queen's Rangers by Lt. Col. Simcoe.* 1968 reprint of 1844 edition (New York: Arno Press), p. 14; omitted from the 1962 edition, John Gellnor ed., (Toronto: Baxter Publishing).

11. The Army List 1776; Strachan, *Uniforms,* p. 180.

12. Riddell, p. 50.

13. EFP, WCSL.

14. AO. Reel 9, item 36, (Milles to Simcoe, 27 Nov. 1768), WCSL.

15. Fryer/HA, p. 257.

16. Burt, A.L. *Guy Carleton — Lord Dorchester, 1724 -1808.* (Canadian Historical Association, Historical Booklet No. 5), pp. 10-14.

CHAPTER 3: The Green Jackets

1. Jenkins, Stephen, *The Story of the Bronx,* pp.162-64, quoted in Mark. M. Boatner III, *Landmarks of the American Revolution.* (New York, Hawthorn Books, 1975), p. 288.

2. Simcoe, *Journal,* 1962 edition, p. 14.

3. Mollo, John, and Malcolm McGregor, *Uniforms of the American Revolution.* (London, Blandford, 1975), pp. 211-212.

4. Rogers, Robert, *Journals (*London: 1769 edition), pp. 50-70.

5. Fryer, Mary Beacock. *King's Men: the soldier founders of Ontario.* (Toronto: Dundurn,1980), pp. 129–30.

6. Ibid., pp., 244–45.

7. Bull, Stewart, *The Queen's York Rangers: an historic regiment.,* revised edition 1993, (Erin, Ontario: Boston Mills Press), pp. 36–37.

8. Talman, J.J. *Loyalist Narratives from Upper Canada.* Toronto, Champlain Society, 1966), "Narrative of Stephen Jarvis" p. 159.

9. Simcoe, *Journal,* 1962 edition, p. 11.

10. Ibid.

11. Ibid., pp. 4-7.

12. Bull, p. 45.

13. Dupuy, Trevor N., Curt Johnson, and David L. Bongard. *The Harper Encyclopedia of Military Biography.* (Edison, N.J., Castle Books,1995), pp. 430-31.

14. Bull, p. 47.

15. Carl Benn, PhD., Curator of Fort York, Toronto.

16. Simcoe, *Journal,* 1962 edition, pp. 20-24; Boatner, *Landmarks,* pp. 194-95.

17. Simcoe, *Journal*, 1787 edition, Appendix.
18. Fryer, *King's Men,* p. 17.
19. Simcoe, *Journal*, 1787 edition, Appendix.

CHAPTER 4: Like a Common Criminal

1. Many copies of this portrait have survived. Simcoe is shown with frizzy brown hair; the portrait is titled "Lieut. Gen. Simcoe" but while he would have worn this coat as Colonel in the Rangers, as a lieutenant general he would have worn a red coat. The green coat was probably made by a London tailor when Simcoe received the command of a new regiment of Queen's Rangers, raised after 1791.
2. Simcoe, *Journal,* 1787 edition, Appendix. Simcoe did not write in sequence. This item is several pages after the following.
3. Ibid., several pages ahead of the previous item.
4. Ibid.
5. Riddell, p. 69.
6. Simcoe, *Journal,* 1787 edition, Appendix.
7. Mealing, S.R., Biography of John McGill, DCB, v. 6, p. 451.
8. "A Narrative of John Peters, Lieutenant Colonel in the Queen's Loyal Rangers in Canada," Toronto *Globe*, 16 July 1877.
9. Simcoe, *Journal,* 1787 edition, Appendix.
10. Seaman, Jordan. "Genealogy of the Seaman Family." Long Island Historical Society.

CHAPTER 5: John André, Edward Drewe and Benedict Arnold

1. Simcoe, *Journal,* 1787 edition, Appendix; Fryer, *King's Men,* pp. 149–54, (an account of the Sullivan expedition).
2. Simcoe, *Journal,* 1787 edition, Appendix.
3. Bull, pp. 53-54.
4. Simcoe, *Journal,* 1962 edition, pp. 47, 72; Bull, p. 54.
5. AO. Reel 9, item193, (Simcoe to Walcot, 8/23/1784), WCSL.
6. Simcoe, *Journal,* 1787 edition, Appdendix; 1962 edition, p. 82.
7. Simcoe, *Journal,* p. 83.
8. Ibid., p. 85; 1787 edition, Appendix.
9. Lancaster, Bruce, and Plumb, J.H., *The American Heritage Book of the Revolution.,* (New York, Dell,1958), p. 264.
10. Simcoe, *Journal,* 1787 edition, Appendix.
11. Simcoe, *Journal,* 1962 edition, p. 85.
12. Ibid., p. 85 (re Burlington); 1787 edition, Appendix (re Billingsport).
13. Drewe, Edward. *Military Sketches by Edward Drewe, Late Major of the 35th Regiment of Foot.,* (Exeter: B. Thorn and So,1784). ()The work, which Chris Dracott found in the West Sussex Record Office along with one of Drewe's letters, was "Dedicated to the British Army."

14. Drewe incorporated extracts from his Court Martial proceedings; photocopy of "The Case of Edward Drewe" etc. West Sussex Record Office.
15. Biographies of Saunders; and Merritt, DCB; Hugh F. Rankin. *Francis Marion: The Swamp Fox* . (New York: Crowell,1973) (Merritt, pp. 145 -147, 172, 176, and Saunders, pp. 166-67. 172).
16. Simcoe, *Journal,* 1962 edition, p. 94.
17. Bull, p. 57.
18. Ibid., p. 58, quotation from Simcoe's *Journal.*
19. Simcoe, *Journal,* 1962 edition, p. 123.

CHAPTER 6: Spencer's Ordinary

1. Simcoe, *Journal,* 1787 Appendix; 1962 edition, p. 130.
2. Simcoe, *Journal,* p. 132.
3. Ibid., pp. 123–34
4. Ibid., p. 134.
5. Ibid., pp. 134–35.
6. Ibid., p. 135.
7. Ibid., p. 137.

CHAPTER 7: "this ill-managed war"

1. Boatner, *Landmarks,* (Arnold's raid on New London, Sept. 1781) p. 55.
2. Simcoe, *Journal,* 1787 edition, Appendix.
3. Simcoe, *Journal,* 1962 edition, pp. 138–39.
4. PRO 30/11 Cornwallis Papers, Simcoe's letter; *Journal,* 1844 and1968 editions refer to the execution; the incident was apparently edited out of the 1962 version.
5. Simcoe, *Journal,* 1962 edition, p. 139.
6. Ibid., 1787 edition, Appendix.
7. Ibid.
8. Simcoe, *Journal,* 1962 edition, p. 147.
9. Hatch, Charles E. Jr. *Yorktown and the siege of 1781.* Historical Handbook Series, No. 14, (National Park Service, 1957), p. 59.
10. Simcoe, *Journal,* 1787 edition, Appendix.
11. Bull, Clinton's letter is quoted on p. 65.

CHAPTER 8: Love in the Blackdown Hills

1. The Army List 1782; Biography of Francis Rawdon-Hastings, DNB.
2. AO. Reel 9, item142, (Rawdon to Simcoe 24 Dec.1781).
3. Riddell, p. 73.
4. Fryer/HA, pp. 255-258.
5. John Ross Robertson, who put together the first edition of Mrs. Simcoe'sCanadian diary, assumed she had been born in 1766. He saw the

grave of Thomas Gwillim at St. Dubricius Church, Whitchurch, near the Gwillim family home, but this Thomas, who died in 1766, was her grandfather.

6. Reel A606 and A607, F30., (several letters of M. Graves to her great niece Eliza Simcoe), NA.

7. Morris, James/Jan. *Heaven's Command: An Imperial Progress.* (Hammondsworth, Middlesex, England: Faber,1973), p. 20.

8. Genealogy of the Drewes of Broadhembury and The Grange, courtesy of Francis Drewe of Ticehurst, Sussex, and Broadhembury, Devon.

9. Biographies of Sir James Bland Burges and Mary Anne Burges, DNB; Reel A606, A607, F29, Simcoe Papers, NA, (letters of Mary Anne Burges to Elizabeth Simcoe); Fryer/HA, p. 266.

10. Simcoe, *Journal,* 1787 edition, Appendix, (close to the end).

11. AO. Reel 9, item 153, (1 July 1782).

12. Fryer, EPS, p. 56.

13. Sparks, J.A. *In the Shadow of the Blackdowns,* (Wiltshire, Moonraker Press,1978), p. 88.

14. AO. Reel 9 items160, 21,12/1782, (Gidley to Simcoe)

15. The Army List 1783.

CHAPTER 9: Wolford Lodge 1783-1787

1. Wright, Esther Clarke. *The Loyalists of New Brunswick.* np,1955, Appendix, p. 255 of alphabetical list.

2. Sim/DRO, (1038M, Box 6, 02 1010), DRO

3. AO.Reel 9 item175, (McGill to Simcoe, 10 July1783; 12 Oct.1783),WCSL.

4. Ibid. Reel 9 item 193, Simcoe to Walcot, 8 Feb.1784.

5. Ibid., Reel 9 item 169, Flood to Simcoe, 10 Nov.1783.

6. EFP, 1 and 8 Jan. 1784. Baring and Simcoe exchanged letters on 6 and 7 Jan., WCSL; AO. Reel 9, items188 and 189, WCSL; Merry making in the Globe, "Devon Documents in honour of Mrs. Margery Rowe," Todd Gray ed., *Devon Notes and Queries,* Exeter, 1754-1809, taken from the journal of Samuel Poole, p. 38, DRO.

7. Reel A606 F29, NA, (Mary Anne Burges to Elizabeth Simcoe, 2 Sept. 1795. She recalled his "despairing" Simcoe was each time Elizabeth was pregnant).

8. AO. Reel 9 item 229, (E. Gwillim to Elizabeth Simcoe, 1785).

9. Reel A607 F32, (Charlotte to Miss Nutcombe, C/O Rev. Hunt, Benefield Sept. 1818), NA.

10. AO. Reel 9 item 231, (JGS to Miss Hunt 7 Dec. 1785), WCSL.

11. Vowler, Simcoe papers, private collection of descendant John Vowler of Holesworthy, Devon.

12. AO. Reel 9 item 232, (Pitfield to Simcoe, 2 Jan.1786), WCSL.

13. Biography of Samuel Badcock, DNB.

14. *Gentleman's Magazine* 1788 — Badcock's *Journal.*

15. Polwhele, Richard, ed., *Poems by Gentlemen of Devon and Cornwall,* v. 2,

(1792, np), p. 333.

16. Reel A605 F23, (poems by JGS and friends), NA.

17. Fryer, EPS, p. 27.

18. EFP, March issues, WCSL.

19. Reel A606 F29, (Mary Anne Burges' letters to Elizabeth Simcoe have many references to the whims of Mrs. Graves), NA.

20. Three different versions of Simcoe's *Journal*, in four editions, have been published and are listed in the bibliography.

21. AO. Reel 9 item 259, (Spencer to JGS, 16 June 1787), WCSL.

22. Fryer, HA, p. 258.

23. Peckham, Howard H., "Sir Henry Clinton's Review of Simcoe's Journal." William and Mary Quarterly (Second series, 2, 1941).

24. AO. Reel 9 item 212, (E. Gwillim to EPS,14 May1785), WCSL.

CHAPTER 10: Into Parliament

1. Genealogy of the Drewe family by Francis Drewe of Ticehurst, Sussex, and Broadhembury; Drewe family tree compiled by Chris Dracott from Burke's landed gentry; Alumni Oxonienses.

2. AO. Reel 9, item 276, (Simcoe to Yonge, 28 Nov.1788), WCSL.

3. Ibid. Reel 9 item 270, (Scadding and Honiton turnpike, 18 Jan.1788).

4. Sheldon, Gilbert, *From Trackway to Turnpike.* (London: Oxford University Press,1928), p. 91.

5. Vancouver, C., *A General Survey of the County of Devon.* (London: 1808), p. 269, quoted in Sheldon, p. 91.

6. Vowler, letter dated 2 Aug. 1789.

7. Cruikshank, Brigadier General Ernest A. ed., *The Correspondence of Lieutenant Governor John Graves Simcoe.* (Ontario Historical Society, 1923-31), 5 vols., vol. 1, pp. 7-8. Abbreviated as Sim/Corresp. For two very different interpretations about Vermont, see Mary Beacock Fryer, *Buckskin Pimpernel.* (Toronto, Dundurn,1981); Frederic F. VanDeWater, *The Reluctant Republic.* (Taftsville, Vermont:1954). Sherwood negotiated a neutral Vermont ahd strove for reunion with Britain.

8. Sim/Corresp. vol. 1, pp. 16-17

9. Biography of Banastre Tarleton, DNB.

10. Page, John L. *An Exploration of Exmoor.* Seeley & Co. 1890, p. 16.

11. Vowler, EPS to Miss Elliott, 10/9/1790.

12. Sim/Corresp. vol. 1 p. 13. Grenville to Dorchester 3 June1790.

CHAPTER 11: The Great Empire Builder

1. Polwhele, Rev. Richard, *History of Devonshire*, published between 1793 and 1806, vol. 2, p. 333; Memoir on the Geological Survey of England and Wales, Explanation of Sheet 331 by W.A.E. Ussher F.G.S., 1906, p. 39.

2. AO. Reel 9, item 319, (Hawker to Simcoe, 26 June1790), WCSL.

3. Martin, Ged. "Simcoes Friends." p. 14.
4. Sim/Corresp, v. 1, p. 16, Simcoe to Dundas, 12 Nov. 1790.
5. The Army List 1791.
6. Sim/Corresp. v. 1, pp. 17-19, Simcoe to Banks, 8 Jan.1791.
7. Ibid. p. 17, Simcoe to Grenville, Simcoe to Grenville, 24 Dec.1790.
8. Fryer, EPS, p. 35.
9. Reels A606 - and A607, F29, NA; AO. Simcoe Collection, B 1-2-, Reel 7-531. Letters of Mary Anne Burges to Elizabeth Simcoe. Those in AO are missing from NA collection, microfilm from DRO. The letters report Eliza's mourning, the girls' illnesses, their joy at receiving letters.
10. *Parliament Register* for 1791.
11. Fryer/HA, p. 258.
12. Sim/Corresp., vol. 1, p. 71, Yonge to Simcoe, War Office, 20 Dec. 1791; Vowler, re the horse Salem; EPS to Miss Elliott, 11 May1791.
13. Innis, Mary Quayle ed., *Mrs. Simcoe's Diary*. (Toronto: MacMillan,1965), p. 92.
14. Reel A606, F29, (undated letter near the beginning of the folder), NA.

CHAPTER 12: Winter at Quebec

1. Sim/Corresp. v. 1, pp 71-73. Formation of what Dundas then called an independent corps, 30 June 1791. Royal assent was given in a letter from Sir George Yonge to Simcoe, vol. 1 p. 75, 7 Oct. 1791.
2. The coat most often shown was the green one, but the portrait in the collection of the Province of Ontario, on the cover of this work, has him in a red coat.
3. The Army List 1792, the Queen's Rangers.
4. Wright, *Loyalists*, Appendix.
5. Biography of Edward Littlehales, DCB.
6. The Army List 1792, garrison list for Upper Canada shows Stephenson and Drewe.
7. Innis, *Diary*, pp. 26-27
8. Ibid. p. 31.
9. Ibid.
10. Ibid., p. 37
11. Fryer, EPS pp. 38-39.
12. Sim/Corresp. v. 1, p. 13; Grenville to Dorchester, 3 June 1790; pp. 27, 29; see Memorandum to Dundas, 30 June 1791. Green uniform reference is p. 75; p. 145, Simcoe to Dundas, 12 Aug. 1791. See also Earle Thomas. *Sir John Johnson: Loyalist Baronet*. (Toronto: Dundurn, 1986), p. 129.
13. Sim/Corresp., v, 1 p. 118, Simcoe to Dundas, 10 Mar. 1792, re Talbot.
14. Innis, *Diary*, p. 47.
15. Ibid., pp. 50-51.
16. Biography of François Baby, DCB.
17. Innis, *Diary*, p. 51.

18. Ibid., p. 58.
19. Ibid.
20. Sim/Corresp. v. 1, p. 27, independent corps; p. 37, royal assent for the Rangers.
21. Fryer, EPS, pp. 51-52.
22. Robertson, *Diary*, p. 89.

CHAPTER 13: A Viceregal Progress and a Royal Visit

1. Innis, pp. 72-80.
2. Leavitt, Thad. W.H. *History of Leeds and Grenville*, (Brockville, 1879), pp. 32-33.
3. Fryer, Mary Beacock, J. William Lamb and Larry Turner. *The Meaning of These Stones*, (Wall Street United Church, Brockville, 1998), pp. 22-26, (early Methodist missionaries in Upper Canada).
4. Innis, pp. 72, 73.
5. Quebec *Gazette,* 12 May 1784, notice of appointment.
6. Sim/Corresp. v. 2, pp. 194-195, (Simcoe to Dorchester, 26 March1794).
7. Fryer, *King's Men*, pp. 131-125, 333.
8. For a comprehensive treatment of the British Indian Department see Robert S. Allen, "The British Indian Department on the Frontier in North America, 1755-1830." Parks Canada, Public Information Branch, Occasional Papers in Archaeology and History. 1975, pp. 49-58 for Simcoe's era.
9. Sim/Corresp. v. 1, p. 205.
10. Innis, p. 77.
11. Ibid., pp. 79.
12. Reel A605, F2, (Simcoe to Eliza, Aug. 1792) NA..
13. Reel A606, F24, (Simcoe to Charlotte, 23 Aug. n. yr), NA.
14. F29, (letter 20 Nov. 1792), NA.
15. Innis, p. 80

CHAPTER 14: Simcoe the Administrator

1. Armstrong, Frederick H. *Handbook of Upper Canadian Chronology*. (Toronto: Dundurn, 1985), pp. 74-75.
2. Riddell, p. 175.
3. Fryer, EPS, p. 66; Armstrong, *Handbook*, pp. 74-75, ridings, members of First Parliament 1792-96.
4. Biography of Sir David William Smith, DCB.
5. Innis, pp. 85, 109.
6. Fryer, EPS, p. 67.
7. Innis, p. 83.
8. Biography of "Thayendanegea" Joseph Brant, DCB.
9. Biography of Hugh Percy 2nd Duke of NOrthumberland, DNB.
10. Innis, p. 83.

11. Reel A606, F24,(section with poetry), NA.
12. Fryer/HA p. 259.
13. Innis, pp. 84-87.
14. Simcoe, *Journal*, 1844 or 1968 edition, p. 328.
15. Riddell, p. 192.
16. Innis, p. 91.
17. Reel A606, F29. letter of 26 September 1792 NA.
18. Innis, p. 89, EPS to Mrs Hunt, 13 March 1793.
19. Ibid., p. 10, from a "Journal of a Treaty held in 1793...." Massachusetts Historical Society, Collections, 3rd series, v. 5 (1936) pp. 123-24.
20. Craig, Gerald M. *Upper Canada : the Formative Years.* Toronto, M. and S., 1963, p. 30.
21. Scott, Duncan Campbell. *John Graves Simcoe.* Toronto, Makers of Canada Series 1910, pp. 89-90.
22. Innis, p. 105.

CHAPTER 15: Simcoe Versus Dorchester

1. Innis, p. 103.
2. Martin, "Simcoes Friends" pp. 104-05.
3. Innis, p. 107.
4. Scadding, Henry. *Toronto of Old*. F.H. Armstrong ed., (Toronto: Oxford, 1987), p. xiii.
5. Innis, p. 15.
6. Sim/Corresp, (account of the journey by Macdonnell), v. 2, p. 70.
7. Ibid. pp. 11-12.
8. Ibid., pp. 109-113, (Simcoe to Dorchester, 2 Dec. 1793).
9. Innis, p. 113.
10. Bull, p. 89, (from letters written in early May).
11. Ibid., p. 89, from Sim/Corresp. v. 2, pp. 182-84, (Simcoe to Dorchester).
12. Bull, p. 89.
13. Innis, pp. 125-26. The letter is quoted in full, dated York, May 1794.
14. Martin, "Simcoe Friends" p. 109 and fn. 26; Reel A606 F30, (last letter in folder), NA.
15. Innis, pp. 120-12.
16. Ibid., pp. 126-130.
17. Biography of William Osgoode, DCB.
18. Innis, p. 131.
19. Sim/Corresp. v. 2, pp. 109-110; AO. Berczy Papers, narrative of Berczy. See also John André, *William Berczy: Co-founder of Toronto.* A Centennial Project of the Borough of York, 1967.
20. AO. Berczy Papers, Berczy to David William Smith, 30 Nov. 1794.
21. Sim/Corresp. v. 2, pp. 403, 404, 407, (Campbell to Wayne; Wayne to Campbell).
22. Ibid., pp. 220-21, Simcoe to Dorchester.

23. Fryer, EPS, pp. 110-111; The Army List 1795. The date on the commission was 3 October 1794.
24. AO, Simcoe Coll. reel 7-531, Simcoe Burges B 1-2, 17 Apr. re Spencer, 20 Apr. re Drewe and Margaret Graves.

CHAPTER 16: Major General

1. Reel A607 F39, (Simcoe to daughters, 22 Oct. 1794; 8 Nov. 1794, Simcoe to Charlotte), NA.
2. Bull, p. 93, from Cruikshank, v. 3, p. 119, Simcoe to R. England.
3. AO. reel 7-631, Simcoe-Burges, B 1-2, letters 8 and 21 Apr. 1795, M.A. Burges to EPS.
4. Ibid., 15 May 1795.
5. Innis, p. 149.
6. Ibid., pp. 150-158.
7. Ibid., p. 155.
8. Ibid., p. 158; Riddell, pp. 273, 276.
9. Sim/Corresp. v. 4, p. 201, (Simcoe to Portland 27 Feb. 1796).
10. Reel A607 F39, (Simcoe to Charlotte, 12 Feb. 1796), NA.
11. Bull, p. 84, quotes part of a letter fro Cartwright to Isaac Todd, from (Cruikshank) Sim/Corresp. v. 2 pp. 87-89.
12. Sim/Corresp. v. 2, pp. 297-98. Nothing came of this hope.
13. Ibid., v. 2, pp. 3, 123, 137, 154, 165, 203; v. 3, p. 28; v. 4, pp. 25, 36, 37, 230, 242-43.
14. Ibid., v. 4, p. 124.
15. Ibid., pp. 155-158.
16. Innis, p. 178.
17. Ibid.
18. Biography of Samuel James Ballard, DNB.
19. Innis, pp. 193-200.
20. Ibid., p. 198.
21. Ibid., pp. 200, 202, 204.
22. Ibid., p. 207.
23. Biography of Sir David Wiliam Smith by S.R. Mealing, DCB.
24. Bradley, A.G., *Guy Carleton (Lord Dorchester)*. Makers of Canada Series. Revised edition, Toronto: Oxford, 1926; A.L. Burt, *Guy Carleton — Lord Dorchester*. Canadian Historical Association Historical Booklet No. 5, 1955.
25. Biography of Simcoe by S. R. Mealing, DCB v. 5, pp. 754–759.
26. Martin, Ged, "Simcoe Friends" p. 105.

CHAPTER 17: San Domingo

1. Swete, Rev. John, "Picturesque Sketches of Devon." 1792-1801, manuscript, v. 9, DRO.
2. AO. Reel 10, p. 34, Bastard to Simcoe 10 Nov. 1796, WCSL.

3. Chatham Papers, 30/8/178, PRO; AO. Reel 10, item 54, WCSL.

4. Riddell, p. 304.

5. Chatham Papers, 30/8/178, PRO.

6. Wilson, Ellen Gibson. *Thomas Clarkson.* Facsimile edition, Wm. Sessions 1996, p. 58.

7. Smith, Donald B.., "Simcoe in Haiti." *Horizon Canada* No. 112, 1987. Background on San Domingo.

8. AO Reel 10, items 37 and 43, (correspondence between Simcoe and Williamson), WCSL.

9. Ibid., item 77, EPS to JGS, 20 Dec. 1797.

10. Ibid., item 96, Northumberland to Simcoe, 18 Aug. 1797.

11. Reel A606 F28, (E. Gwillim to EPS, 19 Nov. 1796), NA.

12. Fryer, EPS p. 172.

13. Will of Eliza Simcoe, #337B/30/1, DRO; also Biography of Sir Adam Williamson, DNB.

14. Mole Valley District Council Archives, Dorking, Surrey. The guns are on display at the Leatherhead Leisure Centre.

15. Ibid.

CHAPTER 18: THREATS FROM FRANCE

1. AO. Reel 10, item 108, (Windham to Simcoe, 19 Jan. 1798), WCSL.

2. Fisher, W.G. *History of the Somerset Yeomanry, Volunteer and Territorial Units.* (Goodman: 1924), p. 25.

3. Watson, Steven. *The Reign of George III 1760-1815,* (London, Oxford, 1960), p. 372.

4. *Gibson, Jeremy, and Mervyn Medlicott, Militia Lists and Musters 1757-1876.* Federation of Family History Societies 1990. Similar lists known as Levee En Masse lists were called for in 1803-04, which were even more detailed.

5. Hemyock Local History Group 1974. "Hemyock v. France."

6. Reel A606 F28, (E. Gwillim to EPS), NA.

7. Vowler, (EPS to Miss Elliott, 13 May1798).

8. Coleridge, Lord, K.C. *The Story of a Devonshire House.* (T. Fisher Unwin, MCMV [1905]), p. 164.

9. Vowler, (EPS to Miss Elliott, 13 May 1798).

10. Clifford, Hugh. *The House of Clifford.* Phillimore, 1987; records in the Clifford Papers at Ugbrooke, and the following articles by Prof. William Revenhill, University of Exeter; "The Honourable Robert Clifford (1788-1817) Officer in Dillon's Regiment. *Journal of the Society of Army Historical Research,* summer 1991, v. LXIX, p. 278; "A Cartographer's Response to Napoleon." *The Geographical Journal,* v. 160, no. 2, 2 July 1994, pp. 159-172; "Skeletons at Ugbrooke Park." *Cartographic Journal* vol. 25, June 1988. WCSL, Sellman, M.A., PhD. "More Notes and Transcripts from Ugrooke Records." (Cliffordiana) Published privately 1981.

11. Biographies of George Henry Lennox and Charles Lennox 4th Duke of

Richmond, DNB; DRO Resolutions of the Devon Standing Committee, pp. 281-89.

12. AO. Reel 16, item 57,)Windham to Simcoe 26 June 1798), WCSL; returns, Reel 10, many items.
13. Reel A606 F30, (M. Graves to Eliza, ? July 1798), NA.
14. Clifford family papers, (Simcoe to Lord Clifford, 10 Sept. 1798).
15. Ibid., Simcoe to Lord Clifford, ? Sept. 1798; DRO AO coll. reel 11, items 41-51.
16. AO. Reel 10, by date, (E. Gwillim to EPS, 13 Oct.1798), WCSL.
17. Ibid., item 407, Nov. 1798.
18. Ibid., item 390, (letter from The King's School, undated).
19. Ibid., item 354, (Samuel Pierce, Clerk to the Trustees, Exeter, 11 Aug. 1798).
20. DRO, Lieut. Papers, 1262M, 16. 20. 98.
21. Clifford papers, (Simcoe to Clifford, 16 Dec. 1798).
22. AO. Reel 16, item 57, WCSL.

CHAPTER 19: Troubled Times

1. AO. Reel 11, item 39, (re gout); Fryer, EPS, pp. 173, 174, WCSL.
2. SRO, Taunton, 9/5/1799; Land Tax; title deeds to new house courtesy of Fairlynch Museum, Budleigh Salterton.
3. AO. Reel 11, item 79, Bastard to Simcoe, 20 May 1799, WCSL.
4. Ibid., item 80.
5. Bailey, Memoir
6. AO. Reel item 102, WCSL.
7. Ibid., items 136, 140, and 143-5.
8. Fryer/HA p. 259.
9. AO. Simcoe coll. (F47), reel 1811, JGS to FGS, 30 Apr. 1800.
10. DRO, Luppitt Land Tax.
11. DRO, Lieut./1262M.
12. AO. Reel 11 item 248, WCSL.
13. Reel A605 F7, (Caroline to Mrs. Hunt, 9 Jan. 1800; should be 1801, she wrote that Henry was learning to walk), NA.
14. Fryer/HA pl 259.
15. AO. Reel 11, item 247, WCSL.
16. Ibid., reel 12, item 213, (Nelson to Addington, 2 Feb. 1801, marked from Sidmouth Papers).
17. Ibid., item 248.
18. Ibid., item 250.
19. Ibid., Reel 16, items 51, 53. (AO. Ref. A-4-3).
20. Ibid., Reel 12, item 213, 1 Feb. 1801.
21. Ibid., Reel 16, item 53. AO Tor. Ref. A-4-3.
22. DRO, Lieut. 1262 ML/45; Bohstedt, J.H., *Riots in England 1790-1810.* (Cambridge, Mass., Dept. of History, Harvard Univ.,1972), p. 381.
23. Biography of William Mudge, DNB; WCSL, quotation from EFP, 28 Aug.

1800; Ravenhill, "Skeletons at Ugbrooke Park" p. 54.

24. Ravenhill, "A Cartographer's Response" pp. 164-65.

25. Ibid., p. 164; recently 77 of Robert Clifford's skeletons were discovered in the archives of Ugbrooke House. Ravenhill's conclusions regarding their origins and purpose were clarified by correspondence between Simcoe and Clifford.

26. Ibid., *Journal of the Society of Army Historical Research*, (exchange of defense plans, JGS and R. Clifford); AO Reel 12, item 315, (marked 1801), WCSL.

27. Ibid, item 323, (marked 1801).

28. Ibid., reel 112, items 11, 322, 326, and 333-4.

29. Clifford papers, Ugbrooke House.

30. Bohstedt, pp. 123 et al.

CHAPTER 20: A BRIEF PEACE

1. DRO, Lieut./1216/L/52.

2. AO. Reel 12, item 33, WCSL.

3. Ibid., reel 11, item 401; reel 12, item 3 (by Simcoe).

4. Ibid., item 40; item 28, 19 Apr.; (re Francis item 133, Geo. Coleridge).

5. DRO, Lieut./1262M. Fortescue.

6. AO. Reel 12, items 26, 13; reel 16, item 27, WCSL.

7. DRO, Lieut./1262M/L.

8. AO, Reel 16, item 164, WCSL.

9. Ibid., reel 12, item 168, (Clifford 1 June); item 242, (4 Aug.); item 264.

10. Ibid., item 264, (26 Sept. 1801); item 291.

11. DRO, Enc. Z/17/3/9, Land Tax for Awliscombe and Hemyock.

12. Vancouver, C. *General Views of the Agriculture of Devon*, general reference.

13. Bailey Memoir.

14. AO. Reel 12, item 340; item 346, WCSL.

15. EFP, 20 May 1802, WCSL.

16. Bull, p. 104.

17. Reel A607 F30, Margaret Graves to Eliza, 23 Aug. 1800, NA; Elizabeth's journal of the visit to Weymouth is from Reel A605 F24, 18-26, NA.

18. Riddell, pp. 320-21.

19. Ibid.

20. Ibid., p. 319; Macdonald Stewart Foundation, Montreal, Simcoe Coll. Simcoe to Rev. Pratt, 19 Aug. 1802. Three copies of the letter are in AO, two dated 1801, correct date 1802, year of JGS' 50th birthday.

21. Reel A605 F7, (Simcoe to Walcot, 11 Nov. 1802), NA.

22. AO. Reel 12, items 356 and 358, WCSL.

23. Ibid. Reel 14, item 269, draft letter dated 23 May.

24. Clifford Archives, Ugbrooke, R. Clifford to his sister, 30 May 1803.

25. AO. Reel 14, item 346B, WCSL.

26. Bailey Memoir.

27. War Office 13, 4280, PRO.

28. AO. Reel 12, item 387, (Mudge); item 399A; Clifford, item 242, WCSL.
29. Ibid., Reel 13, items 11, 17 et al.
30. DRO, Standing Com'ee, July 1803.
31. AO. Reel 13, items 19, 326 on, WCSL.
32. Ibid., item 154.

CHAPTER 21: UNIVERSALLY LAMENTED

1. DRO, Addington Papers.
2. AO. Reel 13, item 195, WCSL,
3. Ibid., Reel 12, item 76.
4. Ibid., Reel 13, items 271; 277 Simcoe to Yorke; 278; 279, Yorke to Simcoe.
5. Ibid., item 348.
6. Fryer/HA, p. 259.
7. AO. Reel 13, item 388, 10 Aug. 1804; item 404, circular 31 Aug. 1804, WCSL.
8. Ibid., item 438,(Gibbs); reel 14, item 12, (Exeter).
9. Clifford Papers, Ugbrooke House, Aug. 1804.
10. Partridge, diary of Eliza Simcoe.
11. AO. F47-12 (new catalogue) FGS to EPS, undated, written before he left London for Ireland.
12. AO. Reels 14, 15, 16 many letters about Rolle, WCSL.
13. Ibid., Reel 14, item 121.
14. Ibid., item 84, (Moira); item 86, (Simcoe).
15. Partridge, Kendall's corresp. with JGS.
16. AO. Reel 14, item 134, WCSL.
17. Ibid., item 177.
18. Ibid., item 186.
19. Ravenhill, "Skeletons" pp. 53-54. ; Palk is AO. Reel 14 item 181.
20. Reel A605 F7, (JGS to EPS, 10 Jan. 1805 incorrectly dated; the funeral was on 9 Jan. 1806), NA.
21. AO. Reel 14 item 209, WCSL.
22. AO. Simcoe F47-12, reel 1812, (Francis to EPS, Eton, 28 June 1806).
23. Bailey Memoir; Deluc vol. 2, p. 10, numbered paragraph 941.
24. AO. Reel 14, item 195, WCSL.
25. Ibid., item 227, Simcoe to Moira 27 and 28 June 1806.
26. Clifford Papers, Ugbrooke Archives; AO. Reel 14, item 252, (Russell), WCSL.
27. Reel A607 F31,(Eliza to Miss Hunt, 30 Nov. 1806), WCSL.
28. AO F47-12, Reel 1812, JGS to Eliza 13 Sept. 1806, Coimbra.
29. DRO, Simcoe Papers, (JGS to EPS, 2 Sept. 1806).
30. Ibid., St. Vincent to Simcoe, 25 Sept. 1806.
31. EFP, 6 Nov. 1806, WCSL.
32. Robertson, *Diary*, p. 412, from Bailey Memoir.
33. Reel A607 F30 n.d., (Margaret Graves to Eliza), NA.

CHAPTER 22: LIFE AFTER THE GENERAL

1. AO. Reel 14, (series of letters starting 8 Nov. 1806).
2. PROB 11/1458, Will of John Graves Simcoe, PRO; DRO, Land Tax Assessment Rolls, Dunkeswell, 1807, Awliscombe 1806. Clifford Papers, Ugbrooke, (Robert Clifford to Lord Clifford, 1 Nov. 1806), EPS' invitation re maps, books.
3. AO. Reel 14, Memorial of EPS, Executrix of JGS'swill; Biography of John McGill by S.R. Mealing, DCB.
4. AO. Reel 14, has these letters back and forth. (See EPS to Greenwood, 14 Sept. 1807; references to commission, cost of JGS' suite to Tagus etc.), WCSL.
5. Scadding, Henry, p. xiii.
6. AO F47-12, reel 1812, (EPS to Moira, 8 Jan. 1808).
7. Ibid., no opening, (Jenkins to EPS, 9 Apr. 1812).
8. The Army List 1813. Lieutenant Simcoe and Captain Johnson died in 1812.
9. Reel A607 F31, (Charlotte to Miss Hunt, 11 and 20 Aug. 1813), NA.
10. Fryer, EPS. pp. 202-210.
11. Hett, Francis Paget. *Georgina*. Facsimile edition, (Sutton West, Ontario: Paget Press, 1978), p. 48.
12. Fryer/HA, p. 259.
13. Ibid., pp. 259-60.
14. Queen's York Rangers. *The Colours of the Queen's Rangers*. Pamphlet, Fort York Armoury, Toronto, undated. Ceremony 18 Apr. 1975, pp 11-12.
15. Gellnor, John. *Simcoe's Military Journal*. (Toronto: Baxter Publishing, 1962), pp. I-II.

BIBLIOGRAPHY

When joint authors, on different sides of the Atlantic, combine, variation in sources is inevitable. Some authors prefer using only primary sources. However, where a secondary source is also available, it should be included for the interested reader. John Graves Simcoe's *A Journal of the operations of the Queen's Rangers from the end of the year 1777 to the conclusion of the late American War* has been published three times. Simcoe's original work, published privately in Exeter, in 1787, appeared on a large format with an unpaged Appendix. An American edition, dated 1844, on a small format, was fully paged. A facsimile edition of the 1844 edition was issued in 1968. A version, in large format, edited by John Gellnor and lacking the Appendix, is dated 1962. We have had recourse to all three versions — 1787, 1844 and 1962 — and have referred to all of them in the documentation.

Another problem arose over whether to use Canadian or British microfilm collections. The main Simcoe papers in the Devon Record Office are available on microfilm from the National Archives, Ottawa. The originals of Simcoe collection that do not relate directly to Canada are in the Archives of Ontario, in Toronto. Microfilms of this collection are in both the Archives of Ontario and in the West Country Studies Library in Exeter, but they are catalogued differently. The reference numbers here apply to the West Country Studies Library microfilm since most sources apply to Devonshire. The finding aid in the Archives of Ontario is Reference Code F47 of the Simcoe Family.

PRIMARY SOURCES

<u>Manuscript</u>
Addington Papers, Devon Record Office. ref. 152M
Arnold, Hilary, for Simcoe genealogy.
Bailey, John. Memoir, property of Margaret Partridge.
Cornwallis Papers, Public Record Office, London.
Chatham Papers, Public Record Office, London.
Clifford Family Papers, Ugbrooke House, Devon.
Drewe Family Papers and Genealogy, property of Francis Drewe.
Simcoe Papers, collections in different places:
Archives of Ontario, Toronto, include Simcoe-Burges B-1-2 and Simcoe Reference Code F47.
Devon Record Office, Exeter, ref. 1038M
National Archives of Canada, Ottawa, microfilm of originals in the Devon Record Office, listed by folder. F29, the letters of Mary Anne Burges to Elizabeth Simcoe. Missing from F29 are letters found in B-1-2, Archives of Ontario.
West Country Studies Library, copies of originals in the Archives of Ontario.
Metropolitan Toronto Reference Library. Wolford-Simcoe Papers.
Still other Simcoe Papers are in the Colonial Williamsburg Collection, Williamsburg, Virginia.

Descendants Margaret Partridge and John Vowler have letters and   diaries which they generously made available.

Devon Record Office, other collections

Devon and Exeter Standing Committee Resolutions. ref. 287-9.

Parish Registers

Land Tax Returns: Dunkeswell, Luppitt, Hemyock, Awliscombe, East Budleigh, Buckerell.

Lord Lieutenant's Papers (Fortescue) ref. 1262M

Dunkeswell Enclosures 1801 Act, ref. 217/3/9

Title Deeds

Swete, Reverend John. "Picturesque Sketches of Devon." 1792-1801, manuscript, vol. 9.

The King's School, Ottery St. Mary, records on Simcoe's sons.

Lincoln's Inn Admission Collection

Mole Valley District Council Records, Dorking, Surrey.

Somerset Record Office, Taunton, Parish Registers, Title Deeds, Land Tax.

Northants. Record Office, Parish Register, Cotterstock

West Sussex Record Office, records of Royal Sussex Regiment.

The Case of Edward Drewe, booklet, original in Metropolitan Toronto Library.

Drewe, Edward, "Military Sketches" 1784.

Drewry's Derby *Mercury*.

Published Primary Sources

Army List, The. Various years.

Armstrong, Fred. H. *Handbook of Upper Canadian Chronology*. Dundurn, Toronto, 1985.

Austen-Leigh, Richard A. ed. *The Eton College Register, 1753-1790.*

Chudley, Ron. *A History of Craft Master Masons in the Province of Devonshire*. 1980, by the author.

Cruikshank, Brigadier E.A. ed., *Simcoe Correspondence*. 5 vols., Ontario Historical Society, Toronto 1923-1931.

Exeter *Flying Post* (Trewan's, Exeter).

Innis, Mary Quayle ed. *Mrs. Simcoe's Diary*. MacMillan, Toronto 1965.

Robertson, John Ross ed. The Diary of *Mrs. John Graves Simcoe*. First edition Toronto 1911, revised, Ontario Publishing, Toronto 1934.

Rogers, Robert. *Journals*. London, 1769 edition.

Seaman, Jordan. "Genealogy of the Seaman Family." Long Island Historical Society, Brookllyn, N.Y.

Toronto Globe. 16 July 1877. "A Narrative of John Peters, Lieutenant Colonel in the Queen's Loyal Rangers in Canada."

Secondary Materials

Allen, Robert S. "The Britisn Indian Department and the Frontier of North America, 1755-1830." *Canadian Historic Sites: Occasional Papers in Archaeology and History.* Ottawa 1875.

Alumni Oxonienses

André, John. *Willialm Berczy: Co-founder of Toronto.* Borough of York, 1967.

Boatner, Mark M. Cassell's *Biographical Dictionary of the American War of Independence 1763-1783.* Cassell, London 1973.

Landmarks of the American Revolution. Hawthorn, New York, 1975.

Bohstedt, J.H. *Riots in England With Special Reference to Devon.* Dept. of History, Harvard University, Cambridge, Mass., 1972.

Boylen, J.C. *The Story of Castle Frank.* Rous & Mann, Toronto 1959.

Bradley, A.G. *Guy Carleton (Lord Dorchester).* Makers of Canada Series, revised edition, Oxford, Toronto, 1926.

Bull, Stewart H. *The Queen's York Rangers. An Historic Regimen*t. Boston Mills Press, Ontario, revised edition 1993.

Burt, A.L. *Guy Carleton-Lord Dorchester, 1724–1808.* Canadian Historical Association, Historical Booklet No. 5, 1955.

Clifford, Hugh. *The House of Clifford from. before the Conquest.* Phillimore, 1987.

Coleridge, Lord, K.C. *The Story of a Devonshire House.* Fisher Unwin MCMV (1905).

Coxhead, J. R. W. *Honiton, A history of the Manor and its Borough.* Devon Books, 1984.

Craig, Gerald M. *Upper Canada: the Formative Years.* M. and S., Toronto, 1963.

Delpratt Harris, J., M. D. The Royal Devon and Exeter Hospital. 1922.

Deluc, Jean André. *Geological Travels.* London 1910,(3 vols., vol. III).

Devon Archaeological Society. *Hembury* (Field Guide No. 5).

Dictionary of Canadian Biography.

Dictionary of National Biography (Great Britain).

Dupuy, Trevor N., Curt Johnson, David L. Bongard. *The Harper Encyclopedia of Military Biography.* Edison, N.J., 1995.

Etoniana. 1914-15.

Fisher, W.G. *History of the Somerset Yeomanry, Volunteer and Territorial Units.* Goodman, 1924.

Fryer, Mary Beacock. *Elizabeth Posthuma Simcoe.* Dundurn, Toronto and Oxford, 1989.

"Our Young Soldier" (Francis Simcoe). Dundurn, Toronto and Oxford, 1996.

King's Men: the soldier founders of Ontario. Dundurn, Toronto 1980.

Buckskin Pimpernel (Justus Sherwood) Dundurn, Toronto, 1981.

Gentleman's Magazine. Sylvanus Urban ed., London 1788.

Gibson, Jeremy, and Mervyn Medlycott. *Militia Lists and Musters 1757-1876.* Federation of Family History Societies. 2nd edition 1990

Gover, J. E. B., A. Mawer, F.M. Stenton. *The Place Names of Devon.* 2 vols. English Place Names Society, Cambridge University, 1931.

Gray, Todd ed. "Devon and Cornwall Notes and Queries" *Devon Documents* 1996.

Hatch, Charles E. Jr. *Yorktown and the Seige of 1781.* National Park Service Historical Handbook Series 14, revised 1957.

Hemyock Local History Group. *Hemyock v. France.* 1974.

Hett, Francis Paget. *Georgina.* Facsimile edition, Paget Press, Sutton West, Ontario, 1978.

History of Parliament Trust. *The House of Commons 1790-1820.* Secker and Warburg, London,1986.

Holmes, G. E. J. *The King's School: A History.* The King's School, Ottery St. Mary, 1963.

Hoskins, W.G. *Devon (A New Survey of England).* Collins, London, 1954.

Lancaster, Bruce, and J. H. Plumb. *The American Heritage Book of the Revolution.* Dell, New York, 1958.

Leavitt, Thad. W. H. *History of Leeds and Grenville.* Brockville, Ont. 1879.

Lyte, C.M. *A History of Eton College 1440-1875.* London 1875.

Martin, Ged. "The Simcoes and Their Friends" *Ontario History.* vol. 69, no. 2 June,1977.

Massachusetts Historical Society. "Journal of a Treaty held in 1793 …" Collections, 3rd series, vol. 5, 1936.

Mealing, S.R. "The Enthusiasms of John Graves Simcoe." Canadian Historical Association,1958.

Morris, James/Jan. *Heaven's Command: An Imperial Progress.* Hammondsworth, Middlesex, England,1973.

Newton, Robert. *Eighteenth Century Exeter.* University of Exeter, 1984.

Page, John L.W. *An Exploration of Exmoor.* Seeley, London 1890.

Parliamentary History of England, The. vols. 98 (1790-1791) and 99 (1791).

Parliamentary Register, The. Vols. 98, 1790-1791, and 99, 1793-1806.

Peckham, Howard H. "Sir Henry Clinton's Review of Simcoe's Journal." *William and Mary Quarterly*, 2nd series, 2, 1941.

Pocock, Tom. *Horatio Nelson.* Knopf, New York, 1988.

Polwhele, the Rev. Richard. *Poems by Gentlemen of Devon and Cornwall.* 1792.

History of Devonshire. Published between 1793 and 1806. vol. 2.

Queen's York Rangers. *The Colours of the Queen's Rangers.* Fort York Armoury, Toronto, undated.

Ravenhill, William, University of Exeter. Articles on the Hon. Robert Clifford.

"The Honourable Robert Clifford (1788-1817) Officer in Dillon's Regiment." *Journal of the Society of Army Historical Research,* Summer 1991, v. LXIX;

"A Cartographer's Response to Napoleon." *The Geographical Journal,* vol. 160, no. 2, 2 July 1994;

"Skeletons at Ugbrooke Park." *Cartographic Journal* vol. 25, June1988.

Readman, A.E. ed. *The Royal Sussex Regiment: A Catalogue of Records.* West Sussex County Council, 1985.

Riddell, William Renwick. *The Life of John Graves Simcoe.* M and S., Toronto 1926

"An Official Record of Slavery in Upper Canada." Ontario Historical Society, *Papers and Records*, vol. 25 1929.

Rowe, M. M. and A. M. Jackson. *Exeter Freemen*. Devon and Cornwall Record Society.

Scadding, Henry. *Toronto of Old*. F. H. Armstrong ed. Oxford, Toronto 1987.

Scott, Duncan Campbell. *John Graves Simcoe*. Maker of Canada Series, Toronto, 1910.

Sellman, M. A. "More Notes and Transcripts from Ugbrooke Records." (Cliffordiana) privately, 1981. Copy in WCSL, Exeter.

Sheldon, Gilbert. *From Trackway to Turnpike*. Oxford, 1928.

Simcoe, Eliza. Diary, property of Margaret Partridge.

Simcoe, John Graves. *A Journal of the Operations of the Queen's Rangers from the end of the year 1777 to the conclusion of the late American War by Lieutenant-Colonel Simcoe, Commander of that Corps*. Exeter, published by the author 1787; *Simcoe's Military Journal*. Bartlett and Welford, New York 1844, facsimile edition Arno Press, N.Y., 1968; *Simcoe's Military Journal*. John Gellnor ed., Baxter, Toronto 1962 (no Appendix).

Smith, Donald B. "Simcoe in Haiti." *Horizon Canada* No. 112, 1987.

Sparks, J.A. *In the Shadow of the Blackdowns*. Moonraker, Wiltshire,1978.

Strachan, Hew. *British Military Uniforms 1768-96*. Arms and Armour, London, 1975.

Talman, J. J. *Loyalist Narratives from Upper Canada*. Champlain Society, Toronto, 1966, "Narrative of Stephen Jarvis."

Ussher, F. G. S. *Memoir of the Geological Survey of England and Wales*. 1906.

Vancouver, C. *A General View of the Agriculture of Devon*. London 1808.

Van Steen, Marcus. *Governor Simcoe and his Lady*. Hodder and Stoughton, Toronto, 1968.

Waldron, Colonel H. *Historical Records of the 1st Devon Militia*. Longmans, 1897.

Watson, J. Steven. *The Reign of George III 1760-1813*. Clarendon, Oxford, 1960.

Wilson, Ellen Gibson. *Thomas Clarkson*. Facsimile edition, Wm. Sessions 1996.

Wise, S.F. "The Indian Diplomacy of John Graves Simcoe." Canadian Historical Association,1957.

Wright, Esther Clarke. *The Loyalists of New Brunswick*. Privately 1955.

APPENDIX
Officers of the Queen's Rangers

1791 from The Army List 1793

		Regiment	Army
Colonel Commandant	John Graves Simcoe	1 Sept. 1791	18 Nov. '90
Captain	David Shank	1 Sept. 1791	25 Dec. '82
	Samuel Smith	do.	25 Dec. '82
Captain Lieut. and Captain	Aeneas Shaw	1 Sept. 1791	25 Dec. '82
	George Spencer	do.	
Lieutenant	Arthur Hen. Brocking	1 Sept. 1791	
	Robert Eyre	do.	
	Rowland Duer	16 Nov. 1791	
	James Givens	30 Nov. 1791	
Ensign	John M'Gill	18 Sept. 1791	
	Leonard Browne	do.	
	J. Whitmarsh Pearce	do.	
	William Mayne	21 Mar. 1792	
Adjutant	John M'Gill	1 Sept. 1791	
Surgeon	David Burns	do.	

The Army List 1803

		Regiment	Army
Lt. Col. Comm.	David Shank	14 Apr. 1798	1 Jan. '98
Major	Samuel Smith	14 Apr. 1798	Lt. Col. 1 Jan. '98
Captain	Aeneas Shaw	1 Sept. 1791	Lt. Col. 1 Jan. '98
	William Fitzgerald	6 June 1798	
Lieutenant	James Givens	30 Nov. 1791	
	Robert Cowell	19 June 1793	25 Mar. '93
	John M'Gill	8 Oct. 1798	
Adjutant	Alexander M'Queen	28 Feb. 1800	

Ensign	Wm. Birds Peters	28 Dec. 1796	21 Apr. '96
	J. Theodore Bryett	1 Nov. 1798	
	Alexander M'Nabb	28 Feb. 1800	
	John Dyne	24 Oct. 1802	1 May 1801
Paymaster	Alexander Burns	17 May 1799	
Adjutant	John M'Gill	1 Sept. 1791	Lt. 8 Oct. '98
Surgeon	John Gamble	9 July 1796	

The Army List 1784,
"On the English Half-Pay"

Simcoe's (Queen's Amer. Rangers) All commissions in the regiment are dated 25 December 1782. "Hussars" are listed first, Infantry follows Major Richard Armstrong

Colonel Commandant	John Graves Simcoe
Captains	John Saunders
	David Shank
	Thomas Ivie Cooke
	M. Robinson
Lieutenants	Allan M'Nab
	George Albies
	John Wilson
	George Spencer
	Wm. Digby Lawler
Cornets	Benj. Thomson
	Thomas Merritt
	Benj. M. Woolsey
	William Jarvis
	Samuel Clayton
Chaplain	John Agnew
Surgeon	Alexander Kelloch
Major	Richard Armstrong

Captains	John Mackay
	Francis Stephenson
	Robert M'Crea
	James Murray
	James Kerr
	Stair Agnew
	John M'Gill
	Samuel Smith
	John Whitlock
	Aeneas Shaw
	Hon. Bennet Wallop *(en Sec.)*
Lieutenants	George Ormond
	William Atkinson
	Thomas Murray
	Alexander Matheson
	George Pendred
	Charles Dunlop
	Hugh Mackay
	Adam Allen
	Caleb Howe
	Andrew M'Can
	Swift Armstrong
	— Potts
Ensigns	Nathaniel Munday
	Charles Hen. Miller
	John Ross
	Andrew Armstrong
	Edward Murray
	Creighton M'Crea
	Christopher Robinson
	Charles Matheson
	J.B. Haight
Adjutant	William Campbell
Quarter Master	George Hamilton

INDEX

Acts, Paliament, defence of realm (Britain), 190; maintenance of poor, 213; Enclosure Act 1801, land allowed to JGS, 224-25

Addington, John, 241

Addington, Henry, Speaker, 111, 189; friend of Pitt, 212; Prime Minister, 214, 215, 254; resigned, Lord Sidmouth, 236, 239, 240, 245

Addison, Rev. Robert, 155, 156

Agnew, Stair, Capt., Q.R., prisoner of war in France, 90; repatriated, settled New Brunswick, 95

Aitken, Alexander, surveyor, 163, 166

Aldwinkle, Northamptonshire, 27-28; birthplace of EPS, 87, 108; plans for sale of, 227-28, 229

Althouse (Althaus), John, Capt., German Jaegers, N.Y. Volunteers, 66, 67

American Revolution (War of Independence), 20; Decl. of Independence, 26, 29; Treaty of Separation, 29, 83, 103

Amiens, Peace of, 195, 223, 225; war resumed, 229

André, John, Major, 39-40, 50, 51; execution, 54-55

Anglican clergy, John Stuart, 147; Addison, 155-56; John Langhorn, 155 Archaeology, Devon, 87, 241; JGS' interest, 98

Arnold, Benedict, Col., attacked Canada, 25-26, 49-50, 51; in Virginia, 54-63

Armstrong, Richard, Major, Q.R., 41-42; takes command of Q.R., 85

Baby, family, Quebec and Detroit, 136, 139, 147, 149

Badcock, Rev. Samuel, biog., influence on JGS, 100-101

Bailey, John, servant of Simcoe family, Memoir he wrote, JGS "very liberal gentlemen," 226; descr. hospitalty to Luppitt artillery, 231, 239, 241, 244

Baltic "problem," expedition to, Denmark, Sweden, Russia. JGS reluctant, 215-16

Banks, Sir Joseph, Bt., JGS wrote to, 119-20

Barnstaple, French shelling, 198

Bastard, Edmund (brother of John P.), 201

Bastard, John Pollexfen, M.P., JGS' friend, 124; Bastard Township, 187, 190, 201, 210, 212, 229, 231; on quartering troops, 234

Bath, spa, 12; M. Graves moved to, 161, 230; Simcoes holiday at, 236; Simcoe daughters moved to, 250

Beacons, signal, Culmstock, Dumpdon, etc., coastal, 232

Beckwith, George, Capt., Col., 52, 174

Bentinck, William, 3rd Duke of Portland, 171; no more sympathetic than Carleton/Dorchester, 181, 182; frigate for San Domingo, 190, 193

Berczy, William, settlers to work on Yonge St., 173; stopped work, 181-82

Billop, Christopher, Col., Staten Is. Militia, 41; prisoner, 45-46, 50

Blackdown Hills, Devon, 86, 89, 207; geology, 118 less unrest in, 223; JGS enclosed, 210 acres, 225; geology, burrow, 241;

Blacks, in U.C., Peter Martin, abduction of Chloe Cooley, 160

Bloxam, armourer, escape plan, 49, 50

Bonaparte, see Napoleon

Borden Town, N.J., 44, 45

Boston, Massacre, Tea Party, 20-21; Bunker/Breed's Hill, 21-23

Bottum (Bothum), Elijah, toast at Johnstown levee, 145

Boudinet, Elisha, N.J. comm. of prisoners, 45, 49-50

Brandywine, Battle of, 28, 36

Brant, Joseph, Mohawk war chief, 134; biog., descr., 156, 158, 174, 193

Brant, Mary (Molly), sister of Joseph, widow of Sir Wm. Johnson, influence of, 132; daughters, 162, 174; cured JGS, 179

Broadhembury, village, 17, 105-06

Buckerell, parish Church of St. Mary and

organised fire fighters, 185; Simcoes'
departure on *Pearl*, Capt. Samuel
Ballard, 184, 185-86
Queenston, lower landing, 150
Queen's York Rangers (1st American
Regiment), 252-253; Colonel in Chief
The Prince Andrew, Duke of York,
253
Quinton's Bridge, skirmish, 39

Rawdon, Francis Lord, see Moira, 2nd
Earl of
Richmond, Va., operations, 61-72
Rogers, Robert, Colonel, ranger tactics,
32; 35-36
Rolle, Lord, 124; quarrels over dung, 211;
property rights, 211, 237; tenants to
reduce prices, 216; challenged JGS to
duel, 237
Roman Catholics, 20, 145; emancipation
rejected, 214
Rosslyn, Lieut. General Sir James St.
Clair, 2nd Earl of, to Portugal, 242
Russell, Peter, receiver general, 126, 141;
sister Elizabeth, 141, 147, 149; re
JGS' accounts in U. Canada, 246
Russell, Robert, of Exeter; 223, corps of
wagoners, 234; 242
Russia, JGS' fear of, 166

St. Lawrence River, Gulf of, 134; rapids
at Lachine, 143, Cascades, Cedars,
Coteau du Lac, Long Sault, 144;
Chimney Is. (Fort Lévis) guns, 144;
bateau channel, 145
St. Vincent, Earl, Sir John Jervis, 215,
230, 231; to Portugal, 242
Salem JGS' horse, 78; to Wolford Lodge,
96, 125
San Domingo, 127; JGS to govern, 190;
historic background, slaves in, 191;
JGS sailed for, left owing to poor
health, lack of support, 192; JGS
resigned, 193; received brass Spanish
guns, 193-94; now at Leatherhead
Leisure Centre, 249, 253
Sandusky, Ohio, U.S. commissioners met
tribes at, 162; returned to U.S., 165
Saunders, John, Capt., Q.R., to
Charleston, 56, 75

Scadding family in Devon, 98
Scadding, John, JGS' estate manager, 98;
102; re Honiton Turnpike, 107-08,
roads in Devon, 108, 125; in U.
Canada, 147; explored Dundas St.,
160, 213, 240; marriage, returned to
York, 3 sons, death, 246
Scadding, Thomas (brother), 80, 147.
178. 224. 225
Scilly Isles, Capt. Lyman asked for
reinforcements, refused, 232
Seven Years' War (French and Indian), 12-
13, 31-32
Shank, David, Capt. Q.R.., 59; at
Spencer's Ordinary, 66-69; settled in
England, 95; to U. Canada, 130, 140;
Colonel of Q.R., in U. Canada, 227
Sherwood, Justus, Capt., on Vermont,
148, 155; and H. Spencer to find
recruits in U.S., 182
Sidmouth, Lord, see Addington
Simcoe, Anne (daughter), birth, 235;
marriage, 248, 250
Simcoe, Caroline (daughter), birth, 104,
178; whooping cough, 209
Simcoe, Charlotte (daughter), birth, 97;
smallpox inoculation, 98; letters to,
151-52, 178; shirt for JGS, 178;
illness, 183; 243, 247
Simcoe, Eliza (daughter), birth, 97;
smallpox inoculation, 98; missed
parents, 126; letters to, 151-52, 242.
243. 245
Simcoe, Elizabeth Posthuma Gwillim,
wife of JGS, biog., 88; wedding, 94;
attitude to her children, 97; visit to
Exmoor, 111-15; plans for U.
Canada, 117; ball gowns, Nankin
china, 122; concern for children, 122-
13; diary, 128, two versions of, 129-
30; sketches, 130; and King George,
132; descr. of voyage, 133-34; happy
in Quebec, 136-39, 154; hut near
Queenston, 160; ill at Fort Niagara,
161; rattlesnakes, 166; Canise,
sketched Great Sail, 167; depression,
171; disapproved of San Domingo,
190; inspection tours with JGS, 200-
201; distress over Portugal, 241;
Francis in diary, 247; evangelical

Vermont, independent republic, 103; JGS
on moving there, 104; need of alliance
with Canada, opinion of Vermonters,
of Gov. Chittenden, 109; Allens and
Fays, 111; became 14th State, 123;
Sherwood negotiations, 148

von Knyphausen, Baron Wilhelm,
division commander, 36, 41, 53

von Steuben, Baron Friedrich, trained
rebel army, 60, 61

Vorhees, Capt. rebel, killed, 45, 49

Walcot, William, cousin of EPS, friend of
JGS, 87, 91, 96; and EPS' estate at
Aldwinkle, 108, 227-28, 229; JGS'
trustee, 234; Henry Simcoe principal
heir, 249

Washington, George, General, 26, 27, 28,
29, 36, 53, 55; U.S. neutral, 166

Wayne, Anthony, General, rebel, 38, in
Virginia, 61-62, 63, 170, 173, Fallen
Timbers, 174-75; did not attack
Detroit, 178

Wemyss, James, Major, 28, 36

West Point, N. Y., Arnold conspiracy, 53-
54

Weymouth, Simcoes; sailing delayed, 132;
yacht racing, 227-28

Whitchurch, Hereford, Gwillim home, 87

White, John, attorney general, 135, 141,
153, 162

Williamsburg, Va., operations near, 60-
63, 65-75

Williamson, Adam, advises JGS, 292

Windham, William, under sec'y, 197, 203

Wolfe, James, General, 12-13

Wolford Chapel, of Cistercian ruins, work
begun, 225; motto in, 229; burial of
JGS, 244; of EPS, 250; Ontario Gov't
assumed ownership, rededicated, 250

Wolford Lodge and estate, origin of name,
Woolford Church, 91; early owners,
JGS' plans for purchase, 91-93; life at,
98; return to, 1796, 186; JGS'
headquarters, 208; library, 238; lodge
burnt, 249

Yonge, Sir George, M.P., Escot county
seat, 94, 119; JGS disappointed by,
13, 143, 253

Yonge St., link York to Lake Simcoe, 170;
strategic road, 182, 253

York, Duke of C in C of the Army, JGS
sent plan to, 107, 127, anger over San
Domingo, 193; praised JGS, 223;
ownership of dung, 237, 242

York, see Toronto

Yorke, Charles, acting home sec'y, advised
ondiscipline, court martial,
punishment, 234

Yorktown, Va., campaign and final defeat,
73-82

ACKNOWLEDGEMENTS

Pride of place must go to two Simcoe descendants, Mrs. Margaret Partridge and John Vowler, who shared original documents in their possession, and were most welcoming. Lord Clifford generously permitted the use of his family papers at Ugbrooke House. Lord Coleridge of Ottery allowed us to photograph the "Simcoe vase" and to use information in the relationship between the Simcoe and Coleridge families. Mr. amd Mrs. Alfred Le Marchant, of Wolford Lodge, gave access to their original copy of Simcoe's journals. Their daughter, Pamela, and her husband the Very Reverend Patrick Mitchell, KCVO have always been encouraging.

This work could not have been completed without the assistance of a host of friends on both sides of the Atlantic. Among them are Hilary Arnold, M.A., of York, who unearthed Mrs. Simcoe's true date and place of birth; Professor Donald Smith of the University of Calgary, Alberta; George Hutchison, former Director of Public Affairs, Government of Ontario in London; Mrs. Paddy Neville who rediscovered the Simcoe cannons; David Hancocks, former manager of the Leatherhead Leisure Centre; Brian Clist of Hemyock; Peter Thomas of the Exeter Cathedral Library; Robin Bush, Somerset Record Office; Paul Dixon of Cotterstock; Mrs. Shaw of Hembury Fort House; Patrick Strong and Mrs. P. Hatfield, for help with Eton College; Rober Highfield of Merton College, Oxford; Michael E. Dunning, The King's School; John Ainsworth of the Royal Sussex Regiment Association; Librarian Christine Mosser, Canadian History, Metropolitan Toronto Library; Deputy Librarian Yvonne McGowan, Lincoln's Inn; Archivist Patricia Gill, West Sussex Record Office; County Archivist Miss R. Watson and P.I. King, Northamptonshire Record Office; the staff of the House of Lords and the British Libraries, and the Public Record Office, Chancery Lane and Kew; Joy Gawne and Anita Jennings, Fairlynch Museum, and Mrs. Coton, former owner of Little Hill (now Simcoe House), Budleigh Salterton; Geoffrey Goodall, former headmaster, and George Ayres, former head of history, Exeter School; Assistant Curator Eileen Parris, Colonial Williamsburg Foundation Library; friends and colleagues of the John Graves Simcoe/Wolford Chapel Committee, England. Fondly remembered as a predecessor of Chris as chairman of the John Graves Simcoe/Wolford Chapel Committee, is the late Wing Commander John F. Sutton, D.S.O., D.F.C., A.F.C.

Most revealing of all is the collection of material in the Archives of Ontario. Archivist Roger Nickerson arranged for this material to be microfilmed and sent to the West Country Studies Library, Exeter, where Librarian Ian Maxted agreed to have the library cover the cost. At the same time a microfilm was made for the Archives of Ontario and entered in the main finding aid on the Simcoes. The Ontario Heritage Foundation has been deeply involved since the province assumed ownership of Wolford Chapel. Heather Broadbent was chairman of the Foundation's Wolford Chapel Advisory Committee. Richard Moorhouse of the Foundation, served as a courier and helped choose photographs taken during the dedication ceremony of 1989. In Toronto, Jim Suderman and Leon Warmski, both of the Archives, also lent interest and encouragement; Gavin Watt, colonel of the recreated King's Royal Yorkers, read the manuscript and made useful suggestions. Dennis Mills was our editor. To Kirk Howard and Barry Jowett of the Dundurn Group, we owe much, and to our spouses, photographer Shirley Dracott and cartographer Geoffrey Fryer.